HEALTHY COOKING
ANNUAL RECIPES

Taste of Home

RDA ENTHUSIAST BRANDS, LLC • MILWAUKEE, WI

HEALTHY COOKING
ANNUAL RECIPES

192

231

© 2019 RDA Enthusiast Brands, LLC.
1610 N. 2nd St., Suite 102, Milwaukee WI 53212-3906

All rights reserved. Taste of Home is a registered trademark of RDA Enthusiast Brands, LLC.

Visit us at **tasteofhome.com** for other Taste of Home books and products.

ISBN:
D 978-1-61765-877-8
U 978-1-61765-878-5
Component Numbers:
D 117900051H
U 117900053H
ISSN: 1944-7736

Deputy Editor: Mark Hagen
Senior Art Director: Raeann Thompson
Editor: Christine Rukavena
Art Director: Maggie Conners
Designer: Arielle Jardine
Copy Editor: Chris McLaughlin
Senior Food Editor: Peggy Woodward, RDN

Cover Photographer: Jim Wieland
Senior Set Stylist: Melissa Franco
Senior Food Stylist: Shannon Roum

Pictured on front cover:
Tequila Lime Shrimp Zoodles, p. 120.

Pictured on title page:
Chicken Tostada Cups, p. 196.

Pictured on back cover:
Mixed Berry French Toast Bake, p. 23; Italian Wedding Soup, p. 47; Pork & Asparagus Sheet-Pan Dinner, p. 125; Chocolate Swirled Cheesecake, p. 252; California Burger Wraps, p. 211.

Printed in USA
1 3 5 7 9 10 8 6 4 2

LIKE US
facebook.com/tasteofhome

TWEET US
@tasteofhome

FOLLOW US
pinterest.com/taste_of_home

SHARE A RECIPE
tasteofhome.com/submit

SHOP WITH US
shoptasteofhome.com

E-MAIL US
bookeditors@tasteofhome.com

VISIT US FOR MORE!
tasteofhome.com

Contents

Eat great and feel great with 350+ amazing heart-healthy dishes. Discover comforting entrees, slow-cooked classics and fiery grilled specialties. You'll also find eye-opening breakfasts, showstopping sweets, heartwarming soups, nutritious sides and much, much more!

77

Here's What "Healthy" Means at *Taste of Home*

We're here to help you navigate the options with *Healthy Cooking Annual Recipes*.

If you think trying to eat healthfully is overwhelming, you're not alone. The concept of healthy eating is really complex: There are a lot of factors to consider, research is constantly uncovering new information, and there's still a lot that science doesn't know about how food and nutrition affect our health. With all this in mind, we at *Taste of Home* have created a set of guardrails to help our health-minded readers keep on track.

Since "healthy" covers such a wide spectrum, we take a middle-of-the-road approach at *Taste of Home*. Organizations that make recommendations rooted in proven science like the USDA, FDA, WHO, NIH plus the American Heart Association, the American Diabetes Association and the Academy of Nutrition and Dietetics help guide us.

WHAT HEALTHY IS
The idea that "healthy" foods should nourish us with vitamins, minerals, protein, fiber and healthy fat is so important that we created a new **"POWER-PACKED" ICON** used throughout this edition of *Healthy Cooking Annual Recipes*. These recipes are made up of multiple healthy ingredients such as vegetables, fruits, whole grains, lean meats, legumes, low-fat or fat-free dairy and healthy fats.

WHAT HEALTHY ISN'T
The big picture isn't just about what's in our food, but what's not in our food, too. It's widely recommended that we limit saturated fat, trans fat and sodium for optimal health and disease prevention, so we steer away from those in our healthy recipes. At the same time, healthy eating doesn't mean cutting out entire food groups, feeling deprived or eating food that doesn't taste good!

IT'S ABOUT BALANCE
Healthy eating is about balance: a recipe that's made mostly of healthy ingredients, a meal that's made up mostly of healthy recipes, a day that includes mostly healthy choices and provides us with all the nutrients we need to function our best. Nutritious recipes can include butter and sugar, just like healthy meals can include an indulgent dessert—it's all about moderation and keeping a healthy big picture in mind.

Use the Test Kitchen-approved dishes from *Healthy Cooking Annual Recipes* to help you find your balance. Whether you're looking for a "power-packed" weeknight dinner, such as **SHEET-PAN PINEAPPLE CHICKEN FAJITAS (P. 199),** or a special-occasion dessert like **LEMON MERINGUE ANGEL CAKE (P. 236),** you'll find a great combination right here that works for you and your family.

Happy Cooking,

Peggy

Peggy Woodward, RDN
Senior Editor/Food

About Our Nutrition Facts

The *Healthy Cooking Annual Recipes* cookbook provides a variety of recipes to fit in a healthy lifestyle. Here's how we arrive at the serving-size nutritional information at the end of each recipe.

- Whenever a choice of ingredients is given (such as ½ cup sour cream or plain yogurt), we use the first ingredient in our calculations.

- When a range is given for an ingredient, we calculate using the first amount.

- Only the amount of a marinade absorbed is calculated.

- Optional ingredients are not included in our calculations.

- Sugars provided in the Nutrition Facts represent both added and naturally occurring sugars.

* HEALTH TIP * Peggy shares her best secrets to help you make healthy eating choices throughout the week.

SPECIAL INDICATORS
- **Power-Packed** Each dish contains a whole grain or legume, a lean protein, and a healthy dose of fruits or vegetables.

- **Meatless** Indicates breakfast, lunch, dinner and snack-time options that don't use meat or meat products.

- **Fast Fix** Dishes are table-ready in 30 minutes or less.

- **Slow Cooker** Dozens of slow-simmered recipes use the favorite appliance.

Power Up with Power-Packed Foods Like These

A great slow-cooked soup has it all: health, convenience, thrift, comfort and amazing taste. 🥘🥕🫙 **SPICY LENTIL & CHICKPEA STEW** from *Melanie MacFarlane* warms up the chilliest day even on Prince Edward Island—and it's loaded with good-for-you and delicious legumes. **P. 226**

While it tastes like pure comfort food, 🫙 **ITALIAN HOT DISH** from Wisconsin cook *Theresa Smith* boasts multigrain pasta, 2 vegetable servings and even 34g of satisfying protein in every portion. This is a family-pleaser that will become part of your regular rotation. **P. 181**

Summertime is the prime time for healthy eating, and Chico, California's *Deena Bowen* grills a fresh and zesty dish that folks will go crazy for! 🕐🫙 **PESTO CORN SALAD WITH SHRIMP** is bursting with ripe garden produce, healthy avocado chunks and flavorful shrimp. **P. 81**

Healthy Food Impostors

These foods may seem like they're "power-packed," but they usually aren't.

1 GRANOLA BARS
We usually equate granola with wholesomeness, but it isn't necessarily, especially when it comes to granola bars. They may contain whole grains and some healthy fats in the form of nuts or seeds, but most are packed with added sugar, more like candy bars than health food. Make your own to control sugar and add good health.

2 BREAKFAST CEREAL
The cereal aisle has become overrun with sweetened flakes, marshmallows and other ingredients you might find in dessert. Check out the ingredient list; if sugar's one of the first, that means it's mostly sugar. Look for whole-grain, low-sugar cereal with satisfying protein-packed ingredients like nuts and seeds.

3 AGAVE NECTAR
Syrup from the agave plant sounds too good to be true–and it probably is. While it might be more "natural" than some sweeteners and lower on the glycemic index, it's still heated and processed, full of fructose—and it's still added sugar. Treat it the same way you would any other sweetener – use it in moderation.

4 SMOOTHIES
While smoothies may seem like health food in a glass, many aren't. In addition to the natural sweetness from fruit, they often have added sugar in the form of fruit juice concentrate, honey or agave nectar. Make your own, leave out the extra sugar, and remember to count the calories from your smoothie in your day's intake.

5 VEGGIE CHIPS
Better than potato chips, right? Well, potatoes are vegetables, too. And just like potato chips, most veggie chips are highly processed with added fat and salt. Some also have preservatives and artificial colors to give them their vibrant color. If you love them, eat them (a few of them, anyway), but don't think it's like eating a serving of raw veggies.

6 LOW-FAT FOODS
Processed foods that are marketed as low-fat or fat-free typically have more of what we don't want—added sugar and processed ingredients to help them taste more like the full-fat versions. Remember that fat isn't off-limits; we need healthy mono- and polyunsaturated fat in our diets to help absorb certain nutrients and provide essential fatty acids.

GOOD MORNINGS

"*Peak-of-freshness strawberries make this drink a summer staple. Garnish the glass with a lime slice.*"
—Elizabeth Johnson, Kemmerer, WY

Savory Apple-Chicken Sausage (p. 13) Denver Omelet Salad (p. 20) Overnight Oatmeal (p. 23)
Vanilla French Toast (p. 11) Strawberry Lime Smoothies (p. 13) Avocado Fruit Salad (p. 25)

PEANUT BUTTER BANANA OATMEAL

The classic flavors of peanut butter and bananas come together in this kid- and adult-friendly oatmeal. We have eaten it many a morning.
—Deborah Purdue, Westland, MI

Takes: 15 min. • **Makes:** 4 servings

- 3 cups fat-free milk or water
- ¼ tsp. salt
- 1½ cups quick-cooking oats
- 2 large bananas, sliced
- 2 Tbsp. peanut butter
- ½ tsp. vanilla extract

Place milk and salt in a large saucepan; bring just to a boil. Stir in oats; cook until thickened, 1-2 minutes, stirring mixture occasionally. Remove from heat; stir in remaining ingredients.

1 cup: 284 cal., 7g fat (1g sat. fat), 4mg chol., 260mg sod., 47g carb. (19g sugars, 5g fiber), 13g pro.

COFFEE LOVER'S COFFEE CAKE

I had this cake at a friend's brunch and she graciously shared the recipe. Now people always request it from me because it's so tasty and such a reliable hit.
—Gale Lalmond, Deering, NH

Prep: 25 min. • **Bake:** 25 min.
Makes: 9 servings

- ⅓ cup sugar
- 4 tsp. instant coffee granules
- 1½ tsp. ground cinnamon

BATTER
- 3 Tbsp. butter, softened
- ½ cup sugar
- 1 large egg
- 1 tsp. vanilla extract
- 1½ cups all-purpose flour
- 1 tsp. baking powder
- ½ tsp. baking soda
- ⅛ tsp. salt
- 1 cup (8 oz.) plain yogurt
- 2 Tbsp. chopped walnuts or pecans

1. Preheat oven to 350°. Mix the sugar, coffee granules and cinnamon. In a large bowl, beat butter and sugar until crumbly, about 2 minutes. Beat in egg and vanilla. In another bowl, whisk together flour, baking powder, baking soda and salt; add to the butter mixture alternately with the yogurt, beating just until blended. (The batter will be thick.)

2. Spread half of the batter evenly into an 8-in. square baking pan coated with cooking spray; sprinkle with half of the coffee mixture. Top with remaining batter; sprinkle with remaining coffee mixture. Cut through batter with a knife to swirl. Sprinkle with nuts.

3. Bake until a toothpick inserted in the center comes out clean, 25-30 minutes. Cool 5 minutes before serving.

1 serving: 220 cal., 6g fat (3g sat. fat), 34mg chol., 207mg sod., 37g carb. (20g sugars, 1g fiber), 4g pro.

PEANUT BUTTER
BANANA OATMEAL

COFFEE LOVER'S
COFFEE CAKE

ROYAL BROCCOLI SOUFFLE

Talk about impressive! This souffle never fails to impress even the toughest of critics—my family.
—Linda Evancoe-Coble, Leola, PA

Prep: 30 min. • **Bake:** 30 min.
Makes: 6 servings

- 4 large egg whites, room temperature
- 2 cups chopped fresh broccoli florets
- ¼ cup water
- 2 Tbsp. butter
- 3 Tbsp. all-purpose flour
- ¼ tsp. cayenne pepper
- ¾ cup fat-free milk
- 2 Tbsp. grated Parmesan cheese
- 1 tsp. ground mustard
- ½ tsp. salt
- ¼ tsp. pepper
- 1 large egg yolk, beaten
- ¼ tsp. cream of tartar

1. Grease a 1½-qt. souffle dish; dust lightly with flour.
2. Preheat oven to 350°. Microwave broccoli and water, covered, on high until the broccoli is tender, 2-3 minutes. Let stand for 5 minutes; drain. Pulse broccoli in a food processor until blended.
3. In a small saucepan, melt butter over medium heat. Stir in flour and cayenne pepper until smooth. Gradually whisk in milk. Bring to a boil, stirring constantly; cook and stir until thickened, 1-2 minutes. Transfer to a large bowl; stir in cheese, mustard, salt, pepper and broccoli. Whisk a small amount of hot mixture into egg yolk; return mixture to the bowl, whisking constantly. Cool slightly.
4. In another bowl, beat egg whites with cream of tartar until stiff but not dry. With a rubber spatula, gently stir a fourth of the egg whites into broccoli mixture until no white streaks remain. Fold in remaining egg whites. Transfer to prepared dish. Bake until top is puffed and center appears set, 30-35 minutes. Serve immediately.
⅔ cup: 100 cal., 5g fat (3g sat. fat), 43mg chol., 318mg sod., 7g carb. (2g sugars, 1g fiber), 6g pro.
Diabetic exchanges: 1 fat, ½ starch.

SWEET POTATO & EGG SKILLET

SWEET POTATO & EGG SKILLET

I like to incorporate nutritious sweet potatoes in my meals as often as possible, especially at breakfast. This recipe originated with the purpose of feeding my family a super healthy and hearty breakfast... and it worked!
—Jeanne Larson
Rancho Santa Margarita, CA

Takes: 25 min. • **Makes:** 4 servings

- 2 Tbsp. butter
- 2 medium sweet potatoes, peeled and shredded (about 4 cups)
- 1 garlic clove, minced
- ½ tsp. salt, divided
- ⅛ tsp. dried thyme
- 2 cups fresh baby spinach
- 4 large eggs
- ⅛ tsp. coarsely ground pepper

1. In a large cast-iron or other heavy skillet, heat butter over low heat. Add sweet potatoes, garlic, ¼ tsp. salt and thyme; cook, covered, until the potatoes are almost tender, 4-5 minutes, stirring occasionally. Stir in the spinach just until wilted, 2-3 minutes.
2. With the back of a spoon, make four wells in potato mixture. Break an egg in each well. Sprinkle eggs with pepper and remaining salt. Cook, covered, on medium-low until the egg whites are completely set and yolks begin to thicken but are not hard, 5-7 minutes.
1 serving: 224 cal., 11g fat (5g sat. fat), 201mg chol., 433mg sod., 24g carb. (10g sugars, 3g fiber), 8g pro.
Diabetic exchanges: 1½ starch, 1½ fat, 1 medium-fat meat.
* HEALTH TIP * With sweet potatoes and spinach, this dish meets the daily requirement for vitamin A.

❋
TEST KITCHEN TIP
Break the eggs into a small dish before adding to the pan. It's easier to remove stray shell pieces if they get into the egg. If you like your eggs sunny-side up, leave the pan uncovered while they cook.

BERRY NECTARINE SALAD

I've been making this recipe for years. Whenever my family has a summer get-together, nearly everyone requests it. The nectarines and berries look beautiful, and the topping is the perfect accent.
—Mindee Myers, Lincoln, NE

....

Prep: 15 min. + chilling
Makes: 8 servings

- 4 **medium nectarines, sliced**
- ¼ **cup sugar**
- 1 **tsp. lemon juice**
- ½ **tsp. ground ginger**
- 3 **oz. reduced-fat cream cheese**
- 2 **cups fresh raspberries**
- 1 **cup fresh blueberries**

1. In a large bowl, toss nectarines with sugar, lemon juice and ginger. Refrigerate, covered, 1 hour, stirring once.

2. Drain nectarines, reserving juices. Gradually beat reserved juices into cream cheese. Gently combine nectarines and berries; serve with cream cheese mixture.
1 serving: 109 cal., 3g fat (2g sat. fat), 8mg chol., 46mg sod., 21g carb. (15g sugars, 4g fiber), 2g pro.
Diabetic exchanges: 1 fruit, ½ starch, ½ fat.

VANILLA FRENCH TOAST

(PICTURED ON P. 6)

We discovered this easy French toast recipe in Mexico. We couldn't figure out what made the French toast so delicious until we learned the secret was vanilla. Since then, we've added a touch of vanilla to our waffle and pancake recipes, and it makes all the difference.
—Joe and Bobbi Schott, Castroville, TX

....

Takes: 15 min. • **Makes:** 6 servings

- 4 **large eggs, lightly beaten**
- 1 **cup 2% milk**
- 2 **Tbsp. sugar**
- 2 **tsp. vanilla extract**
- ⅛ **tsp. salt**
- 12 **slices day-old sandwich bread**
   Optional toppings: butter, maple syrup, fresh berries and confectioners' sugar

1. In a shallow dish, whisk together first five ingredients. Preheat a greased griddle over medium heat.

2. Dip bread in egg mixture, allowing to soak 30 seconds on each side. Cook on griddle until golden brown on both sides. Serve with toppings as desired.
2 slices: 218 cal., 6g fat (3g sat. fat), 127mg chol., 376mg sod., 30g carb. (9g sugars, 1g fiber), 10g pro.
Diabetic exchanges: 2 starch, 1 medium-fat meat.

BERRY NECTARINE SALAD

BLUEBERRY-CINNAMON
CAMPFIRE BREAD

BLUEBERRY-CINNAMON CAMPFIRE BREAD

A neighboring camper made a bread so tempting, I had to ask for the details. Here's my version, best enjoyed with a steaming cup of coffee by the campfire.
—Joan Hallford, North Richland Hills, TX

Prep: 10 min. • **Cook:** 30 min. + standing
Makes: 8 servings

- 1 loaf (1 lb.) cinnamon-raisin bread
- 6 large eggs
- 1 cup 2% milk or half-and-half cream
- 2 Tbsp. maple syrup
- 1 tsp. vanilla extract
- ½ cup chopped pecans, toasted
- 2 cups fresh blueberries, divided

1. Prepare campfire or grill for low heat. Arrange bread slices on a greased double thickness of heavy-duty foil (about 24x18 in.). Bring foil up the sides, leaving the top open. Whisk eggs, milk, syrup and vanilla. Pour over bread; sprinkle with the nuts and 1 cup blueberries. Fold foil edges over top, crimping to seal.
2. Place on a grill grate over campfire or grill until egg mixture is cooked through, 30-40 minutes. Remove from heat; let stand 10 minutes. Sprinkle with remaining blueberries; serve with additional maple syrup if desired.

Oven Directions: Preheat oven to 350°. Place foil packet on a 15x10x1-in. baking pan. Bake 25-30 minutes or until heated through. Let stand for 10 minutes before serving. Sprinkle bread with the remaining blueberries; serve with syrup.

2 slices: 266 cal., 10g fat (2g sat. fat), 142mg chol., 185mg sod., 36g carb. (14g sugars, 5g fiber), 12g pro.
Diabetic exchanges: 2 starch, 1 medium-fat meat, ½ fruit, ½ fat.

STRAWBERRY LIME SMOOTHIES

SAVORY APPLE-CHICKEN SAUSAGE
(PICTURED ON P. 6)

These easy sausages taste great and make an elegant brunch dish. The recipe is also very versatile. It can be doubled or tripled for a crowd, and the sausage freezes well either cooked or raw.
—Angela Buchanan, Longmont, CO

Takes: 25 min. • **Makes:** 8 patties

- 1 large tart apple, peeled and diced
- 2 tsp. poultry seasoning
- 1 tsp. salt
- ¼ tsp. pepper
- 1 lb. ground chicken

1. In a large bowl, combine the apple, poultry seasoning, salt and pepper. Crumble chicken over mixture and mix well. Shape into eight 3-in. patties.
2. In a large, greased cast-iron or other heavy skillet, cook patties over medium heat until no longer pink, 5-6 minutes on each side. Drain if necessary.

1 sausage patty: 92 cal., 5g fat (1g sat. fat), 38mg chol., 328mg sod., 4g carb. (3g sugars, 1g fiber), 9g pro.
Diabetic exchanges: 1 medium-fat meat.

STRAWBERRY LIME SMOOTHIES
(PICTURED ON P. 7)

Peak-of-freshness strawberries make this drink a summer staple. Garnish the glass with a lime slice.
—Elizabeth Johnson, Kemmerer, WY

Takes: 5 min. • **Makes:** 3 servings

- 1 cup (8 oz.) strawberry yogurt
- ½ cup 2% milk
- 2 to 4 Tbsp. lime juice
- 2 Tbsp. honey
- ¼ tsp. ground cinnamon
- 2 cups fresh strawberries, hulled

Process all ingredients in a covered blender until smooth.

1 cup: 172 cal., 2g fat (1g sat. fat), 7mg chol., 61mg sod., 36g carb. (32g sugars, 2g fiber), 5g pro.

FRENCH OMELET

WARM GRAPEFRUIT WITH GINGER-SUGAR

Sweetly broiled grapefruit is a specialty at my bed-and-breakfast. In addition to serving it at breakfast or brunch, try it as a light snack or dessert.
—Stephanie Levy, Lansing, NY

Takes: 15 min. • **Makes:** 2 servings

- 1 large red grapefruit
- 2 to 3 tsp. chopped crystallized ginger
- 2 tsp. sugar

1. Preheat broiler. Cut grapefruit crosswise in half. With a small knife, cut around the membrane in the center of each half and discard. Cut around each section to loosen fruit. Place on a baking sheet, cut side up.
2. Mix ginger and sugar; sprinkle over fruit. Broil 4 in. from heat until sugar is melted, about 4 minutes.
½ grapefruit: 85 cal., 0 fat (0 sat. fat), 0 chol., 3mg sod., 22g carb. (18g sugars, 2g fiber), 1g pro.
Diabetic exchanges: ½ starch, 1 fruit.

DID YOU KNOW?

Crystallized or candied ginger is the root of the ginger plant that has been candied in a sugar syrup. It's used primarily in dips, desserts and Chinese cooking. Many grocery stores carry it in the spice section. In large stores, you can find candied ginger in the Chinese section for a much lower price.

Crystallized ginger is a good emergency stand-in when you don't have fresh ginger for your recipes. Just soak a few slices of ginger in hot water to soften it and remove excess sugar, then chop and use. Use about triple the amount of crystallized ginger in place of fresh.

FRENCH OMELET

This cheesy, full-of-flavor omelet is modeled after one I tasted and loved in a local restaurant. Mine is so hearty and rich-tasting that no one will guess it's lower in fat.
—Bernice Morris, Marshfield, MO

Takes: 20 min. • **Makes:** 2 servings

- 2 large eggs
- 4 large egg whites
- ¼ cup fat-free milk
- ⅛ tsp. salt
- ⅛ tsp. pepper
- ¼ cup cubed fully cooked ham
- 1 Tbsp. chopped onion
- 1 Tbsp. chopped green pepper
- ¼ cup shredded reduced-fat cheddar cheese

1. Whisk together first five ingredients.
2. Place a 10-in. skillet coated with cooking spray over medium heat. Pour in the egg mixture. Mixture should set immediately at edges. As eggs set, push cooked portions toward center, letting uncooked eggs flow underneath. When eggs are thickened and no liquid egg remains, top one side with remaining ingredients. Fold omelet in half. Cut in half to serve.
½ omelet: 186 cal., 9g fat (4g sat. fat), 207mg chol., 648mg sod., 4g carb. (3g sugars, 0 fiber), 22g pro.
Diabetic exchanges: 3 lean meat, 1 fat.

**WARM GRAPEFRUIT
WITH GINGER-SUGAR**

COLORFUL PEPPER FRITTATA

COLORFUL PEPPER FRITTATA

This fluffy breakfast packed with sweet peppers and minced fresh basil is a feast for the eyes. It's so filling and tasty, meat lovers won't notice what's missing.
—Jessie Apfe, Berkeley, CA

Prep: 35 min. • **Bake:** 20 min.
Makes: 6 servings

- 4 large eggs
- 8 large egg whites
- 1 tsp. salt
- ½ tsp. pepper
- 1 cup shredded part-skim mozzarella cheese
- ¼ cup minced fresh basil
- 2 tsp. canola oil
- 1 large onion, chopped
- 2 cups chopped sweet red peppers
- 1 cup chopped sweet yellow pepper
- 1 cup chopped sweet orange pepper
- 3 garlic cloves, minced
- 2 Tbsp. shredded Parmesan cheese

1. Preheat oven to 350°. Whisk together first four ingredients. Stir in mozzarella cheese and basil.
2. In a 10-in. cast-iron or other ovenproof skillet, heat oil over medium heat. Add the onion; cook and stir for 2 minutes. Add peppers; cook and stir until tender, 3-4 minutes. Stir in garlic; cook 1 minute.
3. Pour in egg mixture; remove from heat. Sprinkle with Parmesan cheese. Bake, uncovered, until eggs are completely set, 20-25 minutes. Let stand 5 minutes. Cut into wedges.

1 wedge: 188 cal., 9g fat (4g sat. fat), 137mg chol., 672mg sod., 11g carb. (6g sugars, 2g fiber), 16g pro.
Diabetic exchanges: 2 medium-fat meat, 1 vegetable.

BREAKFAST
SWEET POTATOES

BREAKFAST SWEET POTATOES

Baked sweet potatoes aren't just for dinner anymore. Top them with breakfast favorites to power up your morning.
—*Taste of Home* Test Kitchen

Prep: 10 min. • **Bake:** 45 min.
Makes: 4 servings

- 4 medium sweet potatoes (about 8 oz. each)
- ½ cup fat-free coconut Greek yogurt
- 1 medium apple, chopped
- 2 Tbsp. maple syrup
- ¼ cup toasted unsweetened coconut flakes

1. Preheat oven to 400°. Place potatoes on a foil-lined baking sheet. Bake until tender, 45-60 minutes.
2. With a sharp knife, cut an "X" in each potato. Fluff pulp with a fork. Top with remaining ingredients.

1 stuffed sweet potato: 321 cal., 3g fat (2g sat. fat), 0 chol., 36mg sod., 70g carb. (35g sugars, 8g fiber), 7g pro.

TEST KITCHEN TIP

To microwave the potatoes, scrub and pierce with a fork; place on a microwave-safe plate. Microwave, uncovered, on high until tender, for 12-14 minutes, turning once. If you happen to have a sweet tooth, add some chocolate chips to the topping.

CHICKEN BRUNCH BAKE

Chunks of tender chicken add heartiness to an appealing brunch casserole. This was my son's favorite hot lunch during high school.
—DeLee Jochum, Dubuque, IA

Prep: 15 min. • **Bake:** 1 hour
Makes: 8 servings

- 9 slices day-old bread, cubed
- 3 cups chicken broth
- 4 cups cubed cooked chicken
- ½ cup uncooked instant rice
- ½ cup diced pimientos
- 2 Tbsp. minced fresh parsley
- ½ tsp. salt, optional
- 4 large eggs, beaten

1. In a large bowl, toss bread cubes and broth. Add the chicken, rice, pimientos, parsley and, if desired, salt; mix well. Transfer to a greased 13x9-in. baking dish. Pour eggs over all.

2. Bake, uncovered, at 325° until a knife inserted in the center comes out clean, about 1 hour.

1 serving: 233 cal., 6g fat (2g sat. fat), 62mg chol., 458mg sod., 18g carb. (2g sugars, 3g fiber), 27g pro.
Diabetic exchanges: 3 lean meat, 1 starch.

BLT QUINOA BOWLS

BLT QUINOA BOWLS

I absolutely love a BLT with sliced avocado and an egg. Recently, I've been trying out grain bowls, and I thought the flavors of my favorite sandwich would work really well. My family agreed: I was right!
—Elisabeth Larsen, Pleasant Grove, UT

Prep: 15 min. • **Cook:** 20 min.
Makes: 4 servings

- 1 cup quinoa, rinsed
- ¼ cup olive oil, divided
- 2 Tbsp. minced fresh basil
- 2 Tbsp. white wine vinegar, divided
- 1 Tbsp. lemon juice
- 4 large eggs
- 8 oz. cherry tomatoes
- 3 cups fresh arugula
- 1 small ripe avocado, peeled and sliced
- 4 bacon strips, cooked and crumbled

1. Prepare quinoa according to package directions. Combine 3 Tbsp. olive oil, basil, 1 Tbsp. vinegar and lemon juice. Add to cooked quinoa; stir to combine.

2. Place 2-3 in. of water in a large skillet with high sides; add remaining vinegar. Bring to a boil; adjust heat to maintain a gentle simmer. Break cold eggs, one at a time, into a small cup; holding cup close to surface of water, slip egg into water. Cook, uncovered, until whites are completely set and yolks begin to thicken but are not hard, 3-5 minutes. Using a slotted spoon, lift eggs out of water. Keep warm.

3. In a large skillet, heat remaining oil over medium heat. Cook tomatoes until they begin to release their juices, 8-10 minutes. Add the arugula; cook and stir just until arugula is wilted, 1-2 minutes.

4. To serve, divide quinoa evenly among four bowls. Add cherry tomatoes, arugula, avocado slices and crumbled bacon. Top each with a poached egg.

Note: Look for quinoa in the cereal, rice or organic food aisle.

1 serving: 446 cal., 28g fat (5g sat. fat), 194mg chol., 228mg sod., 33g carb. (2g sugars, 6g fiber), 17g pro.

✱
TEST KITCHEN TIP
Roasting the grape tomatoes really brings out the rich, tomato-y flavor. You get homegrown taste any time of year.

MAKEOVER BISCUITS & GRAVY

We lightened up biscuits and gravy to curb our guilt for eating them the day after having pancakes. Here's a terrific homemade recipe for brunch guests.
—Ellie Martin Cliffe, Milwaukee, WI

Prep: 25 min. • **Cook:** 20 min.
Makes: 6 servings

- 1⅓ cups all-purpose flour
- ⅔ cup whole wheat flour
- 2 tsp. baking powder
- ½ tsp. baking soda
- ¼ tsp. salt
- 3 Tbsp. cold butter
- 1 cup buttermilk

GRAVY
- 1 tsp. olive oil
- ½ lb. bulk chicken sausage
- 1 medium onion, finely chopped
- 1 garlic clove, minced
- 1 tsp. minced fresh thyme
- ⅛ to ¼ tsp. crushed red pepper flakes
- ⅛ tsp. pepper
- 2 cups reduced-sodium chicken broth
- 2 Tbsp. all-purpose flour
- ½ cup 2% milk

1. Preheat oven to 425°. In a large bowl, whisk flours, baking powder, baking soda and salt. Cut in butter until crumbly. Add buttermilk; stir just until moistened.

2. Turn onto a lightly floured surface; knead gently 8-10 times. Pat dough into a 7x5-in. rectangle (about 1 in. thick); cut into six pieces. Place biscuits 2 in. apart on a parchment-lined baking sheet. Bake until golden brown, 8-12 minutes.

3. Meanwhile, in a large skillet, heat oil over medium heat. Add the sausage and onion; cook 4-6 minutes or until sausage is no longer pink and the onion is tender, breaking up sausage into crumbles. Add garlic, thyme, pepper flakes and pepper; cook 30 seconds longer.

4. Add broth to pan. In a small bowl, mix the flour and milk until smooth; stir into sausage mixture. Return to a boil, stirring constantly; cook and stir until thickened, 10-12 minutes.

5. Split biscuits in half; serve warm with gravy.

1 biscuit with ⅓ cup gravy: 308 cal., 10g fat (5g sat. fat), 48mg chol., 854mg sod., 40g carb. (6g sugars, 3g fiber), 15g pro.
Diabetic exchanges: 2½ starch, 1½ fat, 1 lean meat.

MAKEOVER BISCUITS & GRAVY

PECAN WHEAT WAFFLES

2 Tbsp. canola oil
⅓ cup chopped pecans

1. Whisk together first five ingredients. In another bowl, whisk together the egg, egg white, milk and oil; add to the flour mixture, stirring just until moistened. Fold in pecans.
2. Bake in a preheated waffle iron according to manufacturer's directions until golden brown.

1 waffle: 227 cal., 10g fat (1g sat. fat), 32mg chol., 444mg sod., 28g carb. (6g sugars, 2g fiber), 7g pro.
Diabetic exchanges: 2 starch, 2 fat.

DENVER OMELET SALAD

I love this recipe—it's not your typical breakfast but it has all the right elements: easy, healthy and fast! You can make this deconstructed omelet with whatever you have on hand and turn it into a salad.
—Pauline Custer, Duluth, MN

Takes: 25 min. • **Makes:** 4 servings

8 cups fresh baby spinach
1 cup chopped tomatoes
2 Tbsp. olive oil, divided
1½ cups chopped fully cooked ham
1 small onion, chopped
1 small green pepper, chopped
4 large eggs
Salt and pepper to taste

1. Arrange spinach and tomatoes on a platter; set aside. In a large skillet over medium-high heat, heat 1 Tbsp. olive oil. Add ham, onion and green pepper; saute until ham is heated through and vegetables are tender, for 5-7 minutes. Spoon over spinach and tomatoes.
2. In same skillet, heat remaining olive oil over medium heat. Break eggs, one at a time, into a small cup, then gently slide into skillet. Immediately reduce heat to low; season with salt and pepper. To prepare sunny-side up eggs, cover pan; cook until whites are completely set and yolks thicken but are not hard. Top salad with fried eggs.

1 serving: 229 cal., 14g fat (3g sat. fat), 217mg chol., 756mg sod., 7g carb. (3g sugars, 2g fiber), 20g pro.
Diabetic exchanges: 3 lean meat, 2 fat, 1 vegetable.

HOMEMADE YOGURT

Once you try homemade, you won't want to go back to store-bought yogurt.
—*Taste of Home* Test Kitchen

Prep: 5 min. + chilling
Cook: 20 min. + standing
Makes: about 2 qt.

2 qt. pasteurized whole milk
2 Tbsp. plain yogurt with live active cultures

1. In a Dutch oven, heat the milk over medium heat until a thermometer reads 200°, stirring occasionally to prevent scorching. Remove from heat; let stand until a thermometer reads 112°-115°, stirring occasionally. (If desired, place pan in an ice-water bath for faster cooling.)
2. In a small bowl, whisk 1 cup warm milk into yogurt until smooth; return all to pan, stirring gently. Transfer mixture to warm, clean jars, such as 1-qt. canning jars.
3. Cover jars; place in oven. Turn on oven light to keep mixture warm, about 110°. Let stand, undisturbed, until yogurt is set, 6 to 24 hours, tilting jars gently to check. (Yogurt will become thicker and more tangy as it stands.)
4. Refrigerate, covered, until cold. Store in refrigerator up to 2 weeks.

1 cup: 151 cal., 8g fat (5g sat. fat), 25mg chol., 107mg sod., 12g carb. (12g sugars, 0 fiber), 8g pro.
Diabetic exchanges: 1 whole milk.

PECAN WHEAT WAFFLES

Your bunch will say a big "yes" to breakfast when these wonderful waffles are on the menu.
—Susan Bell, Spruce Pine, NC

Takes: 30 min. • **Makes:** 6 servings

1¼ cups all-purpose flour
¼ cup wheat bran
1 Tbsp. sugar
2½ tsp. baking powder
½ tsp. salt
1 large egg
1 large egg white
1½ cups fat-free milk

DENVER OMELET SALAD

OVERNIGHT CHERRY-ALMOND OATMEAL

OVERNIGHT CHERRY-ALMOND OATMEAL

Would you like breakfast ready for you when the sun comes up? If so, try my hot cereal. It's so simple...just place the ingredients in the slow cooker and turn it on before you go to bed. In the morning, enjoy a healthy, warm and satisfying dish.
—Geraldine Saucier, Albuquerque, NM

Prep: 10 min. • **Cook:** 7 hours
Makes: 6 servings

- 4 cups vanilla almond milk
- 1 cup steel-cut oats
- 1 cup dried cherries
- ⅓ cup packed brown sugar
- ½ tsp. salt
- ½ tsp. ground cinnamon
  Additional almond milk, optional

1. In a 3-qt. slow cooker coated with cooking spray, combine all ingredients.

Cook, covered, on low until the oats are tender, 7-8 hours.
2. Stir before serving. If desired, serve with additional milk.
Note: Steel-cut oats are also known as Scotch oats or Irish oatmeal.
¾ cup: 276 cal., 4g fat (0 sat. fat), 0 chol., 306mg sod., 57g carb. (35g sugars, 4g fiber), 5g pro.
* HEALTH TIP * Nutritionally, steel-cut oats are about the same as rolled oats, so take your pick. Skip instant oatmeal mixes, which have a lot of added sugar.

WARM & FRUITY BREAKFAST CEREAL

Sleepyheads will love the heartiness of this nutritious cooked cereal with cinnamon. It's loaded with chopped fruit and nuts. Eat it with plain yogurt and sliced bananas or blueberries.
—John Vale, Long Beach, WA

Prep: 10 min. • **Cook:** 6 hours
Makes: 10 servings

- 2 cups seven-grain hot cereal
- 1 medium apple, peeled and chopped
- ¼ cup dried apricots, chopped
- ¼ cup dried cranberries
- ¼ cup chopped dates
- ¼ cup raisins
- 1 tsp. ground cinnamon
- ½ tsp. salt
- 5 cups water
- 1 cup unsweetened apple juice
- ¼ cup maple syrup
  Chopped walnuts, optional

1. Place first eight ingredients in a 4- or 5-qt. slow cooker coated with cooking spray. Stir in the water, juice and syrup. Cook, covered, on low until thickened and cereal is tender, 6-7 hours. If desired, top with walnuts.
Note: This recipe was tested with Bob's Red Mill 7-Grain Hot Cereal.
1 cup: 185 cal., 3g fat (0 sat. fat), 0 chol., 120mg sod., 37g carb. (18g sugars, 5g fiber), 5g pro.
Diabetic exchanges: 1 starch, 1 fruit, ½ fat.

MIXED BERRY FRENCH TOAST BAKE

I love this recipe. It's perfect for carefree holiday breakfasts or company because it's scrumptious and easy to put together the night before.
—Amy Berry, Poland, ME

....

Prep: 20 min. + chilling • **Bake:** 45 min.
Makes: 8 servings

- 6 large eggs
- 1¾ cups fat-free milk
- 1 tsp. sugar
- 1 tsp. ground cinnamon
- 1 tsp. vanilla extract
- ¼ tsp. salt
- 1 loaf (1 lb.) French bread, cubed
- 1 pkg. (12 oz.) frozen unsweetened mixed berries
- 2 Tbsp. cold butter
- ⅓ cup packed brown sugar

1. Whisk together first six ingredients. Place bread cubes in a 13x9-in. or 3-qt. baking dish coated with cooking spray. Pour egg mixture over top. Refrigerate, covered, 8 hours or overnight.
2. Preheat oven to 350°. Remove berries from the freezer and French toast from refrigerator and let stand while oven heats. Bake, covered, 30 minutes.
3. In a small bowl, cut butter into brown sugar until crumbly. Top the French toast with berries; sprinkle with brown sugar mixture. Bake, uncovered, until a knife inserted in the center comes out clean, 15-20 minutes.

1 serving: 310 cal., 8g fat (3g sat. fat), 148mg chol., 517mg sod., 46g carb. (17g sugars, 3g fiber), 13g pro.

OVERNIGHT OATMEAL
(PICTURED ON P. 7)

Start this breakfast the night before so you can plan on a few extra zzzs in the morning. My husband adds coconut to his, and I stir in dried fruit.
—June Thomas, Chesterton, IN

....

Prep: 10 min. + chilling • **Makes:** 1 serving

- ⅓ cup old-fashioned oats
- 3 Tbsp. fat-free milk
- 3 Tbsp. reduced-fat plain yogurt
- 1 Tbsp. honey
- ½ cup assorted fresh fruit
- 2 Tbsp. chopped walnuts, toasted

In a small container or mason jar, combine oats, milk, yogurt and honey. Top with fruit and nuts. Seal; refrigerate overnight.
Note: To toast nuts, bake in a shallow pan in a 350° oven for 5-10 minutes or cook them in a skillet over low heat until lightly browned, stirring occasionally.

1 serving: 345 cal., 13g fat (2g sat. fat), 4mg chol., 53mg sod., 53g carb. (31g sugars, 5g fiber), 10g pro.

Chocolate-Cherry Oats: Use cherry-flavored yogurt; add 1 Tbsp. cocoa powder, and top with fresh or frozen pitted cherries.

Banana Bread Oats: Replace honey with maple syrup and stir in ½ mashed banana and ½ tsp. cinnamon. Top with toasted pecans.

Carrot Cake Oats: Add 2 Tbsp. grated carrots and substitute spreadable cream cheese for the yogurt.

Pina Colada Oats: Add ½ of a mashed banana, 2 Tbsp. crushed pineapple and 1 Tbsp. shredded coconut to oat mixture.

✳

TEST KITCHEN TIP
Make this dairy-free by using 1/2 cup soy or coconut milk instead of the milk and yogurt.

MIXED BERRY FRENCH TOAST BAKE

AVOCADO FRUIT SALAD

(PICTURED ON P. 7)

This dish is simply delish. I'm glad a friend gave me the recipe. My family loves it and so do I.
—Mildred Sherrer, Fort Worth, TX

Takes: 20 min. • **Makes:** 6 servings

- ½ cup plain yogurt
- 2 Tbsp. honey
- 1 tsp. grated lemon zest
- 1 tsp. plus 2 Tbsp. lemon juice, divided
- 3 medium ripe avocados, peeled and cubed
- 1 medium apple, chopped
- 1 cup halved seedless grapes
- 1 can (11 oz.) mandarin oranges, drained
- 1 medium firm banana, cut into ¼-in. slices

1. For dressing, mix yogurt, honey, lemon zest and 1 tsp. lemon juice. Toss avocados with remaining lemon juice.
2. In a large bowl, combine the remaining ingredients; gently stir in avocados. Serve with dressing.

¾ cup: 231 cal., 11g fat (2g sat. fat), 3mg chol., 22mg sod., 35g carb. (25g sugars, 6g fiber), 3g pro.

SHAKSHUKA

PUMPKIN-FLAVORED PANCAKES

I created these light, pumpkin-flavored pancakes with two kinds of flour and a blend of spices for a delightful taste. Serve them for brunch as a hearty eye-opener.
—Vicki Floden, Story City, IA

Takes: 20 min. • **Makes:** 6 servings

- 1½ cups all-purpose flour
- ½ cup whole wheat flour
- 2 Tbsp. brown sugar
- 2 tsp. baking powder
- 1 tsp. ground cinnamon
- ½ tsp. salt
- ½ tsp. ground ginger
- ½ tsp. ground nutmeg
- 2 cups fat-free milk
- ½ cup canned pumpkin
- 1 large egg white, lightly beaten
- 2 Tbsp. canola oil

1. In a large bowl, combine the first eight ingredients. In a small bowl, combine the milk, pumpkin, egg white and oil; stir into dry ingredients just until moistened.
2. Pour batter by ¼ cupfuls onto a hot griddle coated with cooking spray; turn when bubbles form on top. Cook until second side is golden brown.

2 pancakes: 240 cal., 5g fat (1g sat. fat), 1mg chol., 375mg sod., 41g carb. (9g sugars, 3g fiber), 8g pro.
Diabetic exchanges: 2½ starch, 1 fat.

SHAKSHUKA

Shakshuka is a dish of poached eggs with tomatoes, peppers and cumin. I learned it while traveling through Asia, and it's been my favorite way to eat eggs ever since.
—Ezra Weeks, Calgary, AB

Takes: 30 min. • **Makes:** 4 servings

- 2 Tbsp. olive oil
- 1 medium onion, chopped
- 1 garlic clove, minced
- 1 tsp. ground cumin
- 1 tsp. pepper
- ½ to 1 tsp. chili powder
- ½ tsp. salt
- 1 tsp. Sriracha Asian hot chili sauce or hot pepper sauce, optional
- 2 medium tomatoes, chopped
- 4 large eggs
  Chopped fresh cilantro
  Whole pita breads, toasted

1. In a large skillet, heat oil over medium heat. Add onion; cook and stir 4-6 minutes or until tender. Add garlic, seasonings and, if desired, hot chili sauce; cook 30 seconds longer. Add the tomatoes; cook mixture until thickened, 3-5 minutes, stirring the mixture occasionally.
2. With back of spoon, make four wells in vegetable mixture; break an egg into each well. Cook, covered, until egg whites are completely set and yolks begin to thicken but are not hard, 4-6 minutes. Sprinkle with cilantro; serve with pita bread.

1 serving: 159 cal., 12g fat (3g sat. fat), 186mg chol., 381mg sod., 6g carb. (3g sugars, 2g fiber), 7g pro.
Diabetic exchanges: 1½ fat, 1 medium-fat meat, 1 vegetable.

BAKED BLUEBERRY GINGER PANCAKE

My kids love pancakes, but they can be time consuming. So I came up with this baked version that's such a time-saver. My kids just gobble these ginger-kissed breakfast squares right up.
—Erin Wright, Wallace, KS

Takes: 30 min. • **Makes:** 9 servings

- 2 large eggs
- 1½ cups 2% milk
- ¼ cup butter, melted
- 2 cups all-purpose flour
- 2 Tbsp. sugar
- 3 tsp. baking powder
- 1½ tsp. ground ginger
- ½ tsp. salt
- 2 cups fresh or frozen unsweetened blueberries
   Maple syrup

1. Preheat oven to 350°. Combine the eggs, milk and butter. Whisk the next five ingredients; add to egg mixture. Spoon the batter into a 9-in. square baking pan coated with cooking spray. Sprinkle blueberries over top.

2. Bake until a toothpick inserted in center comes out clean, 20-25 minutes. Cut into squares; serve with warm maple syrup.

1 piece: 213 cal., 7g fat (4g sat. fat), 58mg chol., 368mg sod., 31g carb. (8g sugars, 2g fiber), 6g pro.
Diabetic exchanges: 2 starch, 1½ fat.

✱ TEST KITCHEN TIP

Blueberries make this pancake simply wonderful, but raspberries, blackberries or chopped strawberries would work well, too. Or try a mixture.

ITALIAN CLOUD EGGS

Drop egg yolks on nests of whipped egg whites with Italian seasoning, then bake in a cast-iron skillet. Dreamy!
—Matthew Hass, Ellison Bay, WI

Takes: 25 min. • **Makes:** 4 servings

- 4 large eggs, separated
- ¼ tsp. Italian seasoning
- ⅛ tsp. salt
- ⅛ tsp. pepper
- ¼ cup shredded Parmesan cheese
- 1 Tbsp. minced fresh basil
- 1 Tbsp. finely chopped oil-packed sun-dried tomatoes

1. Preheat oven to 450°. Separate eggs; place whites in a large bowl and yolks in 4 separate small bowls. Beat egg whites, Italian seasoning, salt and pepper until stiff peaks form.

2. In a 9-in. cast-iron skillet generously coated with cooking spray, drop egg white mixture into four mounds. With the back of a spoon, create a small well in the center of each mound. Sprinkle with cheese. Bake until light brown, about 5 minutes. Gently slip an egg yolk into each of the mounds. Bake until yolks are set, 3-5 minutes longer. Sprinkle with basil and tomatoes. Serve immediately.

1 serving: 96 cal., 6g fat (2g sat. fat), 190mg chol., 234mg sod., 1g carb. (0 sugars, 0 fiber), 8g pro.
Diabetic exchanges: 1 medium-fat meat.

BAKED BLUEBERRY GINGER PANCAKE

ITALIAN CLOUD EGGS

STARTERS & SNACKS

"The flavors of mustard and curry blend deliciously in this colorful, appetizing dip. Use your imagination for the raw veggies you serve with it."
—Louise Weyer, Marietta, GA

Four-Tomato Salsa (p. 43) **Pickled Pepperoncini Deviled Eggs** (p. 31) **Roasted Beetroot & Garlic Hummus** (p. 37)
Mini Zucchini Pizzas (p. 40) **Curry Carrot Dip** (p. 40) **Apricot-Apple Cider** (p. 35)

LIGHT ROASTED PUMPKIN SEEDS

LIGHT ROASTED PUMPKIN SEEDS

Try this zippy twist on an old Halloween tradition the next time you find yourself with an abundance of pumpkin seeds. It has just enough heat to take the chill off autumn afternoons and snackers.
—Taste of Home *Test Kitchen*

....

Prep: 10 min. • **Bake:** 45 min. + cooling
Makes: 2 cups

- 2 cups fresh pumpkin seeds
- 5 tsp. butter, melted
- 1 tsp. Worcestershire sauce
- 1 tsp. sugar
- ½ tsp. salt
- ¼ tsp. garlic powder
- ⅛ to ¼ tsp. cayenne pepper

1. Preheat oven to 250°. In a bowl, toss pumpkin seeds with melted butter and the Worcestershire sauce. Mix the remaining ingredients; toss with pumpkin seeds. Spread in a 15x10x1-in. pan coated with cooking spray.
2. Bake until seeds are lightly browned and dry, for 45-60 minutes, stirring occasionally. Cool completely before storing in an airtight container.

¼ cup: 96 cal., 6g fat (2g sat. fat), 6mg chol., 176mg sod., 9g carb. (1g sugars, 3g fiber), 3g pro.
Diabetic exchanges: 1 fat, ½ starch.

SWEET PEA PESTO CROSTINI

I made a healthier spin on my favorite celebrity chef's recipe by using broth instead of oil and less cheese. To top crostini, use less broth for a thick pesto. For use as a pasta sauce, add more broth to thin the consistency.
—Amber Massey, Argyle, TX

....

Takes: 25 min. • **Makes:** 20 pieces

- 12 oz. fresh or frozen peas, thawed
- 4 garlic cloves, halved
- 1 tsp. rice vinegar
- ½ tsp. salt
- ⅛ tsp. lemon-pepper seasoning
- 3 Tbsp. olive oil
- ¼ cup shredded Parmesan cheese
- ⅓ cup vegetable broth
- 1 whole wheat French bread demi-baguette (about 6 oz. and 12 in. long)
- 2 cups cherry tomatoes (about 10 oz.), halved or quartered

1. Preheat broiler. Place the peas, garlic, vinegar, salt and lemon pepper in a blender or food processor; pulse until well blended. Continue processing mixture while gradually adding oil in a steady stream. Add the cheese; pulse just until blended. Add broth; pulse until mixture reaches desired consistency.
2. Cut the baguette into 20 slices, each ½ in. thick. Place on ungreased baking sheet. Broil 4-5 in. from heat until golden brown, 45-60 seconds per side. Remove to wire rack to cool.
3. To assemble crostini, spread each slice with about 1 Tbsp. pesto mixture; top with tomato pieces.

1 crostini: 77 cal., 2g fat (trace sat. fat), 1mg chol., 190mg sod., 11g carb. (2g sugars, 1g fiber), 3g pro.
Diabetic exchanges: ½ starch, ½ fat.

REALLY GOOD SNACK MIX

I grew tired of my family picking through a snack mix for their favorite bits and leaving the rest. And so I experimented using only their favorites and came up with this recipe. Now they eat all of it, and there's never any left!
—Lori Genske, Waldo, WI

....

Prep: 10 min. • **Bake:** 45 min.
Makes: about 7 cups

- 3 Tbsp. butter, melted
- 4 tsp. Worcestershire sauce
- 1 Tbsp. canola oil
- 1 tsp. seasoned salt
- ½ tsp. garlic powder
- 2 cups Corn Chex
- 2 cups Crispix
- 2 cups bite-sized Shredded Wheat
- 1½ cups salted cashews

1. Preheat oven to 250°. Mix first five ingredients; toss with the cereals and cashews, coating the mixture evenly. Spread snack mix into a 15x10x1-in. pan coated with cooking spray.
2. Bake for 45 minutes, stirring every 15 minutes. Cool completely before storing in airtight containers.

½ cup: 180 cal., 11g fat (3g sat. fat), 7mg chol., 269mg sod., 18g carb. (2g sugars, 2g fiber), 4g pro.
Diabetic exchanges: 1 starch, 2 fat.

REALLY GOOD SNACK MIX

PICKLED PEPPERONCINI DEVILED EGGS

(PICTURED ON P. 28)

It's hard to resist these adorable deviled trees on our Christmas buffet table. The avocado filling has pepperoncini and cilantro to add a little extra zip.
—Carmell Childs, Clawson, UT

....

Takes: 30 min. • **Makes:** 1 dozen

- 6 hard-boiled large eggs
- 1 jar (16 oz.) garlic and dill pepperoncini
- 1 medium ripe avocado, peeled and pitted
- 1 Tbsp. minced fresh cilantro, divided
- ¼ tsp. salt
- ⅛ tsp. pepper
- 1 Tbsp. minced sweet red pepper
- ¼ tsp. chili powder

1. Cut eggs lengthwise in half. Remove yolks, reserving whites. Mash the yolks. Stir in 1 tsp. of minced garlic from the pepperoncini jar and 2 tsp. pepperoncini juice. Add 3 Tbsp. minced pepperoncini and the whole avocado; mash with a fork until smooth. Stir in 2 tsp. cilantro, salt and pepper.
2. Cut a small hole in the tip of a pastry bag or in a corner of a food-safe plastic bag; insert a medium star tip. Transfer avocado mixture to bag. Pipe into egg whites, swirling it upward to resemble Christmas trees. Sprinkle the swirls with minced red pepper, chili powder and the remaining cilantro.
3. Cut open one larger pepperoncini; seed and slice into 12 small diamond shapes and top the Christmas trees. Refrigerate, covered, until serving. Save remaining pepperoncini for another use.

1 egg half: 59 cal., 4g fat (1g sat. fat), 93mg chol., 125mg sod., 1g carb. (0 sugars, 1g fiber), 3g pro.

TEST KITCHEN TIP

Can't find garlic and dill pepperoncini? Use regular pepperoncini, or add a clove of garlic to a jar of pepperoncini a few days ahead of time.

SMOKED SALMON NEW POTATOES

PINEAPPLE ICED TEA

We have a large family so we go through beverages quickly at our house. This thirst-quenching tea is simple to mix up and has a sparkling pineapple and citrus flavor we all enjoy.
—K. Kittell, Lenexa, KS

Prep: 10 min. + chilling • **Cook:** 5 min.
Makes: 6 servings

- 4 cups water
- 7 individual tea bags
- 2 Tbsp. sugar
- 1 cup unsweetened pineapple juice
- ⅓ cup lemon juice
  Optional garnishes: pineapple wedges, lemon slices and fresh mint leaves

1. In a large saucepan, bring water to a boil; remove from heat. Add tea bags; steep, covered, 3-5 minutes according to taste. Discard tea bags. Stir in sugar until dissolved. Transfer tea to a pitcher; cool slightly. Stir in fruit juices.
2. Refrigerate, covered, overnight. Serve over ice. Garnish as desired.
¾ cup: 43 cal., 0 fat (0 sat. fat), 0 chol., 6mg sod., 11g carb. (9g sugars, 0 fiber), 0 pro.
Diabetic exchanges: ½ starch.

TEST KITCHEN TIP

Go for freshly squeezed lemon juice when preparing this summery sipper. Bottled lemon juice, which is from concentrate, won't provide the same bright, fresh flavor. Buy two lemons to get the job done.

SMOKED SALMON NEW POTATOES

Give twice-baked potatoes a rest this year and try these stuffed spuds. Simply pipe smoked salmon and cream cheese blended with lemon juice and dill into small red potatoes. If you have any leftovers, serve with eggs for breakfast.
—*Taste of Home* Test Kitchen

Prep: 30 min. • **Cook:** 20 min.
Makes: 3 dozen

- 36 baby red potatoes (1½ in. wide, about 1½ lbs.)
- 1 pkg. (8 oz.) reduced-fat cream cheese, cubed
- 2 pkg. (3 oz. each) smoked salmon or lox
- 2 Tbsp. chopped green onion
- 2 Tbsp. snipped fresh dill or 2 tsp. dill weed
- 2 tsp. lemon juice
- ⅛ tsp. salt
- ⅛ tsp. pepper
  Fresh dill sprigs

1. Place potatoes in a large saucepan; add water to cover. Bring to a boil. Reduce heat; cook, covered, until tender, 15-20 minutes. Drain potatoes; immediately drop in ice water. Drain; pat dry.
2. Cut a thin slice off the bottom of each potato to allow them to lie flat. Using a melon baller, remove a small portion from the top of each potato.
3. For the filling, place all the remaining ingredients except dill sprigs in a food processor; process until smooth. To serve, pipe or spoon about 2 tsp. filling into each potato. Top with dill sprigs.
1 potato: 35 cal., 2g fat (1g sat. fat), 6mg chol., 67mg sod., 4g carb. (0 sugars, 0 fiber), 2g pro.

ASIAN WRAPS

This recipe is just like any other Asian wrap, but with more delicious and healthy flavor. Instead of ordering carryout Chinese, you'll be making these yourself!
—Melissa Hansen, Ellison Bay, WI

Prep: 30 min. • **Cook:** 3½ hours
Makes: 1 dozen

- 2 lbs. boneless skinless chicken breast halves
- ¼ cup reduced-sodium soy sauce
- ¼ cup ketchup
- ¼ cup honey
- 2 Tbsp. minced fresh gingerroot
- 2 Tbsp. sesame oil
- 1 small onion, finely chopped
- 2 Tbsp. cornstarch
- 2 Tbsp. cold water
- 12 round rice papers (8 in.)
- 3 cups broccoli coleslaw mix
- ¾ cup crispy chow mein noodles

1. Place chicken in a 3-qt. slow cooker. In a small bowl, whisk soy sauce, ketchup, honey, ginger and oil; stir in onion. Pour over chicken. Cook, covered, on low until the chicken is tender, 3-4 hours. Remove chicken; shred with two forks. Refrigerate until assembly.
2. In a small bowl, mix cornstarch and water until smooth; gradually stir into honey mixture. Cook, covered, on high until sauce is thickened, 20-30 minutes. Toss chicken with ¾ cup sauce; reserve remaining sauce for serving.
3. Fill a large shallow dish partway with water. Dip a rice paper wrapper into the water just until pliable, about 45 seconds (do not soften completely); allow excess water to drip off.
4. Place wrapper on a flat surface. Layer ¼ cup coleslaw, ⅓ cup chicken mixture and 1 Tbsp. noodles across bottom third of the wrapper. Fold in both sides of wrapper; fold bottom over filling, then roll up tightly. Place on a serving plate, seam side down. Repeat with remaining ingredients. Serve with reserved sauce.
1 wrap: 195 cal., 5g fat (1g sat. fat), 42mg chol., 337mg sod., 21g carb. (8g sugars, 1g fiber), 17g pro.
Diabetic exchanges: 2 lean meat, 1½ starch, ½ fat.

SLOW-COOKER CHAI TEA

A wonderful sweet and spicy aroma wafts from the slow cooker as this pleasant chai tea cooks.
—Crystal Jo Bruns, Iliff, CO

Prep: 20 min. • **Cook:** 8 hours
Makes: 12 servings (3 qt.)

- 15 slices fresh gingerroot (about 3 oz.)
- 3 cinnamon sticks (3 in.)
- 25 whole cloves
- 15 cardamom pods, lightly crushed
- 3 whole peppercorns
- 3½ qt. water
- 8 black tea bags
- 1 can (14 oz.) sweetened condensed milk

1. Place the first five ingredients on a double thickness of cheesecloth. Gather corners of cloth to enclose seasonings; tie securely with string. Place spice bag and water in a 5- or 6-qt. slow cooker. Cook the spice bag, covered, on low 8 hours. Discard spice bag.
2. Add the tea bags; steep, covered, for 3-5 minutes according to taste. Discard tea bags. Stir in milk and heat through. Serve warm.
1 cup: 109 cal., 3g fat (2g sat. fat), 11mg chol., 50mg sod., 19g carb. (18g sugars, 0 fiber), 3g pro.

★ ★ ★ ★ ★ **READER REVIEW**

"Absolutely wonderful! I like it a little sweeter, so I put in more condensed milk. But the combination of spices was perfect."
BNCOX TASTEOFHOME.COM

ASIAN WRAPS

NUTTY APPLE BUTTER

APRICOT-APPLE CIDER
(PICTURED ON P. 29)

Dried apricots give this cider a delicious twist. Add cranberries, cinnamon, allspice and cloves, and you've got the perfect hot drink to sip on chilly nights.
—Ginnie Busam, Pewee Valley, KY

Prep: 20 min. • **Cook:** 3 hours
Makes: 13 servings (2½ qt.)

- 8 cups unsweetened apple juice
- 1 can (12 oz.) ginger ale
- ½ cup dried apricots, halved
- ½ cup dried cranberries
- 2 cinnamon sticks (3 in.)
- 1 Tbsp. whole allspice
- 1 Tbsp. whole cloves

1. In a 5-qt. slow cooker, combine apple juice and ginger ale. Place the apricots, cranberries, cinnamon sticks, allspice and cloves on a double layer of cheesecloth;

bring up corners of cloth and tie with string to form a bag. Place bag in the slow cooker; cover.
2. Cook on high until heated through, 3-4 hours. Discard spice bag.
¾ cup: 79 cal., 0 fat (0 sat. fat), 0 chol., 8mg sod., 20g carb. (17g sugars, 0 fiber), 0 pro.

NUTTY APPLE BUTTER

As a New England native, I love apple-picking season. Grab some apples and peanut butter to make your own spicy riff on a PB&J. Of course it's great on a sandwich, but you can dunk sliced fruit or graham crackers in it, too.
—Brandie Cranshaw, Rapid City, SD

Prep: 20 min. • **Cook:** 8 hours
Makes: 5 cups

- 4 lbs. apples (about 8 large), peeled and chopped
- ¾ to 1 cup sugar

- ¼ cup water
- 3 tsp. ground cinnamon
- ¼ tsp. ground nutmeg
- ¼ tsp. ground cloves
- ¼ tsp. ground allspice
- ¼ cup creamy peanut butter

1. In a greased 5-qt. slow cooker, combine the first seven ingredients. Cook the mixture, covered, on low until the apples are tender, 8-10 hours.
2. Whisk in peanut butter until the apple mixture is smooth. Cool the apple butter to room temperature. Store in an airtight container in the refrigerator.
2 Tbsp.: 43 cal., 1g fat (0 sat. fat), 0 chol., 7mg sod., 9g carb. (8g sugars, 1g fiber), 0 pro.
Diabetic exchanges: ½ starch.
* HEALTH TIP * Looking to lift your spirits? Including cinnamon in your diet can help increase attention and enhance cognitive processing, which are both mood lifters.

GREEK VEGGIE TARTLETS

GREEK VEGGIE TARTLETS

This recipe started out as a salad that I re-created after a trip to Greece. But when my husband suggested I serve the mixture in phyllo cups, it became my most-requested appetizer!
—Radelle Knappenberger, Oviedo, FL

Takes: 25 min. • **Makes:** 45 tartlets

- 3 pkg. (1.9 oz. each) frozen miniature phyllo tart shells
- ¾ cup finely chopped seeded peeled cucumber
- ¾ cup finely chopped red onion
- ¾ cup finely chopped seeded plum tomatoes
- ¾ cup finely chopped pitted Greek olives
- ½ cup Greek vinaigrette
- ¾ cup crumbled feta cheese

1. Preheat oven to 350°. Place shells on two 15x10x1-in. pans. Bake until lightly browned, 7-10 minutes. Cool completely.
2. Toss the vegetables and olives with vinaigrette. To serve, spoon about 1 Tbsp. mixture into each tart shell. Sprinkle with feta cheese.

1 tartlet: 43 cal., 3g fat (0 sat. fat), 1mg chol., 93mg sod., 3g carb. (0 sugars, 0 fiber), 1g pro.

ROASTED BEETROOT & GARLIC HUMMUS

(PICTURED ON P. 29)

This beetroot hummus is so tasty and healthy, and what's more, it's the prettiest pink snack I've ever seen. Nothing looks or tastes like it on any buffet table. But I like to make batches of it to keep in the fridge for super lunches and snacks throughout the week.
—Elizabeth Worndl, Toronto, ON

Prep: 25 min. • **Bake:** 45 min.
Makes: 4 cups

- 3 fresh medium beets (about 1 lb.)
- 1 whole garlic bulb
- ½ tsp. salt, divided
- ½ tsp. coarsely ground pepper, divided
- 1 tsp. extra virgin olive oil plus ¼ cup olive oil, divided
- 1 can (15 oz.) garbanzo beans or chickpeas, rinsed and drained
- 3 to 4 Tbsp. lemon juice

SPICY MIXED NUTS

- 2 Tbsp. tahini
- ½ tsp. ground cumin
- ½ tsp. cayenne pepper
- ¼ cup plain Greek yogurt, optional
  Minced fresh dill weed or parsley
  Assorted fresh vegetables
  Sliced or torn pita bread

1. Preheat oven to 375°. Pierce beets with a fork; place in a microwave-safe bowl and cover loosely with plastic. Microwave the beets on high for 4 minutes, stirring halfway. Cool beets slightly. Wrap beets in individual foil packets.
2. Remove papery outer skin from garlic bulb, but do not peel or separate cloves. Cut in half crosswise. Sprinkle halves with ¼ tsp. salt and ¼ tsp. pepper; drizzle with 1 tsp. oil. Wrap in individual foil packets. Roast beets and garlic until cloves are soft, about 45 minutes.
3. Remove from oven; unwrap. Rinse beets with cold water; peel when cool enough to handle. Squeeze garlic from skins. Place beets and garlic in food processor. Add garbanzo beans, lemon juice, tahini, cumin, cayenne pepper and the remaining olive oil, salt and pepper. Process until smooth.
4. If desired, pulse 2 Tbsp. Greek yogurt with beet mixture, dolloping remaining yogurt over finished hummus. Sprinkle with dill or parsley. Serve with assorted vegetables and pita bread.

¼ cup: 87 cal., 5g fat (1g sat. fat), 0 chol., 131mg sod., 8g carb. (3g sugars, 2g fiber), 2g pro.
Diabetic exchanges: ½ starch, 1 fat.

SPICY MIXED NUTS

Cumin and chili powder give some extra oomph to the classic homemade nut mix. It's perfect for both holiday snacking and gift giving.
—Delores Hill, Helena, MT

Prep: 5 min. • **Cook:** 10 min. + cooling
Makes: 3 cups

- 3 Tbsp. butter
- 1 can (15 to 16 oz.) mixed nuts
- ¼ tsp. Worcestershire sauce
- ½ tsp. salt
- ¼ tsp. paprika
- ¼ tsp. cayenne pepper
- ¼ tsp. chili powder
- ⅛ tsp. ground cumin

In a large skillet, melt butter over low heat. Add nuts and Worcestershire sauce; cook and stir 5-7 minutes. Drain on paper towels. Place the nuts in a large bowl. Combine remaining ingredients; sprinkle over nuts, tossing to coat. Cool. Store in an airtight container at room temperature.

¼ cup: 225 cal., 19g fat (2g sat. fat), 0 chol., 232mg sod., 10g carb. (2g sugars, 3g fiber), 7g pro.

CREAMY THAI CHICKEN DIP

CAPRESE SALAD KABOBS

Trade in your usual veggie party platter for these fun kabobs. I often make them as snacks for my family, and the kids love helping make them.
—Christine Mitchell, Glendora, CA

Takes: 10 min. • **Makes:** 12 kabobs

- 24 grape tomatoes
- 12 cherry-size fresh mozzarella cheese balls
- 24 fresh basil leaves
- 2 Tbsp. olive oil
- 2 tsp. balsamic vinegar

On each of 12 appetizer skewers, alternately thread two tomatoes, one cheese ball and two basil leaves. Whisk oil and vinegar; drizzle over kabobs.

1 kabob: 44 cal., 4g fat (1g sat. fat), 5mg chol., 10mg sod., 2g carb. (1g sugars, 0 fiber), 1g pro.
Diabetic exchanges: 1 fat.

CREAMY THAI CHICKEN DIP

Guests are sure to be quick to dig into this delectable dip. With tender chunks of chicken and Asian seasoning plus a little peanut and carrot crunch, it's a nice switch from traditional taco dip.
—Bonnie Mazur, Reedsburg, WI

Prep: 20 min. + chilling
Makes: 20 servings

- 1 cup chopped cooked chicken breast
- ½ cup shredded carrot
- ¼ cup chopped unsalted peanuts
- 3 Tbsp. chopped green onions
- 1 Tbsp. minced fresh parsley
- 1 tsp. toasted sesame seeds
- 3 Tbsp. reduced-sodium soy sauce, divided
- 1 garlic clove, minced
- 1½ tsp. cornstarch
- ½ cup water
- 2 Tbsp. brown sugar
- 2 Tbsp. ketchup
- 1½ tsp. Worcestershire sauce
- ½ tsp. cider vinegar
- 2 drops hot pepper sauce
- 1 pkg. (8 oz.) reduced-fat cream cheese
  Assorted rice crackers

1. In a bowl, combine the first six ingredients. Mix 2 Tbsp. soy sauce and garlic; toss with the chicken mixture. Refrigerate, covered, several hours.
2. For sauce, in a small saucepan, mix cornstarch and water until smooth; stir in brown sugar, ketchup, Worcestershire sauce, vinegar and pepper sauce. Bring to a boil; cook and stir until thickened, 1-2 minutes. Cool slightly. Refrigerate, covered, until cold.
3. To serve, mix the cream cheese and remaining soy sauce until blended; transfer to a serving plate, spreading evenly. Top with chicken mixture. Drizzle with sauce. Serve with crackers.

1 serving: 61 cal., 4g fat (2g sat. fat), 13mg chol., 165mg sod., 3g carb. (2g sugars, 0 fiber), 4g pro.
Diabetic exchanges: 1 fat.

ORANGE SHRIMP MOJO

A bright salsa and an irresistible orange-kissed glaze make every bite of this dish spicy, tangy and fresh.
—Don Thompson, Houston, OH

Prep: 25 min. • **Cook:** 45 min.
Makes: 8 servings

- 1 Tbsp. cumin seeds
- 1 Tbsp. whole peppercorns
- 1 Tbsp. grated orange or tangerine zest
- ½ tsp. dried oregano
- ½ tsp. salt
- 1 lb. uncooked jumbo shrimp, peeled and deveined
- 4 tsp. olive oil
- 3 cups orange juice
- 3 Tbsp. rum or chicken broth
- 1 garlic clove, minced
- 1 large navel orange, peeled, sectioned and chopped
- ½ cup chopped sweet onion
- 1 cup cubed avocado
- ½ cup minced fresh cilantro, divided
- 1 tsp. chopped seeded jalapeno pepper

1. In a small dry skillet over medium heat, toast cumin seeds and peppercorns until aromatic, 1-2 minutes. Remove from the skillet. Crush seeds using a spice grinder or mortar and pestle.

2. In a small bowl, combine the orange zest, oregano, salt and crushed spices. Sprinkle 1 Tbsp. of the spice mixture over the shrimp.

3. In a large skillet, cook shrimp in oil over medium-high heat 1 minute; turn shrimp. Add orange juice, rum, garlic and 1 Tbsp. spice mixture. Cook and stir until shrimp turn pink, 1-2 minutes longer; remove and keep warm.

4. Bring liquid in the skillet to a boil. Cook until reduced to ⅔ cup, about 35 minutes. Meanwhile, for the salsa, combine the orange, onion, avocado, ¼ cup cilantro, jalapeno and remaining spice mixture in a small bowl.

5. Stir shrimp and remaining cilantro into sauce; heat through. Serve with salsa.

Note: Wear disposable gloves when cutting hot peppers; the oils can burn skin. Avoid touching your face.

1 serving: 172 cal., 6g fat (1g sat. fat), 69mg chol., 218mg sod., 16g carb. (11g sugars, 2g fiber), 11g pro.
Diabetic exchanges: 1 starch, 1 lean meat, 1 fat.

ROASTED EGGPLANT SPREAD

Black pepper and garlic perk up this out-of-the-ordinary spread that hits the spot. Whether on a crisp cracker or slice of toasted bread, it's excellent!
—Barbara McCalley, Allison Park, PA

Prep: 20 min. • **Bake:** 45 min.
Makes: 2 cups

- 3 Tbsp. olive oil
- 3 garlic cloves, minced
- ½ tsp. salt
- ½ tsp. pepper
- 2 large sweet red peppers, cut into 1-in. pieces
- 1 medium eggplant, cut into 1-in. pieces
- 1 medium red onion, cut into 1-in. pieces
- 1 Tbsp. tomato paste
  Toasted baguette slices or assorted crackers

1. Preheat oven to 400°. Mix first four ingredients. Place vegetables in a large bowl; toss with oil mixture. Transfer to a 15x10x1-in. pan coated with cooking spray. Roast vegetables until softened and lightly browned, 45-50 minutes, stirring mixture once.

2. Transfer to a food processor; cool slightly. Add tomato paste; pulse just until blended (mixture should be chunky).

3. Transfer to a bowl; cool completely. Serve with toasted baguette.

¼ cup: 84 cal., 5g fat (1g sat. fat), 0 chol., 153mg sod., 9g carb. (5g sugars, 3g fiber), 1g pro.
Diabetic exchanges: 1 vegetable, 1 fat.

ORANGE SHRIMP MOJO

MINI SAUSAGE BUNDLES

MINI SAUSAGE BUNDLES

These savory hors d'oeuvres are baked, cutting the fat as well as the cleanup by eliminating the need for a deep fryer. You don't need chive ties, but they're cute.
—*Taste of Home* Test Kitchen

Prep: 25 min. **Bake:** 10 min.
Makes: 1 dozen

- ½ lb. turkey Italian sausage links, casings removed
- 1 small onion, finely chopped
- ¼ cup finely chopped sweet red pepper
- 1 garlic clove, minced
- ½ cup shredded cheddar cheese
- 12 sheets phyllo dough (14x9-in. size)
  Cooking spray
- 12 whole chives, optional

1. Preheat oven to 425°. In a large skillet, cook and crumble sausage with onion, red pepper and garlic over medium-high heat until no longer pink, 4-6 minutes. Stir in cheese; cool slightly.
2. Place one sheet of phyllo dough on a work surface; spritz with cooking spray. Layer with two additional phyllo sheets, spritzing each layer. (Keep the remaining phyllo sheets covered with a damp towel to prevent it from drying out.) Cut the dough crosswise into three strips (about 4½-in. wide).
3. Place a rounded tablespoon of sausage mixture near the end of each strip. Fold end of strip over filling, then fold in sides and roll up. Place on an ungreased baking sheet, seam side down. Repeat with the remaining phyllo and filling.
4. Bake appetizers until lightly browned, 8-10 minutes. If desired, tie bundles with chives. Serve warm.
1 bundle: 74 cal., 3g fat (1g sat. fat), 12mg chol., 154mg sod., 7g carb. (1g sugars, 0 fiber), 4g pro. **Diabetic exchanges::** 1 lean meat, ½ starch.

MINI ZUCCHINI PIZZAS
(PICTURED ON P. 28)

This simple snack recipe is an appealing and perfect low-carb way to satisfy your pizza cravings.
—*Taste of Home* Test Kitchen

Takes: 20 min. • **Makes:** about 2 dozen

- 1 large zucchini (about 11 oz.), cut diagonally into ¼ in.-slices
- ⅛ tsp. salt
- ⅛ tsp. pepper
- ⅓ cup pizza sauce
- ¾ cup shredded part-skim mozzarella cheese
- ½ cup miniature pepperoni slices
  Minced fresh basil

1. Preheat broiler. Arrange zucchini in a single layer on a greased baking sheet. Broil slices 3-4 in. from the heat just until crisp-tender, 1-2 minutes per side.
2. Sprinkle the zucchini slices with salt and pepper; top with sauce, cheese and pepperoni. Broil until cheese is melted, about 1 minute. Sprinkle with basil.
1 appetizer: 29 cal., 2g fat (1g sat. fat), 5mg chol., 108mg sod., 1g carb. (1g sugars, 0 fiber), 2g pro.

CURRY CARROT DIP

The flavors of mustard and curry blend deliciously in this colorful, appetizing dip. Use your imagination for the raw veggies you serve with it.
—Louise Weyer, Marietta, GA

Takes: 30 min. • **Makes:** 1 cup

- 1 small onion, chopped
- 2 tsp. canola oil
- 4 medium carrots, sliced
- ⅓ cup water
- ¼ tsp. salt
- ¼ tsp. pepper
- ¼ tsp. curry powder
- 2 Tbsp. reduced-fat mayonnaise
- 2 tsp. prepared mustard
  Assorted raw vegetables

1. In a nonstick skillet, saute onion in oil. Add the carrots, water, salt, pepper and curry. Bring to a boil. Reduce heat; cover and simmer for 6 minutes or until the vegetables are tender. Uncover; cook mixture 8 minutes or until the liquid has evaporated. Cool.
2. Transfer mixture to a food processor or blender; cover and process until smooth. Add mayonnaise and mustard; mix well. Serve with vegetables.
2 Tbsp.: 40 cal., 3g fat (0 sat. fat), 1mg chol., 133mg sod., 4g carb. (2g sugars, 1g fiber), 0 pro.

CURRY CARROT DIP

WARM SPICED CIDER PUNCH

This is such a nice warm-up punch. I like to serve it when there is a nip in the air. The aroma is wonderful as the punch simmers in the slow cooker.
—Susan Smith, Forest, VA

Prep: 5 min. • **Cook:** 4 hours
Makes: 8 servings

- 4 cups apple cider or unsweetened apple juice
- 2¼ cups water
- 1 can (6 oz.) frozen orange juice concentrate, thawed
- ¾ tsp. ground nutmeg
- ¾ tsp. ground ginger
- 3 whole cloves
- 2 cinnamon sticks
  Orange slices and additional cinnamon sticks, optional

1. In a 3-qt. slow cooker, combine apple cider, water, orange juice concentrate, nutmeg and ginger. Place cloves and cinnamon sticks on a double thickness of cheesecloth; bring up corners of cloth and tie with string to form a bag. Place bag in slow cooker.

2. Cover and cook on low for 4-5 hours or until heated through. Discard the spice bag. Garnish with the orange slices and additional cinnamon sticks if desired.

¾ cup: 94 cal., 0g fat (0g sat. fat), 0 chol., 14mg sod., 23g carb. (19 sugars, 0g fiber), 1g pro.

CRISP CUCUMBER SALSA

CRISP CUCUMBER SALSA

Here's a fantastic way to use cucumbers. You'll love the creamy, crunchy texture and super-fresh flavors.
—Charlene Skjerven, Hoople, ND

Takes: 20 min. • **Makes:** 2½ cups

- 2 cups finely chopped cucumber, peeled and seeded
- ½ cup finely chopped seeded tomato
- ¼ cup chopped red onion
- 2 Tbsp. minced fresh parsley
- 1 jalapeno pepper, seeded and chopped
- 4½ tsp. minced fresh cilantro
- 1 garlic clove, minced
- ¼ cup reduced-fat sour cream
- 1½ tsp. lemon juice
- 1½ tsp. lime juice
- ¼ tsp. ground cumin
- ¼ tsp. seasoned salt
  Baked tortilla chip scoops

In a small bowl, combine the first seven ingredients. In another bowl, combine the sour cream, lemon juice, lime juice, cumin and seasoned salt. Pour over cucumber mixture and toss gently to coat. Serve immediately with chips.

Note: Wear disposable gloves when cutting hot peppers; the oils can burn skin. Avoid touching your face.

¼ cup: 16 cal., 1g fat (0 sat. fat), 2mg chol., 44mg sod., 2g carb. (1g sugars, 0 fiber), 1g pro.

Diabetic exchanges: Free food.

✳

TEST KITCHEN TIP

Don't skip seeding the cucumber. If you do, you may end up with watery salad. Make seeding a breeze by halving the cucumbers lengthwise and using a spoon to scoop out the pulpy centers.

RISOTTO BALLS (ARANCINI)

My Italian grandma made these for me. I still ask for them when I visit her, and so do my children. They freeze well, so when I'm making them, I do it ahead of time.
—Gretchen Whelan, San Francisco, CA

Prep: 35 min. • **Bake:** 25 min.
Makes: about 3 dozen

- 1½ cups water
- 1 cup uncooked arborio rice
- 1 tsp. salt
- 2 large eggs, lightly beaten
- ⅔ cup sun-dried tomato pesto
- 2 cups panko (Japanese) bread crumbs, divided
  Marinara sauce, warmed

1. Preheat oven to 375°. In a large saucepan, combine water, rice and salt; bring to a boil. Reduce heat; simmer, covered, 18-20 minutes or until liquid is absorbed and rice is tender. Let stand, covered, 10 minutes. Transfer to a large bowl; cool slightly. Add eggs and pesto; stir in 1 cup bread crumbs.
2. Place remaining bread crumbs in a shallow bowl. Shape rice mixture into 1¼-in. balls. Roll in bread crumbs, patting to help coating adhere. Place on greased 15x10x1-in. baking pans. Bake until golden brown, 25-30 minutes. Serve arancini with marinara sauce.

1 ball: 42 cal., 1g fat (0 sat. fat), 10mg chol., 125mg sod., 7g carb. (1g sugars, 0 fiber), 1g pro.
Diabetic exchanges: ½ starch.

FOUR-TOMATO SALSA
(PICTURED ON P. 28)

A variety of tomatoes, onions and peppers makes this chunky salsa extra good. Whenever I try to take a batch to a get-together, it's hard to keep my family from finishing it off first! It's a super snack served with tortilla chips or as a relish with meat.
—Connie Siese, Wayne, MI

Takes: 30 min. • **Makes:** 14 cups

- 7 plum tomatoes, chopped
- 7 medium red tomatoes, chopped
- 3 medium yellow tomatoes, chopped
- 3 medium orange tomatoes, chopped
- 1 tsp. salt
- 2 Tbsp. lime juice
- 2 Tbsp. olive oil
- 1 medium white onion, chopped
- 1 medium red onion, chopped
- 2 green onions, chopped
- ½ cup each chopped green, sweet red, orange and yellow pepper
- 3 pepperoncini, chopped
- ⅓ cup mild pickled pepper rings, chopped
- ½ cup minced fresh parsley
- 2 Tbsp. minced fresh cilantro
- 1 Tbsp. dried chervil
  Tortilla chips

1. In a colander, combine the tomatoes and salt. Let drain for 10 minutes.
2. Transfer to a large bowl. Stir in the lime juice, oil, onions, peppers, parsley, cilantro and chervil. Serve with the tortilla chips. Refrigerate any leftovers for up to 1 week.
Note: Look for pepperoncini (pickled peppers) in the pickle and olive section of your grocery store.
¼ cup: 15 cal., 1g fat (0 sat. fat), 0 chol., 62mg sod., 2g carb. (1g sugars, 1g fiber), 0 pro.
Diabetic exchanges: Free food.

RISOTTO BALLS (ARANCINI)

SOUPS & SANDWICHES

"We eat fish on Fridays, so I like to experiment with different types. I pulled salmon, spinach and avocado from the fridge for these wraps. My kids loved them, and I love them, too, because they're delicious and they contain all the food groups right in one hand-held meal."
—Jennifer Krey, Clarence, NY

Vegetable Lentil Soup (p.54) **Butternut Squash & Carrot Soup** (p. 51) **Grilled Bean Burgers** (p. 58)
Apple-Swiss Turkey Sandwiches (p.60) **Grilled Salmon Wraps** (p.60) **Rotini Chicken Soup** (p. 63)

LOADED POTATO-LEEK SOUP

When I was growing up, my mother made potato and onion soup because it was affordable and fast. I've trimmed the calories, and it's still a comforting family favorite.

—Courtney Stultz, Weir, KS

Prep: 20 min. • **Cook:** 6 hours
Makes: 6 servings

- 1 medium leek
- 1½ lbs. potatoes (about 2 large), peeled and finely chopped
- 2 cups fresh cauliflowerets
- ¾ tsp. rubbed sage
- ½ tsp. salt
- ¼ tsp. pepper
- 4 cups reduced-sodium chicken or vegetable broth
- 2 tsp. olive oil
- 2 tsp. lemon juice
  Sour cream, optional

1. Finely chop white portion of leek. Cut leek greens into thin strips; reserve for the topping. In a 3- or 4-qt. slow cooker, combine the potatoes, cauliflowerets, seasonings, broth and chopped leek. Cook, covered, on low until vegetables are tender, 6-8 hours.

2. In a small skillet, heat oil over medium-high heat. Add reserved leek greens; cook until light golden, 3-5 minutes. Puree the soup using an immersion blender. Or cool slightly and puree the soup in batches in a blender. Stir in lemon juice. Top with leek greens and if desired, sour cream.

1 cup: 108 cal., 2g fat (0 sat. fat), 0 chol., 593mg sod., 20g carb. (3g sugars, 2g fiber), 4g pro.
Diabetic exchanges: 1 starch, ½ fat.

FAMILY-PLEASING SLOPPY JOES

My grandma gave this recipe to me years ago, but I made a few changes to give her yummy supper some more pizzazz.

—Jill Zosel, Seattle, WA

Takes: 30 min. • **Makes:** 6 servings

- 1 lb. lean ground turkey
- 1 small onion, chopped
- 2 garlic cloves, minced
- 1 Tbsp. sugar
- 1 Tbsp. all-purpose flour
- ¼ tsp. pepper
- 1 cup ketchup
- 1 Tbsp. Worcestershire sauce
- 1 Tbsp. prepared mustard
- 1 Tbsp. barbecue sauce
- 6 hamburger buns, split

1. In a large skillet, cook turkey and onion over medium heat 6-8 minutes or until the turkey is no longer pink, breaking up turkey into crumbles; drain if necessary. Add garlic; cook 1 minute longer. Stir in sugar, flour and pepper until blended.

2. Stir in ketchup, Worcestershire sauce, mustard and barbecue sauce. Bring to a boil. Reduce heat; simmer the mixture, covered, 10 minutes to allow flavors to blend. Spoon sloppy joe mixture onto the bun bottoms; replace tops.

Freeze option: Freeze cooled meat mixture in freezer containers. To use, partially thaw in refrigerator overnight. Heat through in a saucepan, stirring occasionally and adding a little water if necessary.

1 sandwich: 297 cal., 8g fat (2g sat. fat), 52mg chol., 846mg sod., 38g carb. (17g sugars, 1g fiber), 19g pro.
Diabetic exchanges: 2½ starch, 2 lean meat.

FAMILY-PLEASING SLOPPY JOES

ITALIAN WEDDING SOUP

SLOW-COOKER PEA SOUP

This slow-cooker soup is one of my favorite meals to make during a busy workweek. When I get home, I just add the milk...and supper is served!
—Deanna Waggy, South Bend, IN

....

Prep: 10 min. • **Cook:** 4 hours
Makes: 9 servings

- 1 pkg. (16 oz.) dried split peas
- 2 cups cubed fully cooked ham
- 1 cup diced carrots
- 1 medium onion, chopped
- 2 garlic cloves, minced
- 2 bay leaves
- ½ tsp. salt
- ½ tsp. pepper
- 5 cups boiling water
- 1 cup hot whole milk

In a 5-qt. slow cooker, layer the first nine ingredients in order listed (do not stir). Cover and cook on high for 4-5 hours or until vegetables are tender. Stir in milk. Discard bay leaves before serving.

1 cup: 244 cal., 3g fat (1g sat. fat), 21mg chol., 537mg sod., 36g carb. (7g sugars, 14g fiber), 20g pro.
Diabetic exchanges: 2½ starch, 2 lean meat.

ITALIAN WEDDING SOUP

I first simmered up a batch of this soup when it was featured in a local newspaper. You can also substitute chicken or other sausage, rolled up into little balls, for the meatballs here.
—Amy McGowen, Jupiter, FL

....

Prep: 30 min. • **Cook:** 40 min.
Makes: 7 servings

- 1 large egg white
- ¼ cup panko (Japanese) bread crumbs
- 1 tsp. Italian seasoning
- ½ lb. ground pork
- 2 medium carrots, chopped
- 2 celery ribs, chopped
- 1 medium parsnip, peeled and chopped
- 1 small onion, finely chopped
- 2 Tbsp. olive oil
- 6 cups reduced-sodium chicken broth
- 3 tsp. herbes de Provence
- ½ tsp. crushed red pepper flakes
- ½ tsp. pepper
- 1 cup uncooked orzo pasta
- 1 pkg. (6 oz.) fresh baby spinach
- ¼ cup shredded Parmesan cheese
- ¼ cup minced fresh parsley

1. In a large bowl, combine the egg white, bread crumbs and Italian seasoning.

Crumble pork over mixture and mix well. Shape into ¾-in. balls.
2. Place meatballs on a greased rack in a foil-lined 15x10x1-in. baking pan. Bake at 350° until a thermometer reads 160°, 15-18 minutes.
3. Meanwhile, in a Dutch oven, saute the carrots, celery, parsnip and onion in oil until tender. Stir in the broth, herbes de Provence, pepper flakes and pepper.
4. Drain meatballs on paper towels. Bring soup to a boil; add meatballs. Reduce heat; simmer, uncovered, for 20 minutes. Add the orzo; cook until pasta is tender, 8-10 minutes longer, stirring soup occasionally. Add spinach; cook and stir until spinach is wilted. Sprinkle with cheese and parsley.

Freeze option: Do not add the orzo or spinach. Cool soup; transfer to freezer containers and freeze up to 3 months. To use, thaw in the refrigerator overnight. Transfer to a large saucepan; bring to a boil. Add orzo, then proceed with recipe as directed.

Note: Look for herbes de Provence in the spice aisle.

1 cup: 281 cal., 10g fat (3g sat. fat), 24mg chol., 615mg sod., 32g carb. (5g sugars, 3g fiber), 16g pro.
Diabetic exchanges: 2 starch, 1 high-fat meat, ½ fat.

LAMB PITAS WITH YOGURT SAUCE

The spiced lamb in these stuffed pita pockets goes perfectly with cool cucumber and yogurt. It's like having your own Greek gyro stand in the kitchen!
—Angela Leinenbach, Mechanicsville, VA

Prep: 35 min. • **Cook:** 6 hours
Makes: 8 servings

- 2 Tbsp. olive oil
- 2 lbs. lamb stew meat (¾-in. pieces)
- 1 large onion, chopped
- 1 garlic clove, minced
- ⅓ cup tomato paste
- ½ cup dry red wine
- 1¼ tsp. salt, divided
- 1 tsp. dried oregano
- ½ tsp. dried basil
- 1 medium cucumber
- 1 cup (8 oz.) plain yogurt
- 16 pita pocket halves, warmed
- 4 plum tomatoes, sliced

1. In a large skillet, heat oil over medium-high heat; brown lamb in batches. Transfer lamb to a 3- or 4-qt. slow cooker, reserving drippings in skillet.
2. In drippings, saute onion over medium heat until tender, 4-6 minutes. Add garlic and tomato paste; cook and stir 2 minutes. Stir in wine, 1 tsp. salt, oregano and basil. Add to lamb. Cook, covered, on low until lamb is tender, 6-8 hours.
3. To serve, dice enough cucumber to measure 1 cup; thinly slice remaining cucumber. Combine diced cucumber with yogurt and remaining salt. Fill pitas with lamb mixture, tomatoes, sliced cucumbers and yogurt mixture.

Freeze option: Freeze cooled lamb mixture in freezer containers. To use, partially thaw in refrigerator overnight. Heat through in a saucepan, stirring occasionally and adding a little broth or water if necessary.

2 filled pita halves: 383 cal., 11g fat (3g sat. fat), 78mg chol., 766mg sod., 39g carb. (5g sugars, 3g fiber), 31g pro.
Diabetic exchanges: 3 lean meat, 2½ starch, 1 fat.

SPRING PEA QUINOA SOUP

SPRING PEA QUINOA SOUP

This soup is low in fat, high in fiber, and has a fantastically fresh flavor with wonderful texture. Best of all, it's so simple to make.
—Jane Hacker, Milwaukee, WI

Prep: 10 min. • **Cook:** 25 min.
Makes: 6 servings

- 1 cup water
- ½ cup quinoa, rinsed
- 2 tsp. canola oil
- 1 medium onion, chopped
- 2½ cups frozen peas (about 10 oz.)
- 2 cans (14½ oz. each) reduced-sodium chicken broth or vegetable broth
- ½ tsp. salt
- ¼ tsp. pepper
  Optional toppings: plain yogurt, croutons, shaved Parmesan cheese and cracked pepper

1. In a small saucepan, bring water to a boil. Add quinoa. Reduce heat; simmer quinoa, covered, until water is absorbed, 12-15 minutes.
2. Meanwhile, in a large saucepan, heat oil over medium-high heat; saute onion until tender. Stir in peas and broth; bring to a boil. Reduce the heat; simmer, uncovered, until peas are tender, about 5 minutes.
3. Puree the soup using an immersion blender, or cool slightly and puree soup in a blender; return to pan. Stir in quinoa, salt and pepper; heat through. Serve the soup with toppings as desired.

1 cup: 126 cal., 3g fat (0 sat. fat), 0 chol., 504mg sod., 19g carb. (4g sugars, 4g fiber), 7g pro.
Diabetic exchanges: 1 starch, ½ fat.
* HEALTH TIP * Quinoa is a good source of trace minerals, including manganese and copper, that are important in turning carbohydrates into energy.

PUREED BUTTERNUT SQUASH SOUP

For several years, we've been enjoying this velvety, healthy soup at Thanksgiving. Butternut squash isn't the easiest thing to cut up, so I buy mine already chopped.
—Christen Chalmers, Houston, TX

Takes: 30 min. • **Makes:** 2 servings

- 1 tsp. butter
- 1 tsp. olive oil
- ¼ cup chopped onion
- ¼ cup chopped carrot
- 1 garlic clove, minced
- 1½ cups cubed peeled butternut squash
- 1½ cups chicken stock
- ¼ tsp. dried sage leaves
- ¼ tsp. salt
- ⅛ tsp. pepper
  Pinch crushed red pepper flakes

1. In a small saucepan, heat butter and oil over medium heat. Add onion and carrot; cook and stir until tender. Add garlic; cook 1 minute longer.
2. Stir in the squash, stock, sage, salt and pepper; bring to a boil. Reduce the heat; simmer, covered, 10-15 minutes or until squash is tender. Remove from heat; cool slightly. Process in a blender until smooth. Sprinkle servings with pepper flakes.

1 cup: 126 cal., 4g fat (2g sat. fat), 5mg chol., 710mg sod., 20g carb. (5g sugars, 3g fiber), 5g pro.

TURKEY WHITE CHILI

TURKEY WHITE CHILI

Growing up in Pennsylvania Dutch country, I was surrounded by excellent cooks and wonderful foods. I enjoy experimenting with new recipes, like this change-of-pace chili.
—Kaye Whiteman, Charleston, WV

Prep: 15 min. • **Cook:** 70 min.
Makes: 6 servings

- 2 Tbsp. canola oil
- ½ cup chopped onion
- 3 garlic cloves, minced
- 2½ tsp. ground cumin
- 1 lb. boneless skinless turkey breast, cut into 1-in. cubes
- ½ lb. ground turkey
- 3 cups chicken broth
- 1 can (15 oz.) garbanzo beans or chickpeas, rinsed and drained
- 1 Tbsp. minced jalapeno pepper
- ½ tsp. dried marjoram
- ¼ tsp. dried savory
- 2 tsp. cornstarch
- 1 Tbsp. water
  Shredded Monterey Jack cheese and sliced red onion, optional

1. In a large saucepan or Dutch oven, heat canola oil over medium heat. Add onion; saute until tender, about 5 minutes. Add garlic and cook 1 minute longer. Stir in cumin; cook 5 minutes. Add turkey; cook until no longer pink. Add broth, beans, jalapeno, marjoram and savory. Bring to a boil. Reduce heat; simmer, covered, for 45 minutes, stirring occasionally.
2. Uncover; cook 15 minutes longer. Dissolve cornstarch in water; stir into chili. Bring to a boil. Cook and stir 2 minutes. If desired, serve with cheese and red onion.
Note: Wear disposable gloves when cutting hot peppers; the oils can burn skin. Avoid touching your face.

1 cup: 288 cal., 12g fat (2g sat. fat), 73mg chol., 635mg sod., 15g carb. (3g sugars, 3g fiber), 29g pro.

Diabetic exchanges: 3 lean meat, 1 starch, 1 fat.

HOMEMADE CHICKEN STOCK

Peppercorns and a handful of herbs add the perfect seasoning to this low-sodium chicken stock.
—*Taste of Home* Test Kitchen

Prep: 10 min. • **Cook:** 3¾ hours
Makes: about 2 qt.

- 1 Tbsp. canola oil
- 1 broiler/fryer chicken (3 to 4 lbs.), cut up
- 2 medium carrots, cut into chunks
- 1 medium onion, cut into chunks
- 2½ qt. water
- 1 celery rib with leaves, cut into chunks
- 3 sprigs fresh parsley
- 1 bay leaf
- ½ tsp. dried thyme
- ¼ tsp. dried rosemary, crushed
- ¼ tsp. whole peppercorns

1. In a large stockpot, heat oil over medium heat. Brown chicken on both sides in batches. Remove from pot.

Add carrots and onion to the same pot; cook and stir 3-4 minutes or until onion is tender.

2. Return chicken to pot. Add remaining ingredients; bring to a boil. Reduce heat; simmer, uncovered, until chicken juices run clear, 30 minutes. Skim off foam. Remove chicken from pot; let stand until cool enough to handle. Remove chicken from bones (save meat for another use); return bones and skin to pot.

3. Slowly return stock to a boil. Reduce heat; simmer, uncovered, for 3-4 hours longer. Strain chicken stock through a cheesecloth-lined colander; discard the vegetables, bones, skin and spices. If using immediately, skim fat. Or cool stock, then refrigerate 8 hours or overnight; remove fat from surface before using. (Stock may be refrigerated up to 3 days or frozen for 4-6 months.)

1 cup: 33 cal., 0 fat (0 sat. fat), 1mg chol., 89mg sod., 6g carb. (0 sugars, 1g fiber), 2g pro.
Diabetic exchanges: 1 vegetable.

HOMEMADE CHICKEN STOCK

BUTTERNUT SQUASH & CARROT SOUP

(PICTURED ON P. 44)

I got the recipe for this beautifully golden soup from a friend. Sometimes I add a few slices of red pepper to change up the flavor and color a bit.
—Pat Roberts, Thornton, ON

Prep: 25 min. • **Cook:** 7 hours
Makes: 8 servings (2 qt.)

- 1 Tbsp. canola oil
- 1 medium onion, chopped
- 2 garlic cloves, sliced
- ¼ tsp. minced fresh gingerroot
- 1 small butternut squash (about 2 lbs.), peeled and cut into 1-in. cubes (about 5 cups)
- 1 lb. fresh baby carrots
- ⅛ tsp. ground nutmeg
- ½ tsp. salt
- 1 carton (32 oz.) chicken broth
- ½ cup half-and-half cream
  Sliced green onions, optional

1. In a large skillet, heat oil over medium-high heat; saute onion, garlic and ginger until tender, 4-5 minutes. Transfer to a 5-qt. slow cooker.

2. Add all remaining ingredients except cream and green onions. Cook, covered, on low until vegetables are soft, 7-9 hours.

3. Puree the soup using an immersion blender, or cool slightly and, in batches, puree in a blender and return to slow cooker. Stir in cream; heat through. If desired, top with green onions.

Freeze option: Freeze cooled soup in freezer containers. To use, partially thaw in refrigerator overnight. Heat through in a saucepan, stirring occasionally and adding a little broth or milk if necessary.

1 cup: 121 cal., 4g fat (1g sat. fat), 10mg chol., 695mg sod., 20g carb. (7g sugars, 5g fiber), 3g pro.
Diabetic exchanges: 1 starch, 1 fat.

TEST KITCHEN TIP

Fresh ginger adds bright flavor, but ground ginger can be used instead. Add just a dash of dry ginger for the 1/4 tsp. of fresh ginger the recipe calls for.

BETTER THAN EGG SALAD

3 to 4 Tbsp. minced fresh gingerroot
2 Tbsp. minced fresh parsley
2 tsp. chili powder
1 carton (32 oz.) chicken stock
1 can (11.8 oz.) coconut water
3 Tbsp. lemon juice
2 lbs. uncooked skinless turkey breast, cut into 1-in. cubes
2 tsp. pepper
½ tsp. salt
2 Tbsp. canola oil
1 cup frozen corn (about 5 oz.), thawed
1 cup frozen peas (about 4 oz.), thawed
8 oz. rice noodles or thin spaghetti

1. Place first eight ingredients in a 4- or 5-qt. slow cooker.
2. Toss turkey with pepper and salt. In a large skillet, heat oil over medium-high heat; brown turkey in batches. Add turkey to slow cooker.
3. Cook, covered, on low until carrots and turkey are tender, 4-5 hours. Stir in corn and peas; heat through.
4. Cook noodles according to package directions; drain. Add noodles to soup just before serving.

1½ cups: 351 cal., 6g fat (1g sat. fat), 65mg chol., 672mg sod., 41g carb. (5g sugars, 4g fiber), 33g pro.
Diabetic exchanges: 3 starch, 3 lean meat.

* HEALTH TIP * Research supports the idea that chicken noodle soup can help you feel better faster. This turkey soup can do the same and more: ginger can also help to soothe an upset stomach.

*

TEST KITCHEN TIP

This soup is equally as good prepared with chicken instead of turkey. If you know you're not going to eat the soup in one sitting, it's best to cook and store the noodles separately to add later. Otherwise, they'll soak up most of the liquid and pretty much fall apart.

BETTER THAN EGG SALAD

Tofu takes the taste and texture of egg salad in this quick-fix sandwich. The salad is high in protein and has almost no cholesterol.
—Lisa Renshaw, KS City, MO

Takes: 20 min. • **Makes:** 4 servings

¼ cup reduced-fat mayonnaise
¼ cup chopped celery
2 green onions, chopped
2 Tbsp. sweet pickle relish
1 Tbsp. Dijon mustard
¼ tsp. ground turmeric
¼ tsp. salt
⅛ tsp. cayenne pepper
1 pkg. (12.3 oz.) silken firm tofu, cubed
8 slices whole wheat bread
4 lettuce leaves
Coarsely ground pepper, optional

Mix first eight ingredients; stir in tofu. Line four slices of bread with lettuce. Top with tofu mixture. If desired, sprinkle top with pepper; close sandwiches.

1 sandwich: 266 cal., 9g fat (2g sat. fat), 5mg chol., 692mg sod., 31g carb. (7g sugars, 4g fiber), 14g pro.
Diabetic exchanges: 2 starch, 1 lean meat, 1 fat.

TURKEY GINGER NOODLE SOUP

I was looking for a soup that's both healthy and tasty. Ginger is my favorite spice, making this recipe a shoo-in.
—Adina Monson, Nanaimo, BC

Prep: 20 min. • **Cook:** 4¼ hours
Makes: 8 servings (about 3 qt.)

2 medium carrots, sliced
2 cans (8 oz. each) sliced water chestnuts, drained

TURKEY GINGER NOODLE SOUP

FIREHOUSE CHILI

VEGETABLE LENTIL SOUP

(PICTURED ON P. 44)

Here's a healthy soup that's ideal for vegetarians and those watching their weight. Butternut squash and lentils make it filling, while herbs and other veggies round out the flavor.

—Mark Morgan, Waterford, WI

Prep: 20 min. • **Cook:** 4½ hours
Makes: 6 servings (about 2 qt.)

- 3 cups cubed peeled butternut squash
- 1 cup chopped carrot
- 1 cup chopped onion
- 1 cup dried lentils, rinsed
- 2 garlic cloves, minced
- 1 tsp. dried oregano
- 1 tsp. dried basil
- 4 cups vegetable broth
- 1 can (14½ oz.) Italian diced tomatoes, undrained
- 2 cups frozen cut green beans (about 8 oz.)

1. Place first eight ingredients in a 5-qt. slow cooker. Cook, covered, on low until lentils are tender, about 4 hours.
2. Stir in the tomatoes and beans. Cook, covered, on high until heated through, about 30 minutes.

1⅓ cups: 217 cal., 1g fat (0 sat. fat), 0 chol., 685mg sod., 45g carb. (11g sugars, 8g fiber), 11g pro.

FIREHOUSE CHILI

As one of the cooks at the firehouse, I used to prepare meals for 10 firefighters. This chili was among their favorites. It's tasty, and it gives the energy you might need.

—Richard Clements, San Dimas, CA

Prep: 20 min. • **Cook:** 1½ hours
Makes: 16 servings (4 qt.)

- 2 Tbsp. canola oil
- 4 lbs. lean ground beef (90% lean)
- 2 medium onions, chopped
- 1 medium green pepper, chopped
- 4 cans (16 oz. each) kidney beans, rinsed and drained
- 3 cans (28 oz. each) stewed tomatoes, cut up
- 1 can (14½ oz.) beef broth
- 3 Tbsp. chili powder
- 2 Tbsp. ground coriander
- 2 Tbsp. ground cumin
- 4 garlic cloves, minced
- 1 tsp. dried oregano

In a Dutch oven, heat the canola oil over medium heat. Brown beef in batches, crumbling meat, until no longer pink; drain and set aside. Add the onions and green pepper; cook until tender. Return meat to Dutch oven. Stir in remaining ingredients. Bring to a boil. Reduce heat; simmer, covered, until flavors are blended, about 1½ hours.

1 cup: 354 cal., 12g fat (4g sat. fat), 71mg chol., 657mg sod., 32g carb. (10g sugars, 8g fiber), 31g pro.
Diabetic exchanges: 5 lean meat, 2½ starch, ½ fat.

ITALIAN GRILLED STEAK SANDWICH

If you are going to feed a hungry crowd, you can't go wrong with steak sandwiches. They're so easy to make—especially this way— and most people love them.
—Gilda Lester, Millsboro, DE

Prep: 35 min. + marinating
Grill: 15 min. + chilling
Makes: 8 servings

- ½ cup reduced-sodium teriyaki sauce
- 2 Tbsp. lemon juice
- 2 Tbsp. olive oil
- 2 Tbsp. Worcestershire sauce
- 1 beef flank steak (1 lb.)
- 1 round loaf Italian bread (about 2 lbs.), unsliced
- 4 plum tomatoes, chopped
- 4 green onions, thinly sliced
- ¼ cup Greek olives, coarsely chopped
- ¼ cup sliced pepperoni
- 1 Tbsp. thinly sliced fresh basil leaves
- 2 Tbsp. plus ¼ cup prepared Italian salad dressing, divided
- 2 cups fresh arugula

1. Place first four ingredients in a large bowl or shallow dish. Add steak and turn to coat. Refrigerate, covered, for 8 hours or overnight.
2. Remove steak, discarding marinade. Grill steak, covered, over medium heat or broil 4 in. from heat until meat reaches desired doneness (for medium-rare, a thermometer should read 135°; medium, 140°; medium-well 145°), 6-8 minutes per side. Cool completely.
3. Cut the bread loaf horizontally in half. Hollow out both halves, leaving a ½-in. shell (save removed bread for another use). Cut steak across the grain into thin slices. In a bowl, toss tomatoes with green onions, olives, pepperoni, basil and 2 Tbsp. dressing. In another bowl, toss the arugula with remaining dressing.
4. Place half of the arugula in the bread bottom. Layer with steak, tomato mixture and remaining arugula; replace top. Wrap in foil; refrigerate at least 1 hour. Cut into wedges to serve.

1 wedge: 260 cal., 10g fat (3g sat. fat), 30mg chol., 567mg sod., 24g carb. (4g sugars, 2g fiber), 16g pro.
Diabetic exchanges: 2 lean meat, 1½ starch, 1 fat.

HAZELNUT ASPARAGUS SOUP

My heart is happy when bundles of tender local asparagus start to appear at my grocery store in spring. No one would ever guess this restaurant-quality vegetarian soup can be prepared in not much more than half an hour.
—Cindy Beberman, Orland Park, IL

Prep: 20 min. • **Cook:** 15 min.
Makes: 4 servings

- 1 Tbsp. olive oil
- ½ cup chopped sweet onion
- 3 garlic cloves, sliced
  Dash crushed red pepper flakes
- 2½ cups cut fresh asparagus (about 1½ lbs.), trimmed
- 2 cups vegetable broth
- ⅓ cup whole hazelnuts, toasted
- 2 Tbsp. chopped fresh basil
- 2 Tbsp. lemon juice
- ½ cup unsweetened almond milk
- 2 tsp. gluten-free reduced-sodium tamari soy sauce
- ¼ tsp. salt
  Shaved asparagus, optional

1. In a large saucepan, heat the oil over medium heat. Add the onion, garlic and pepper flakes; cook and stir until onion is softened, 4-5 minutes. Add asparagus and broth; bring to a boil. Reduce heat; simmer, covered, until asparagus is tender, 6-8 minutes. Remove from the heat and cool slightly.
2. Place nuts, basil and lemon juice in a blender. Add asparagus mixture. Process until smooth and creamy. Return to the saucepan. Stir in almond milk, tamari sauce and salt. Heat through, taking care not to boil soup. If desired, top servings with shaved asparagus.

Note: Reduced-sodium soy sauce may be used in place of the tamari soy sauce.
¾ cup: 164 cal., 13g fat (1g sat. fat), 0 chol., 623mg sod., 11g carb. (4g sugars, 4g fiber), 5g pro.
Diabetic exchanges: 2½ fat, ½ starch.

ITALIAN GRILLED STEAK SANDWICH

GREAT GRAIN BURGERS

GREAT GRAIN BURGERS

I've experimented with many combinations of ingredients to make a good meatless burger...and this is our favorite. These patties cook up golden brown and crispy. They make delicious sandwiches.
—Pat Whitaker, Alsea, OR

Prep: 45 min. + chilling • **Cook:** 30 min.
Makes: 12 servings

- ½ cup uncooked brown rice
- ½ cup uncooked bulgur
- 1 Tbsp. salt-free seasoning blend
- ¼ tsp. poultry seasoning
- 2 cups water
- ¼ cup egg substitute
- ½ cup fat-free cottage cheese
- 2 cups finely chopped fresh mushrooms
- ¾ cup old-fashioned oats
- ⅓ cup finely chopped onion
- 2 Tbsp. minced fresh parsley
- 1 tsp. salt
- ½ tsp. dried basil
- ⅛ tsp. celery seed
- 1 cup shredded part-skim mozzarella cheese
- ¼ cup shredded reduced-fat cheddar cheese
- 3 tsp. canola oil, divided
- 12 sandwich rolls
  Optional toppings: watercress and tomato, red onion and avocado slices

1. Place first five ingredients in a large saucepan; bring to a boil. Reduce heat; simmer, covered, until rice is tender, about 30 minutes. Remove to a bowl and cool slightly. Refrigerate, covered, until cold.
2. Place the egg substitute and cottage cheese in a blender; cover and process until smooth. Transfer to a large bowl. Stir in mushrooms, oats, onion, parsley and seasonings. Add the mozzarella cheese, cheddar cheese and rice mixture; mix well. Refrigerate, covered, 2 hours or overnight before shaping.
3. Shape ½ cups of mixture into patties, pressing to adhere. In a large nonstick skillet, heat 1 tsp. oil over medium heat; cook four patties until lightly browned, about 5 minutes per side. Repeat with remaining patties and oil. Serve on rolls with toppings as desired.

1 burger: 335 cal., 9g fat (3g sat. fat), 8mg chol., 701mg sod., 51g carb. (6g sugars, 3g fiber), 14g pro.

SHRIMP GAZPACHO

Here's a refreshing take on the classic chilled tomato soup. Our twist features shrimp, lime and plenty of avocado.
—*Taste of Home* Test Kitchen

Prep: 15 min. + chilling
Makes: 12 servings (about 3 qt.)

- 6 cups spicy hot V8 juice
- 2 cups cold water
- ½ cup lime juice
- ½ cup minced fresh cilantro
- ½ tsp. salt
- ¼ to ½ tsp. hot pepper sauce
- 1 lb. peeled and deveined cooked shrimp (31-40 per lb.), tails removed
- 1 medium cucumber, seeded and diced
- 2 medium tomatoes, seeded and chopped
- 2 medium ripe avocados, peeled and chopped

In a large nonreactive bowl, mix first six ingredients. Gently stir in the remaining ingredients. Refrigerate, covered, 1 hour before serving.

Note: This recipe is best served the same day it's made.

1 cup: 112 cal., 4g fat (1g sat. fat), 57mg chol., 399mg sod., 9g carb. (5g sugars, 3g fiber), 10g pro.

Diabetic exchanges: 1 lean meat, 2 vegetable, 1 fat.

★ ★ ★ ★ ★ **READER REVIEW**

"Five stars, but I didn't use V8. I used a good bloody mix (Daily's Thick & Spicy), and Cholula hot sauce on the side for those who like an extra kick."

BNRUDY TASTEOFHOME.COM

SHRIMP GAZPACHO

GRILLED BEAN BURGERS

These juicy veggie patties have major flavor with cumin, garlic and a little chili powder. They can hold their own against any veggie burger you'd buy at the supermarket.
—Marguerite Shaeffer, Sewell, NJ

Prep: 25 min. • **Grill:** 10 min.
Makes: 8 servings

- 1 Tbsp. olive oil
- 1 large onion, finely chopped
- 4 garlic cloves, minced
- 1 medium carrot, shredded
- 1 to 2 tsp. chili powder
- 1 tsp. ground cumin
- ¼ tsp. pepper
- 1 can (15 oz.) pinto beans, rinsed and drained
- 1 can (15 oz.) black beans, rinsed and drained
- 2 Tbsp. Dijon mustard
- 2 Tbsp. reduced-sodium soy sauce
- 1 Tbsp. ketchup
- 1½ cups quick-cooking oats
- 8 whole wheat hamburger buns, split
- 8 lettuce leaves
- ½ cup salsa

1. In a large nonstick skillet, heat oil over medium-high heat; saute onion 2 minutes. Add garlic; cook and stir 1 minute. Stir in carrot and spices; cook and stir until the carrot is tender, 2-3 minutes. Remove from heat.
2. In a large bowl, mash pinto and black beans using a potato masher. Stir in the mustard, soy sauce, ketchup and carrot mixture. Add oats, mixing well. Shape into eight 3½-in. patties.
3. Place burgers on an oiled grill rack over medium heat or on a greased rack of a broiler pan. Grill, covered, or broil 4 in. from heat until lightly browned and heated through, 4-5 minutes per side. Serve on buns with lettuce and salsa.

1 burger: 305 cal., 5g fat (1g sat. fat), 0 chol., 736mg sod., 54g carb. (8g sugars, 10g fiber), 12g pro.
Diabetic exchanges: 3½ starch, 1 lean meat.

How To Quickly Peel Garlic

Put garlic cloves in a hard-sided bowl with a similar-sized bowl over the top. Metal is best, but you can use glass or even a firm plastic food storage container with a lid. Shake vigorously for 10-15 seconds and the peels will come right off. A jar works, too, but it takes longer to shake.

TOMATO CRAB SOUP

With crab and bits of vegetables in every bite, this rich dish is sure to please all the seafood fans in your family. Fresh basil gives the soup a brighter flavor.
—Clinton Liu, Edmonds, WA

Prep: 20 min. • **Cook:** 30 min.
Makes: 10 servings (2½ qt.)

- 1 small onion, chopped
- ¼ cup chopped sweet red pepper
- 4 garlic cloves, minced
- 3 Tbsp. butter
- 4 plum tomatoes, finely chopped
- ¼ cup all-purpose flour
- ½ tsp. pepper
- ⅛ tsp. salt
- 3 cans (14½ oz. each) reduced-sodium chicken broth
- 1 can (6 oz.) tomato paste
- 2 cans (6 oz. each) crabmeat, drained, flaked and cartilage removed
- 3 Tbsp. minced fresh basil
- 1 cup whole milk

1. In a large saucepan, saute onion, red pepper and garlic in butter for 3 minutes. Stir in tomatoes; cook 2-3 minutes longer or until onion is tender.
2. Whisk in the flour, pepper and salt until blended. Gradually stir in the broth and tomato paste. Bring to a boil; cook and stir for 2 minutes or until thickened. Stir in crab and basil. Gradually stir in the milk; heat through.

1 cup: 126 cal., 5g fat (3g sat. fat), 43mg chol., 526mg sod., 11g carb. (6g sugars, 2g fiber), 11g pro.
Diabetic exchanges: 1 lean meat, 1 vegetable, ½ starch, ½ fat.

GRILLED BEAN BURGERS

CREAMY CAULIFLOWER PAKORA SOUP

VEGETABLE STEAK SOUP

Your crew will chase away winter's chill with a spoon when you cook up this hearty soup. It has such a rich flavor, and it's full of nutritious vegetables and chunks of tender steak.
—Brigitte Schultz, Barstow, CA

Prep: 15 min. • **Cook:** 30 min.
Makes: 7 servings

- 1 lb. beef top sirloin steak, cut into ½-in. cubes
- ¼ tsp. pepper, divided
- 2 tsp. olive oil
- 2 cans (14½ oz. each) beef broth
- 2 cups cubed peeled potatoes
- 1¼ cups water
- 2 medium carrots, sliced
- 1 Tbsp. onion soup mix
- 1 Tbsp. dried basil
- ½ tsp. dried tarragon
- 2 Tbsp. cornstarch
- ½ cup white wine or additional beef broth

1. Sprinkle steak with ⅛ tsp. pepper. In a Dutch oven, brown steak in batches in oil over medium heat. Add the broth, potatoes, water, carrots, onion soup mix, basil, tarragon and remaining pepper; bring to a boil. Reduce heat; cover and simmer until the vegetables are tender, 20-25 minutes.
2. In a small bowl, combine cornstarch and wine until smooth; stir into the soup. Bring soup to a boil; cook and stir until thickened, 2 minutes.

1 cup: 175 cal., 4g fat (1g sat. fat), 26mg chol., 660mg sod., 14g carb. (1g sugars, 2g fiber), 16g pro.
Diabetic exchanges: 1 starch, 2 lean meat.

CREAMY CAULIFLOWER PAKORA SOUP

My husband and I often crave pakoras, deep-fried fritters from India. I wanted to get the same flavors but use a healthier cooking technique, so I created a soup using all the classic spices and our favorite veggie, cauliflower!
—Melody Johnson, Pulaski, WI

Prep: 20 min. • **Cook:** 20 min.
Makes: 8 servings (3 qt.)

- 1 large head cauliflower, cut into small florets
- 5 medium potatoes, peeled and diced
- 1 large onion, diced
- 4 medium carrots, peeled and diced
- 2 celery ribs, diced
- 1 carton (32 oz.) vegetable stock
- 1 tsp. garam masala
- 1 tsp. garlic powder
- 1 tsp. ground coriander
- 1 tsp. ground turmeric
- 1 tsp. ground cumin
- 1 tsp. pepper
- 1 tsp. salt
- ½ tsp. crushed red pepper flakes
    Water or additional vegetable stock
    Fresh cilantro leaves
    Lime wedges, optional

In a Dutch oven over medium-high heat, bring first 14 ingredients to a boil. Cook and stir until vegetables are tender, about 20 minutes. Remove from the heat; cool slightly. Process in batches in a blender or food processor until smooth. Adjust the consistency as desired with more water or additional stock. Sprinkle with fresh cilantro. Serve soup hot, with lime wedges if desired.

Freeze option: Before adding cilantro, freeze cooled soup in freezer containers. To use, partially thaw in refrigerator overnight. Heat through in a saucepan, stirring occasionally and adding a little water if necessary. Sprinkle with cilantro. If desired, serve with lime wedges.

Note: Look for garam masala in the spice or Indian food aisle.

1½ cups: 135 cal., 1g fat (0 sat. fat), 0 chol., 645mg sod., 30g carb. (6g sugars, 5g fiber), 4g pro.
Diabetic exchanges: 1½ starch, 1 vegetable.

DILL CHICKEN SOUP

2 medium apples, thinly sliced
8 slices multigrain bread, toasted
3 Tbsp. honey mustard
8 oz. thinly sliced cooked turkey breast
½ cup thinly sliced cucumber
8 slices reduced-fat Swiss cheese

1. Place apples on a microwave-safe plate; microwave, uncovered, on high 1 minute or until slightly softened.
2. Lightly spread the toast with mustard. Layer half of the toast with the turkey, cucumber, cheese and apples; top with remaining toast.

1 sandwich: 415 cal., 13g fat (5g sat. fat), 88mg chol., 412mg sod., 41g carb. (15g sugars, 6g fiber), 38g pro.
Diabetic exchanges: 3 lean meat, 2 starch, 1 fat, ½ fruit.

GRILLED SALMON WRAPS

We eat fish on Fridays, so I like to experiment with different types. I pulled salmon, spinach and avocado from the fridge for these wraps. My kids loved them, and I love them, too, because they're delicious and they contain all the food groups right in one hand-held meal.
—Jennifer Krey, Clarence, NY

Takes: 25 min. • **Makes:** 4 servings

1 lb. salmon fillet (about 1 in. thick)
½ tsp. salt
¼ tsp. pepper
½ cup salsa verde
4 whole wheat tortillas (8 in.), warmed
1 cup chopped fresh spinach
1 medium tomato, chopped
½ cup shredded Monterey Jack cheese
½ medium ripe avocado, peeled and thinly sliced

1. Sprinkle salmon with salt and pepper; place on an oiled grill rack over medium heat, skin side down. Grill the salmon, covered, 8-10 minutes or until fish just begins to flake easily with a fork.
2. Remove from grill. Break salmon into bite-sized pieces, removing skin if desired. Toss gently with salsa; serve in tortillas. Top with remaining ingredients.

1 wrap: 380 cal., 18g fat (5g sat. fat), 69mg chol., 745mg sod., 27g carb. (2g sugars, 5g fiber), 27g pro.
Diabetic exchanges: 3 lean meat, 2 starch, 2 fat.

DILL CHICKEN SOUP

I could eat soup for every meal of the day, all year long. I particularly like dill and spinach—they add brightness and color to this light and healthy soup.
—Robin Haas, Jamaica Plain, MA

Takes: 30 min. • **Makes:** 6 servings (2 qt.)

1 Tbsp. canola oil
2 medium carrots, chopped
1 small onion, coarsely chopped
2 garlic cloves, minced
½ cup uncooked whole wheat orzo pasta
1½ cups shredded rotisserie chicken
6 cups reduced-sodium chicken broth
1½ cups frozen peas (about 6 oz.)
8 oz. fresh baby spinach (about 10 cups)
2 Tbsp. chopped fresh dill or 1 Tbsp. dill weed
2 Tbsp. lemon juice
Coarsely ground pepper, optional

1. In a 6-qt. stockpot, heat oil over medium heat. Add carrots, onion and garlic; saute until the carrots are tender, 4-5 minutes.
2. Stir in orzo, chicken and broth; bring to a boil. Reduce heat; simmer, uncovered, 5 minutes. Stir in the peas, spinach and dill; return to a boil. Reduce the heat; simmer, uncovered, until orzo is tender, for 3-4 minutes. Stir in lemon juice. If desired, top servings with coarsely ground pepper.

1⅓ cups: 198 cal., 6g fat (1g sat. fat), 31mg chol., 681mg sod., 20g carb. (4g sugars, 5g fiber), 18g pro.
Diabetic exchanges: 2 lean meat, 1 starch, 1 vegetable, ½ fat.

APPLE-SWISS TURKEY SANDWICHES

(PICTURED ON P. 44)

Honey mustard adds a sweet tang to this hearty sandwich. Apple slices, Swiss cheese, cucumber and turkey are layered between slices of nutritious multigrain bread. These sandwiches pack well to take to the office or on the trail.
—Gloria Updyke, Front Royal, VA

Takes: 15 min. • **Makes:** 4 servings

GRILLED SALMON WRAPS

THE SOUTH IN A POT SOUP

With black-eyed peas, sweet potatoes, ground beef and zesty spices, this soup has every wonderful memory from my childhood simmered together in one tasty, nutritious pot.
—Stephanie Rabbitt-Schapp, Cincinnati, OH

Prep: 15 min. • **Cook:** 45 min.
Makes: 8 servings (2½ qt.)

- 1 Tbsp. canola oil
- 1½ lbs. lean ground beef (90% lean)
- 1 large sweet potato, peeled and diced
- 1 large sweet onion, diced
- 1 medium sweet pepper (any color), diced
- 1 can (15½ oz.) black-eyed peas, rinsed and drained
- 1 Tbsp. ground cumin
- 1 Tbsp. curry powder
- ¾ tsp. salt
- ½ tsp. coarsely ground pepper
- 2 cans (14½ oz. each) reduced-sodium beef broth
- 4 cups chopped collard greens or chopped fresh spinach

1. In a Dutch oven, heat oil over medium heat. Cook and stir the ground beef, crumbling meat, until no longer pink, 8-10 minutes. Add sweet potato, onion and pepper; saute until onion and pepper are slightly softened, 4-5 minutes.
2. Add black-eyed peas, cumin, curry, salt and pepper; stir in broth and bring to a boil. Reduce heat; simmer until sweet potato is almost tender, 15-18 minutes.
3. Add collard greens; cook until tender, 15-18 minutes. If desired, add more cumin and curry.

For slow cooker: In a 4- to 5-qt. slow cooker, crumble ground beef; add next eight ingredients. Pour in enough broth to reach desired consistency. Cook, covered, on low 6-8 hours. A half-hour before serving, skim off any fat; add greens.

1¼ cups: 267 cal., 9g fat (3g sat. fat), 55mg chol., 544mg sod., 23g carb. (8g sugars, 5g fiber), 22g pro.
Diabetic exchanges: 2 lean meat, 1 starch, 1 vegetable, ½ fat.

BLACK BEAN & PUMPKIN CHILI

BLACK BEAN & PUMPKIN CHILI

This is my kind of chili — thick and hearty. Try sweet potato or butternut squash instead of pumpkin, and serve over quinoa, barley, brown rice or farro.
—Jean Ecos, Hartland, WI

Prep: 20 min. • **Cook:** 1 hour
Makes: 8 servings (2½ qt.)

- 1 Tbsp. olive oil
- 1 medium sweet yellow pepper, chopped
- 1 medium onion, chopped
- 3 garlic cloves, minced
- 3 cups reduced-sodium chicken broth
- 1 can (15 oz.) solid-pack pumpkin
- 1 can (14½ oz.) diced tomatoes, undrained
- 2 tsp. chili powder
- 1½ tsp. ground cumin
- 1½ tsp. dried oregano
- ½ tsp. salt
- ½ tsp. smoked paprika
- 2 cans (15 oz. each) black beans, rinsed and drained
- 1½ cups shredded cooked chicken
- ¼ cup chopped fresh cilantro or parsley

1. In a 6-qt. stockpot, heat the oil over medium heat. Add pepper and onion; cook and stir 6-8 minutes or until tender. Stir in garlic; cook 1 minute longer.
2. Stir in broth, pumpkin, tomatoes and seasonings. Mash one can of beans. Add mashed beans and remaining can of whole beans to pot; bring to a boil. Reduce heat; simmer, covered, 45 minutes to allow flavors to blend, stirring occasionally. Stir in chicken and cilantro; heat through.

1¼ cups: 200 cal., 4g fat (1g sat. fat), 23mg chol., 698mg sod., 26g carb. (5g sugars, 8g fiber), 15g pro.
Diabetic exchanges: 2 lean meat, 1 starch, 1 vegetable.

GRILLED WATERMELON GAZPACHO

This is the perfect starter for a summer dinner or as a light lunch. It's cool and tangy with a whole lot of great grilled flavor. If you like a little more heat, just add more jalapeno peppers.
—George Levinthal, Goleta, CA

Prep: 10 min. + chilling • **Grill:** 10 min.
Makes: 4 servings

- 2 Tbsp. olive oil, divided
- ¼ seedless watermelon, cut into three 1½-in.-thick slices
- 1 large beefsteak tomato, halved
- ½ English cucumber, peeled and halved lengthwise
- 1 jalapeno pepper, seeded and halved lengthwise
- ¼ cup plus 2 Tbsp. diced red onion, divided
- 2 Tbsp. sherry vinegar
- 1 Tbsp. lime juice
- ½ tsp. kosher or sea salt
- ¼ tsp. pepper
- 1 small ripe avocado, peeled, pitted and diced

1. Brush 1 Tbsp. olive oil over watermelon slices, tomato, cucumber and jalapeno; grill, covered, on a greased grill rack over medium-high direct heat until seared, for 5-6 minutes on each side. Remove from heat, reserving one watermelon slice.
2. When cool enough to handle, remove rind from remaining watermelon slices; cut flesh into chunks. Remove skin and seeds from tomato and jalapeno; chop. Coarsely chop cucumber. Combine grilled vegetables; add ¼ cup onion, vinegar, lime juice and seasonings. Process in batches in a blender until smooth, adding remaining olive oil during final minute. If desired, strain through a fine-mesh strainer; adjust seasonings as needed. Refrigerate soup, covered, until chilled.
3. To serve, pour gazpacho into bowls or glasses. Top with diced avocado and the remaining onion. Cut the reserved watermelon slice into wedges. Garnish bowls or glasses with wedges.

1 cup: 181 cal., 12g fat (2g sat. fat), 0 chol., 248mg sod., 19g carb. (13g sugars, 4g fiber), 2g pro.
Diabetic exchanges: 2 fat, 1 vegetable, 1 fruit.

ROTINI CHICKEN SOUP
(PICTURED ON P. 45)

I created this recipe for a dinner I hosted for a group of friends. The main course was Italian, and I needed a good soup, so I converted a favorite tortilla soup recipe by substituting pasta and adding different, more Italian, seasonings.
—Maxine Pierson, San Ramon, CA

Prep: 10 min. • **Cook:** 1 hour 25 min.
Makes: 9 servings (about 2 qt.)

- 1 lb. boneless skinless chicken breasts, cut into ½-in. pieces
- 1 large onion, chopped
- 4 celery ribs, sliced
- 2 medium carrots, sliced
- 4 garlic cloves, minced
- 2 Tbsp. butter
- 2 Tbsp. olive oil
- 1 tsp. dried basil
- ½ tsp. dried oregano
- ⅛ tsp. pepper
- 3 cans (14½ oz. each) reduced-sodium chicken broth, divided
- 1 can (14½ oz.) diced tomatoes, undrained
- 6 oz. uncooked tricolor spiral pasta
- ¼ cup all-purpose flour

1. In a large saucepan, saute the chicken, onion, celery, carrots and garlic in butter and oil for 5 minutes. Stir in basil, oregano and pepper until blended.
2. Set aside 1 cup broth. Gradually add remaining broth to the pan. Stir in the tomatoes. Bring to a boil. Reduce heat; cover and simmer for 45-60 minutes.
3. Return to a boil; stir in the pasta. Reduce heat; simmer, uncovered, for 10-13 minutes or until pasta is almost tender. Combine the flour and reserved broth until smooth. Stir into pan. Bring to a boil; cook and stir for 2 minutes or until thickened.

1 cup: 223 cal., 7g fat (2g sat. fat), 35mg chol., 537mg sod., 24g carb. (4g sugars, 2g fiber), 16g pro.
Diabetic exchanges: 1½ starch, 1 lean meat, 1 vegetable, 1 fat.

GRILLED WATERMELON GAZPACHO

BUTTERNUT SQUASH CHILI

BUTTERNUT SQUASH CHILI

Add butternut squash to chili for a tasty, filling, energy-packed dish your whole family will love. Mine does!
—Jeanne Larson
Rancho Santa Margarita, CA

....

Prep: 20 min. • **Cook:** 30 min.
Makes: 8 servings (2 qt.)

- 1 lb. ground beef or turkey
- ¾ cup chopped red onion
- 5 garlic cloves, minced
- 3 Tbsp. tomato paste
- 1 Tbsp. chili powder
- 1 tsp. ground cumin
- ½ to 1 tsp. salt
- 1¾ to 2 cups water
- 1 can (15 oz.) black beans, rinsed and drained
- 1 can (15 oz.) pinto beans, rinsed and drained
- 1 can (14½ oz.) diced tomatoes
- 1 can (14½ to 15 oz.) tomato sauce
- 3 cups cubed peeled butternut squash, (½-in. cubes)
- 2 Tbsp. cider vinegar
  Chopped avocado, plain Greek yogurt and shredded mozzarella cheese, optional

1. In a Dutch oven over medium heat, cook beef and onion, crumbling meat, until beef is no longer pink and onion is tender, 6-8 minutes.
2. Add the next five ingredients; cook for 1 minute longer. Stir in water, both types of beans, diced tomatoes and tomato sauce. Bring to a boil; reduce heat. Stir in squash; simmer, covered, until squash is tender, 20-25 minutes. Stir in vinegar.
3. If desired, serve the chili with chopped avocado, Greek yogurt and shredded mozzarella cheese.

1 cup: 261 cal., 8g fat (3g sat. fat), 35mg chol., 704mg sod., 32g carb. (6g sugars, 8g fiber), 18g pro.
Diabetic exchanges: 2 starch, 2 lean meat.

❄

TEST KITCHEN TIP
Unexpected company? Ladle the chili over spiral pasta or macaroni to stretch the servings.

CHICKEN CORN SOUP WITH RIVELS

CHICKEN CORN SOUP WITH RIVELS

Traditional chicken soup gets an interesting twist from a dumpling-like broth-stretcher called rivels. This soup is so chock-full of chicken, vegetables and herbs that you won't be able to resist it.
—Elissa Armbruster, Medford, NJ

....

Takes: 25 min. • **Makes:** 7 servings

- 1 cup chopped carrots
- 1 celery rib, chopped
- 1 medium onion, chopped
- 2 tsp. canola oil
- 2 cans (14½ oz. each) reduced-sodium chicken broth
- 2 cups fresh or frozen corn
- 2 cups cubed cooked chicken breast
- ½ tsp. minced fresh parsley
- ¼ tsp. salt
- ¼ tsp. dried tarragon
- ¼ tsp. pepper
- ¾ cup all-purpose flour
- 1 large egg, beaten

1. In a large saucepan, saute the carrots, celery and onion in oil until tender. Add the broth, corn, chicken, parsley, salt, tarragon and pepper. Bring to a boil.
2. Meanwhile, for rivels, place the flour in a bowl; mix in the egg with a fork just until blended. Drop dough by teaspoonfuls into boiling soup, stirring constantly. Cook and stir for 1-2 minutes or until the rivels are cooked through.

1 cup: 191 cal., 4g fat (1g sat. fat), 57mg chol., 482mg sod., 22g carb. (5g sugars, 2g fiber), 17g pro.
Diabetic exchanges: 1½ starch, 2 lean meat.

LAUREN'S BOUILLABAISSE

This golden-colored soup is brimming with an assortment of seafood. The savory sourdough croutons with red pepper mayo take it over the top.
—Lauren Covas, NB, NJ

Prep: 30 min. • **Cook:** 20 min.
Makes: 12 servings (5 qt.)

- ⅔ cup chopped roasted sweet red pepper, drained
- ¼ cup reduced-fat mayonnaise

CROUTONS
- 6 slices sourdough bread
- 1 garlic clove, halved

BOUILLABAISSE
- 1 medium onion, chopped
- 1 Tbsp. olive oil
- 2 garlic cloves, minced
- 2 plum tomatoes, chopped
- ½ tsp. saffron threads or 2 tsp. ground turmeric
- 3½ cups cubed red potatoes
- 2½ cups thinly sliced fennel bulb
- 1 carton (32 oz.) reduced-sodium chicken broth
- 3 cups clam juice
- 2 tsp. dried tarragon
- 24 fresh littleneck clams
- 24 fresh mussels, scrubbed and beards removed
- 1 lb. red snapper fillet, cut into 2-in. pieces
- ¾ lb. uncooked large shrimp, peeled and deveined
- ¼ cup minced fresh parsley

1. Place red pepper and mayonnaise in a food processor; cover and process until smooth. Refrigerate until serving.
2. For the croutons, rub one side of each bread slice with garlic; discard garlic. Cut bread slices in half. Place on an ungreased baking sheet. Bake at 400 for on each side until lightly browned, 4-5 minutes.
3. In a stockpot, saute onion in oil until tender. Add garlic; cook 1 minute longer. Reduce heat; stir in tomatoes and saffron. Add the potatoes, fennel, broth, clam juice and tarragon. Bring to a boil. Reduce heat; simmer, uncovered, until potatoes are almost tender,10-12 minutes.
4. Add the clams, mussels, snapper and shrimp. Cook, stirring occasionally, until clams and mussels open and fish flakes easily with a fork, 10-15 minutes. Discard any unopened clams or mussels. Spoon

LAUREN'S BOUILLABAISSE

into bowls; sprinkle with parsley. Spread pepper mayo over croutons; serve with the bouillabaisse.

1⅔ cups with 1 crouton: 239 cal., 5g fat (1g sat. fat), 70mg chol., 684mg sod., 23g carb. (3g sugars, 2g fiber), 24g pro.
Diabetic exchanges: 3 lean meat, 1½ starch, ½ fat.

HEARTY BACKYARD BURGERS

I like to toast rye rolls or whole wheat hamburger buns on the grill for a few minutes while the burgers finish cooking. Then I top the burgers with ketchup and pickle planks right before serving. But even plain, these are mighty fine.
—Paula LeFevre, Garden, MI

Takes: 25 min. • **Makes:** 6 servings

- ½ cup finely chopped onion
- ¼ cup beer or nonalcoholic beer
- 1 Tbsp. Worcestershire sauce
- 2 garlic cloves, minced
- 1 tsp. salt
- ¼ tsp. pepper
- 1½ lbs. lean ground beef (90% lean)
- 6 rye rolls or whole wheat hamburger buns, split
- 6 lettuce leaves
- 12 tomato slices

1. In a large bowl, combine the first six ingredients. Crumble beef over mixture and mix well. Shape into six patties.
2. Lightly oil the grill rack. Place patties on rack; cover and grill over medium-high heat or broil 4 in. from the heat until a thermometer reads 160° and juices run clear, 4-5 minutes on each side.
3. Serve burgers on rolls with lettuce and tomato slices.

1 burger: 305 cal., 11g fat (4g sat. fat), 71mg chol., 725mg sod., 24g carb. (3g sugars, 3g fiber), 27g pro.
Diabetic exchanges: 3 lean meat, 2 starch.

CAMPFIRE BEAN & HAM SOUP

These are the best beans and ham you'll ever taste—bar none! Friends rave about this hearty soup that I serve hot off the grill. For easy cleanup, consider covering the outside of your Dutch oven with heavy-duty foil first.
—Tom Greaves, Carrollton, IL

Prep: 15 min. + standing • **Grill:** 1½ hours
Makes: 12 servings (3 qt.)

- 1 lb. dried navy beans
- 2 small onions
- 8 cups water
- 4 cups cubed fully cooked lean ham (1½ lbs.)
- 2 smoked ham hocks
- 2 cups chopped celery
- 1 cup chopped carrots
- ½ tsp. dried basil
- ½ tsp. pepper

1. Place beans in an ovenproof Dutch oven; add enough water to cover by 2 in. Bring to a boil; boil for 2 minutes. Remove from the heat; cover and let stand until beans are softened, 1 to 4 hours.

2. Chop one onion; slice second onion and separate into rings. Set onions aside. Drain and rinse beans, discarding liquid. Return beans to the pan. Add reserved onions; stir in the remaining ingredients. Cover pan and place on the grill rack over indirect medium heat.

3. Cover grill; cook for 1 hour or until beans are almost tender. Uncover Dutch oven; cover grill and cook 30 minutes longer or until beans are tender. Discard ham hocks.

1 cup: 197 cal., 3g fat (1g sat. fat), 28mg chol., 612mg sod., 26g carb. (3g sugars, 7g fiber), 19g pro.

Diabetic exchanges: 3 lean meat, 1½ starch.

HEARTY BEEF BARLEY SOUP

My entire family just loves this delicious and comforting soup. Loaded with chunks of tender beef, the rich broth also includes plenty of fresh mushrooms, sliced carrots and quick-cooking barley.
—Barbara Beattie, Glen Allen, VA

Prep: 10 min. • **Cook:** 30 min.
Makes: 4 servings

- 2 Tbsp. all-purpose flour
- ½ tsp. salt
- ¼ tsp. pepper, divided
- 1 lb. lean beef top sirloin steak, cut into ½-in. cubes
- 1 Tbsp. canola oil
- 2 cups sliced fresh mushrooms
- 2 cans (14½ oz. each) reduced-sodium beef broth
- 2 medium carrots, sliced
- ¼ tsp. garlic powder
- ¼ tsp. dried thyme
- ½ cup quick-cooking barley

1. In a shallow dish, combine the flour, salt and ⅛ tsp. pepper. Add beef a few pieces at a time and toss to coat. In a Dutch oven, brown the beef in oil over medium heat or until the meat is no longer pink. Remove beef and set aside.

2. In the same pan, saute mushrooms until tender. Add the broth, carrots, garlic powder, thyme and the remaining pepper; bring to a boil. Add the barley and beef. Reduce the heat; cover and simmer until meat, vegetables and barley are tender, for 20-25 minutes.

1¼ cups: 306 cal., 9g fat (2g sat. fat), 50mg chol., 748mg sod., 25g carb. (3g sugars, 5g fiber), 31g pro.

Diabetic exchanges: 3 lean meat, 1½ starch, 1 vegetable, ½ fat.

CAMPFIRE BEAN & HAM SOUP

SALADS

"I developed this recipe for a friend who needed a potato salad that could withstand Fourth of July weather. The vinaigrette was a safe and delicious alternative to traditional mayonnaise-based potato salads. I've also substituted fresh thyme for the basil. Any fresh herbs would be great!"
—Melanie Cloyd, Mullica Hill, NJ

Mango & Jicama Salad (p. 82) Holiday Rice Salad (p. 91) Mango Barley Salad (p. 70)
Apple Sausage Salad with Cinnamon Vinaigrette (p. 74) Lemon Vinaigrette Potato Salad (p. 94)
Shrimp & Spinach Salad with Hot Bacon Dressing (p. 83)

MANGO BARLEY SALAD

MANGO BARLEY SALAD

I made this fresh, colorful mango salad on the fly and it was a big hit! The bright flavor is perfect for a spring or summer picnic, served right away or chilled.
—Dan Wellberg, Elk River, MN

....

Takes: 25 min. • **Makes:** 6 servings

- 1¾ cups water
- 1 cup quick-cooking barley
- 2 medium limes
- ¼ cup olive oil
- 1 Tbsp. Dijon mustard
- 1 Tbsp. honey
- ½ tsp. salt
- ¼ tsp. ground cumin
- ¼ tsp. pepper
- ½ cup chopped sweet red pepper
- ½ cup chopped green pepper
- ¼ cup chopped red onion
- 1 medium mango, peeled and chopped
- ¼ cup minced fresh cilantro

1. In a small saucepan, bring water to a boil. Stir in barley. Reduce the heat; simmer, covered, until barley is tender, 10-12 minutes. Remove from heat; let stand 5 minutes.

2. Finely grate enough zest from limes to measure 1 tsp. Cut the limes crosswise in half; squeeze juice from limes. In a small bowl, whisk lime juice, lime zest, oil, mustard, honey, salt, cumin and pepper until blended.

3. In a large bowl, combine barley, peppers, onion, mango and cilantro. Add dressing; toss to coat. Refrigerate until serving.

¾ cup: 185 cal., 10g fat (1g sat. fat), 0 chol., 261mg sod., 25g carb. (9g sugars, 5g fiber), 2g pro.
Diabetic exchanges: 2 fat, 1½ starch.

TEST KITCHEN TIP
We call for barley in this recipe, but you can also try making it with quinoa, farro or other grains. Whatever you choose, it's going to be delicious!

CUCUMBER SHELL SALAD

Ranch dressing is the mild coating for this pleasant pasta salad chock-full of crunchy cucumber, onion and green peas. Wherever I take it, I'm always asked for the recipe.
—Paula Ishii, Ralston, NE

....

Prep: 20 min. + chilling
Makes: 16 servings

- 1 pkg. (16 oz.) medium pasta shells
- 1 pkg. (16 oz.) frozen peas, thawed
- 1 medium cucumber, halved and sliced
- 1 small red onion, chopped
- 1 cup ranch salad dressing

Cook pasta shells according to package directions; drain and rinse in cold water. In a large bowl, combine the pasta, peas, cucumber and onion. Add dressing; toss to coat. Cover and chill at least 2 hours before serving.

¾ cup: 165 cal., 1g fat (0 sat. fat), 0 chol., 210mg sod., 33g carb. (0 sugars, 3g fiber), 6g pro.
Diabetic exchanges: 2 starch.

SESAME BEEF & ASPARAGUS SALAD

Cooking is one of my favorite hobbies—especially when it comes to experimenting with fresh ingredients like these. This meaty salad is wonderful at the start of asparagus season.

—Tamara Steeb, Issaquah, WA

....

Takes: 30 min. • **Makes:** 6 servings

1 beef top round steak (1 lb.)
4 cups cut fresh asparagus
   (2-in. pieces)
3 Tbsp. reduced-sodium soy sauce
2 Tbsp. sesame oil
1 Tbsp. rice vinegar
½ tsp. grated gingerroot
   Sesame seeds
   Lettuce leaves, julienned carrot and
     radishes, cilantro leaves and lime
     wedges, optional

1. Preheat broiler. Place steak on a broiler pan. Broil 2-3 in. from heat until meat reaches desired doneness (for medium-rare, a thermometer should read 135°), 6-7 minutes per side. Let stand 5 minutes before slicing.

2. In a large saucepan, bring ½ in. water to a boil. Add asparagus; cook, uncovered, just until crisp-tender, 3-5 minutes. Drain and cool.

3. Mix soy sauce, sesame oil, vinegar and ginger; toss with beef and asparagus. Sprinkle with sesame seeds. If desired, serve over lettuce with carrot, radishes, cilantro and lime wedges.

1 cup: 160 cal., 7g fat (1g sat. fat), 42mg chol., 350mg sod., 5g carb. (2g sugars, 2g fiber), 19g pro.
Diabetic exchanges: 2 lean meat, 1 vegetable, 1 fat.

SESAME BEEF & ASPARAGUS SALAD

TUNA & WHITE BEAN LETTUCE WRAPS

Say bye-bye to ho-hum tuna salad. This is a version we actually look forward to eating! It's great for a quick dinner or work lunch.

—Heather Senger, Madison, WI

....

Takes: 20 min.
Makes: 4 servings

1 can (12 oz.) light tuna in water, drained and flaked
1 can (15 oz.) cannellini beans, rinsed and drained
¼ cup chopped red onion
2 Tbsp. olive oil
1 Tbsp. minced fresh parsley
⅛ tsp. salt
⅛ tsp. pepper
12 Bibb or Boston lettuce leaves (about 1 medium head)
1 medium ripe avocado, peeled and sliced

In a small bowl, combine the first seven ingredients; toss lightly to combine. Serve in lettuce leaves; top with avocado.

3 wraps: 279 cal., 13g fat (2g sat. fat), 31mg chol., 421mg sod., 19g carb. (1g sugars, 7g fiber), 22g pro.
Diabetic exchanges: 3 lean meat, 2 fat, 1 starch.

CURRIED QUINOA SALAD

PORK & BALSAMIC STRAWBERRY SALAD

Serving this entree salad in early spring gives me hope that warmer days aren't too far off. If strawberries aren't in season yet, use thawed frozen in place of fresh.
—Laurie Lufkin, Essex, MA

Prep: 20 min. + marinating • **Bake:** 15 min.
Makes: 4 servings

  1 pork tenderloin (1 lb.)
  ½ cup Italian salad dressing
1½ cups halved fresh strawberries
  2 Tbsp. balsamic vinegar
  2 tsp. sugar
  ¼ tsp. salt
  ¼ tsp. pepper
  2 Tbsp. olive oil
  ¼ cup chicken broth
  1 pkg. (5 oz.) spring mix salad greens
  ½ cup crumbled goat cheese

1. Place pork in a shallow dish. Add the salad dressing; turn to coat. Refrigerate, covered, at least 8 hours. Combine the strawberries, vinegar and sugar; cover and refrigerate.
2. Preheat oven to 425°. Drain and wipe off pork, discarding marinade. Sprinkle with salt and pepper. In a large ovenproof skillet, heat oil over medium-high heat. Add pork; brown on all sides.
3. Bake until a thermometer reads 145°, 15-20 minutes. Remove from skillet; let stand 5 minutes. Meanwhile, add broth to skillet; cook over medium heat, stirring to loosen browned bits from pan. Bring to a boil. Reduce heat; add strawberry mixture. Heat through.
4. Place greens on a serving platter; sprinkle with cheese. Slice pork; arrange over greens. Top with strawberry mixture.
2 cups: 291 cal., 16g fat (5g sat. fat), 81mg chol., 444mg sod., 12g carb. (7g sugars, 3g fiber), 26g pro.
Diabetic exchanges: 3 lean meat, 3 fat, 1 vegetable.

CURRIED QUINOA SALAD

Quinoa is such a fantastic salad base— it's full of protein, adds a nutty flavor, and is the perfect vehicle to soak up any kind of dressing. If you like a little more heat, add more cayenne or curry to the dressing.
—Shannon Dobos, Calgary, AB

Prep: 35 min. + chilling
Makes: 6 servings

  1 cup quinoa, rinsed
  1 tsp. ground turmeric
  ¼ tsp. ground cumin
  1 can (14½ oz.) vegetable or chicken broth
1½ cups grape tomatoes, halved
  1 small cucumber, diced
  ⅓ cup diced red onion
DRESSING
  2 Tbsp. lemon juice
  2 Tbsp. olive oil
  1 Tbsp. honey

  1 tsp. yellow mustard
  ½ tsp. curry powder
  ¼ tsp. salt
  ⅛ tsp. cayenne pepper

1. In a small saucepan, combine first four ingredients; bring to a boil. Reduce heat; simmer, covered, until liquid is absorbed, 12-15 minutes. Remove from heat; let stand, covered, 15 minutes. Transfer to a large bowl; cool slightly.
2. Add tomatoes, cucumber and onion to quinoa. In a small bowl, whisk together dressing ingredients; toss with salad. Refrigerate, covered, until cold, about 2 hours. Stir before serving.
¾ cup: 176 cal., 6g fat (1g sat. fat), 0 chol., 320mg sod., 25g carb. (5g sugars, 3g fiber), 5g pro.
Diabetic exchanges: 1½ starch, 1 fat.

**PORK & BALSAMIC
STRAWBERRY SALAD**

CRANBERRY TURKEY BURGERS WITH ARUGULA SALAD

These healthy burgers taste like the holidays in just one bite. They're a little sweet, a little savory and extremely delicious over a bed of bright arugula.
—Nicole Stevens, Mount Pleasant, SC

Takes: 25 min. • **Makes:** 4 servings

- ¾ lb. ground turkey
- ⅓ cup dried cranberries
- ⅓ cup gluten-free soft bread crumbs
- 3 green onions, finely chopped
- 2 to 3 Tbsp. crumbled goat cheese
- 2 Tbsp. pepper jelly
- 3 garlic cloves, minced
- 1 large egg yolk
- ¼ tsp. salt
- ¼ tsp. pepper
- 4 cups fresh arugula
- 1 Tbsp. grapeseed oil or olive oil
- 1 Tbsp. honey

1. Preheat oven to 375°. Combine the first 10 ingredients, mixing lightly but thoroughly. Shape into four ½-in.-thick patties; transfer to a greased baking sheet. Bake until no longer pink, 10-12 minutes. Heat broiler; broil until a thermometer inserted in burgers reads 165°, about 5 minutes.
2. Meanwhile, toss the arugula with oil. Drizzle with honey; toss to combine. Top salad with turkey burgers.

1 burger with 1 cup salad: 281 cal., 12g fat (3g sat. fat), 107mg chol., 240mg sod., 26g carb. (21g sugars, 2g fiber), 19g pro.

APPLE SAUSAGE SALAD WITH CINNAMON VINAIGRETTE
(PICTURED ON P. 68)

Making croutons with cinnamon-raisin bread is sweet genius. Toss together the rest of the salad while they toast.
—Kim Van Dunk, Caldwell, NJ

Prep: 25 min. • **Bake:** 10 min.
Makes: 6 servings

- 4 slices cinnamon-raisin bread
- ⅓ cup olive oil
- 3 Tbsp. cider vinegar
- 2 tsp. honey
- ½ tsp. ground cinnamon
- ⅛ tsp. sea salt
  Dash pepper
- 1 pkg. (12 oz.) fully cooked apple chicken sausage links, cut diagonally in ½-in.-thick slices
- 2 pkg. (5 oz. each) spring mix salad greens
- 2 cups sliced fresh Bartlett pears
- ½ cup chopped walnuts, toasted
- ½ cup dried sweet cherries

1. Preheat oven to 375°. Cut each slice of bread into 12 cubes; scatter over a 15x10-in. pan. Bake until toasted, 8-10 minutes, stirring halfway. Cool 5 minutes.
2. Meanwhile, combine next six ingredients in a jar with a tight-fitting lid. Shake until blended. In a large nonstick skillet, cook sausage over medium heat until browned and heated through, 2-3 minutes per side.
3. Divide salad greens among six dinner-size plates; add sausage to each plate. Top with pear slices, walnuts, cherries and croutons. Shake dressing again; spoon over salad and serve immediately.

Note: To toast nuts, bake in a shallow pan in a 350° oven for 5-10 minutes or cook in a skillet over low heat until lightly browned, stirring occasionally.

1 serving: 404 cal., 23g fat (4g sat. fat), 40mg chol., 441mg sod., 39g carb. (23g sugars, 5g fiber), 14g pro.

CRANBERRY TURKEY BURGERS WITH ARUGULA SALAD

TARRAGON ASPARAGUS SALAD

NECTARINE & BEET SALAD

Beets and nectarines sprinkled with feta cheese make a scrumptious flavor combination over a mixed green salad. The grouping of ingredients may seem unlikely, but I think it will become a favorite.
—Nicole Werner, Ann Arbor, MI

....

Takes: 10 min. • **Makes:** 8 servings

- 2 pkg. (5 oz. each) spring mix salad greens
- 2 medium nectarines, sliced
- ½ cup balsamic vinaigrette
- 1 can (14½ oz.) sliced beets, drained
- ½ cup crumbled feta cheese

On a serving dish, toss salad greens and nectarines with vinaigrette. Top with beets and cheese; serve immediately.
1 cup: 84 cal., 4g fat (1g sat. fat), 4mg chol., 371mg sod., 10g carb. (6g sugars, 3g fiber), 3g pro.
Diabetic exchanges: 2 vegetable, ½ fat.

TARRAGON ASPARAGUS SALAD

I love asparagus, and I love it even more when drizzled with my light, lemony vinaigrette dressing with a touch of tarragon. It's perfect as a side for fresh spring meals.
—Linda Lacek, Winter Park, FL

....

Prep: 15 min. + chilling • **Cook:** 5 min.
Makes: 4 servings

- 2 Tbsp. lemon juice
- 2 Tbsp. olive oil
- 1 tsp. minced fresh tarragon or ¼ tsp. dried tarragon
- 1 garlic clove, minced
- ½ tsp. Dijon mustard
- ¼ tsp. pepper
  Dash salt
- 1 lb. fresh asparagus, cut into 2-in. pieces

1. Place first seven ingredients in a jar with a tight-fitting lid; shake well. Refrigerate at least 1 hour.
2. In a large skillet, bring ½ in. of water to a boil. Add asparagus; cook, covered, until crisp-tender, 1-3 minutes. Remove asparagus and immediately drop into ice water. Drain and pat dry. Refrigerate, covered, until serving.
3. To serve, shake dressing again. Spoon over asparagus.
1 serving: 77 cal., 7g fat (1g sat. fat), 0 chol., 387mg sod., 3g carb. (1g sugars, 1g fiber), 2g pro.
Diabetic exchanges: 1½ fat, 1 vegetable.

BLACK BEAN BULGUR SALAD

BLACK BEAN BULGUR SALAD

The only cooking in this easy bulgur salad is heating up the vegetable broth in the microwave. You can adapt the recipe to your preference; if you want to add chopped, cooked chicken for a protein boost, use chicken broth instead.

—Carole Resnick, Cleveland, OH

Takes: 30 min. • **Makes:** 4 servings

- 1 cup bulgur
- 2 cups vegetable broth
- ¼ cup orange juice
- ¼ cup lime juice
- 1 jalapeno pepper, seeded and minced
- 2 Tbsp. olive oil
- ¼ tsp. ground cumin
- 1 cup shredded carrots
- 3 Tbsp. minced fresh cilantro
- 1 can (15 oz.) black beans, rinsed and drained
- 1 cup frozen corn, thawed
- ¾ cup shredded Monterey Jack cheese
  Sliced jalapeno pepper, optional

1. Place bulgur and broth in a small saucepan; bring to a boil. Reduce heat; simmer bulgur, covered, until tender, 12-15 minutes. Transfer to a large bowl; cool slightly.
2. For dressing, whisk together citrus juices, minced jalapeno, oil and cumin. Add ⅓ cup dressing to bulgur; stir in carrots and cilantro.
3. To serve, divide bulgur mixture among four bowls. Top with beans, corn, cheese and, if desired, sliced jalapeno. Drizzle with remaining dressing.

1 serving: 402 cal., 14g fat (5g sat. fat), 19mg chol., 688mg sod., 56g carb. (6g sugars, 10g fiber), 16g pro.

TEST KITCHEN TIP

Bulgur is sometimes called cracked wheat. It's a whole grain that's been boiled, dried and ground. Since it's been precooked, it cooks up faster than most whole grains.

ROASTED GREEN BEAN SALAD

ROASTED GREEN BEAN SALAD

This easy-to-fix recipe turns homegrown green beans into something special. A tangy dill and Dijon vinaigrette coats the crisp-tender beans without overpowering them so the fresh-picked flavor comes through.

—Kathy Shell, San Diego, CA

Prep: 10 min. • **Bake:** 30 min.
Makes: 6 servings

- 2 lbs. fresh green beans, trimmed
- 3 Tbsp. olive oil, divided
- ¾ tsp. salt, divided
- 2 Tbsp. white wine vinegar
- 2 Tbsp. snipped fresh dill or 2 tsp. dill weed
- 1½ tsp. Dijon mustard
- 1½ tsp. sugar
- ¼ tsp. pepper

1. Preheat oven to 400°. In a large bowl, toss beans with 1 Tbsp. oil and ½ tsp. salt. Transfer to two ungreased 15x10x1-in. baking pans.
2. Roast 30-35 minutes or until beans are tender and lightly browned, stirring occasionally.
3. In a small bowl, whisk vinegar, dill, mustard, sugar, pepper and the remaining oil and salt until blended. Transfer beans to a large bowl. Drizzle with vinaigrette and toss to coat.

1 serving: 108 cal., 7g fat (1g sat. fat), 0 chol., 335mg sod., 11g carb. (4g sugars, 5g fiber), 3g pro.
Diabetic exchanges: 1½ fat, 1 vegetable.

★ ★ ★ ★ ★ **READER REVIEW**

"Zippy flavor, and you must like dill. We eat it as a warm side dish. We also make the sauce for roasted Brussels sprouts or asparagus. Definitely tasty and recommended."

SAL865 TASTEOFHOME.COM

SOUTH-OF-THE-BORDER CITRUS SALAD

Orange, grapefruit and jicama add color and texture to this out-of-the-ordinary fruit salad. Sometimes I'll toss in slices of mango and cucumber for extra fun.
—Mary Fuller, SeaTac, WA

Prep Time: 20 min. + chilling
Makes: 6 servings

- 3 medium pink grapefruit
- 3 medium oranges
- 1 cup julienned peeled jicama
- 2 Tbsp. minced fresh cilantro
- 2 Tbsp. lime juice
- ¼ tasp. ground cinnamon

1. Cut a thin slice from the top and bottom of each grapefruit and orange; stand fruit upright on a cutting board. With a knife, cut the peel and the outer membrane from fruit. Cut fruit crosswise into slices; place in a large bowl.
2. Add remaining ingredients; toss to combine. Transfer to a platter; refrigerate, covered, until serving.
¾ cup: 70 cal., 0 fat (0 sat. fat), 0 chol., 2mg sod., 17g carb. (13g sugars, 3g fiber), 1g pro.
Diabetic exchanges: 1 fruit.

POTATO-BEAN SALAD WITH HERB DRESSING

POTATO-BEAN SALAD WITH HERB DRESSING

My veggie garden inspired this creamy combo of beans, potatoes and fresh herbs. I toss them with a ranch-style dressing sparked up with Creole mustard.
—Christopher Cummer, Rincon, GA

Prep: 15 min. • **Cook:** 20 min. + chilling
Makes: 6 servings

- 1 lb. potatoes (about 2 medium), peeled and cubed
- ½ lb. fresh green beans, trimmed and cut into 2-in. pieces

DRESSING
- ⅓ cup buttermilk
- 2 Tbsp. mayonnaise
- 2 Tbsp. sour cream
- 1 Tbsp. Creole mustard
- 1 Tbsp. minced chives
- 1 Tbsp. minced fresh parsley or 1 tsp. dried parsley flakes
- 1½ tsp. snipped fresh dill or ½ tsp. dill weed
- 1½ tsp. cider vinegar
- 1 garlic clove, minced
- ½ tsp. salt
- ⅛ tsp. celery seed
- ⅛ tsp. pepper

1. Place potatoes in a large saucepan; add water to cover. Bring to a boil. Reduce heat; cook, uncovered, 10-15 minutes or until tender, adding green beans during the last 4 minutes of cooking. Drain; cool completely.
2. In a small bowl, combine the dressing ingredients. Pour over the potato mixture and toss to coat. Refrigerate, covered, until cold.
⅔ cup: 109 cal., 5g fat (1g sat. fat), 6mg chol., 305mg sod., 14g carb. (3g sugars, 2g fiber), 2g pro.
Diabetic exchanges: 1 starch, 1 fat.

EASY PEASY SLAW

I get tons of compliments when I bring out this slaw brightened up with peas, peanuts and poppy seed dressing. It's fresh and colorful with a satisfying crunch.
—Sue Ort, Des Moines, IA

Takes: 5 min.
Makes: 12 servings (⅔ cup each)

- 4 cups frozen peas (about 16 oz.), thawed
- 1 pkg. (14 oz.) coleslaw mix
- 4 green onions, chopped
- 1 cup poppy seed salad dressing
- 1 cup sweet and crunchy peanuts or honey-roasted peanuts

Place the peas, coleslaw mix and green onions in a large bowl. Pour dressing over salad and toss to coat. Stir in peanuts just before serving.

⅔ cup: 202 cal., 12g fat (2g sat. fat), 7mg chol., 178mg sod., 20g carb. (14g sugars, 4g fiber), 4g pro.
Diabetic exchanges: 2 fat, 1 starch, 1 vegetable.

RASPBERRY-WALNUT PORK SALAD

Raspberry, rosemary, Gorgonzola and walnuts combine to make a pork dish that's bursting with flavor.
—Virginia Anthony, Jacksonville, FL

Prep: 30 min. • **Cook:** 20 min.
Makes: 6 servings

- 1½ lbs. pork tenderloins, cut into 1-in. slices
- ⅓ cup ground walnuts
- 2 Tbsp. all-purpose flour
- ½ tsp. salt, divided
- ½ tsp. coarsely ground pepper, divided
- 4½ tsp. walnut oil
- ⅓ cup chopped shallot
- 1 medium pear, chopped
- ¾ cup reduced-sodium chicken broth
- ¾ cup seedless raspberry preserves
- ½ cup raspberry vinegar
- 2 tsp. minced fresh rosemary or ½ tsp. dried rosemary, crushed
- 2 tsp. minced fresh sage
- 2 pkg. (6 oz. each) fresh baby spinach
- ½ cup crumbled Gorgonzola cheese
- ½ cup chopped walnuts, toasted

1. Flatten pork slices to ½-in. thickness. In a shallow dish, combine the ground walnuts, flour, ¼ tsp. salt and ¼ tsp. pepper. Add pork, a few pieces at a time, and turn to coat.

2. In a large skillet over medium heat, cook pork in oil in batches for 2-3 minutes on each side or until meat is no longer pink. Remove and keep warm.

3. In the same skillet, saute shallot until tender. Add pear; cook 1 minute longer. Add the broth, preserves and vinegar. Bring to a boil; cook for 6-8 minutes or until slightly thickened. Stir in the rosemary, sage and remaining salt and pepper. Remove from the heat.

4. Place spinach in a large bowl. Add pear mixture; toss to coat. Divide among six plates; top each with pork. Sprinkle with cheese and chopped walnuts.

1 serving: 398 cal., 17g fat (4g sat. fat), 71mg chol., 415mg sod., 34g carb. (25g sugars, 2g fiber), 30g pro.

EASY PEASY SLAW

STRAWBERRY SPINACH SALAD WITH POPPY SEED DRESSING

I love to make this spinach salad in the spring when I have fresh yummy strawberries. Everyone loves this pretty, healthy side.
—Erin Loughmiller, Ridgecrest, CA

Prep: 25 min. + chilling
Makes: 10 servings

- ⅓ cup olive oil
- ¼ cup sugar
- 3 Tbsp. white or balsamic vinegar
- 2 Tbsp. sesame seeds
- 1 Tbsp. poppy seeds
- 1 Tbsp. chopped onion
- ¼ tsp. paprika
- ¼ tsp. Worcestershire sauce
- 1 pkg. (9 oz.) fresh spinach, trimmed
- 4 cups fresh strawberries, sliced
- ¼ cup chopped pecans, toasted

1. Place the first eight ingredients in a jar with a tight-fitting lid; shake well. Refrigerate for 1 hour.
2. Just before serving, combine the remaining ingredients in a large bowl. Shake dressing and drizzle over salad; toss to coat.

1 cup: 141 cal., 11g fat (1g sat. fat), 0 chol., 23mg sod., 11g carb. (8g sugars, 2g fiber), 2g pro.
Diabetic exchanges: 1½ fat, ½ starch.

How To Get the Most Juice

This simple trick will help you get the most juice from your citrus. Firmly roll the fruit on the counter, using the palm of your hand, for 20-30 seconds. You can also microwave the fruit on high for 10-20 seconds just before cutting.

SUMMERTIME TOMATO SALAD

Here is the best of summer in one cool, refreshing salad. Cherry tomatoes make it pretty and colorful, and the blueberry surprise sweetens it up along with a hint of mint.
—Thomas Faglon, Somerset, NJ

Prep: 25 min. + chilling
Makes: 12 servings

- 4 medium ears sweet corn, husks removed
- 2 lbs. cherry tomatoes (about 6 cups), halved
- 1 small yellow summer squash, halved lengthwise and sliced
- 1 cup fresh blueberries
- 1 small red onion, halved and thinly sliced
- ¼ cup olive oil
- 2 Tbsp. lemon juice
- 1 Tbsp. minced fresh mint
- ½ tsp. salt
- ½ tsp. freshly ground pepper

1. In a 6-qt. stockpot, bring 8 cups water to a boil. Add corn; cook, uncovered, until crisp-tender, 2-4 minutes. Remove corn and immediately drop into ice water to cool; drain well.
2. Cut corn from cobs and place in a bowl. Add remaining ingredients; toss to combine. Refrigerate, covered, until cold, about 30 minutes.

¾ cup: 95 cal., 5g fat (1g sat. fat), 0 chol., 108mg sod., 12g carb. (6g sugars, 2g fiber), 2g pro.
Diabetic exchanges: 1 vegetable, 1 fat, ½ starch.

STRAWBERRY SPINACH SALAD WITH POPPY SEED DRESSING

HERBED TUNA & WHITE BEAN SALAD

Canned tuna makes this quick, delicious salad economical, but you can also make it special for dinner guests by grilling fresh tuna steaks if you like.
—Charlene Chambers, Ormond Beach, FL

Takes: 15 min. • **Makes:** 4 servings

- 4 cups fresh arugula
- 1 can (15 oz.) no-salt-added cannellini beans, rinsed and drained
- 1 cup grape tomatoes, halved
- ½ small red onion, thinly sliced
- ⅓ cup chopped roasted sweet red peppers
- ⅓ cup pitted Nicoise or other olives
- ¼ cup chopped fresh basil
- 3 Tbsp. extra virgin olive oil
- ½ tsp. grated lemon zest
- 2 Tbsp. lemon juice
- 1 garlic clove, minced
- ⅛ tsp. salt
- 2 cans (5 oz. each) albacore white tuna in water, drained

Place first seven ingredients in a large bowl. Whisk together oil, lemon zest, lemon juice, garlic and salt; drizzle over salad. Add tuna; toss gently to combine.
2 cups: 319 cal., 16g fat (2g sat. fat), 30mg chol., 640mg sod., 20g carb. (3g sugars, 5g fiber), 23g pro.
Diabetic exchanges: 3 fat, 2 lean meat, 1 starch, 1 vegetable.

✱
TEST KITCHEN TIP
Kalamata olives, though stronger in flavor, would be a good substitute for Nicoise olives.

PESTO CORN SALAD WITH SHRIMP

PESTO CORN SALAD WITH SHRIMP

This recipe showcases the beautiful bounty of summer with its fresh corn, tomatoes and delicious basil. Prevent browning by placing plastic wrap directly on the salad or spritzing with lemon juice.
—Deena Bowen, Chico, CA

Takes: 30 min. • **Makes:** 4 servings

- 4 medium ears sweet corn, husked
- ½ cup packed fresh basil leaves
- ¼ cup olive oil
- ½ tsp. salt, divided
- 1½ cups cherry tomatoes, halved
- ⅛ tsp. pepper
- 1 medium ripe avocado, peeled and chopped
- 1 lb. uncooked shrimp (31-40 per lb.), peeled and deveined

1. In a pot of boiling water, cook corn until tender, about 5 minutes. Drain; cool slightly. Meanwhile, in a food processor, pulse basil, oil and ¼ tsp. salt until blended.
2. Cut corn from cob and place in a bowl. Stir in tomatoes, pepper and remaining salt. Add the avocado and 2 Tbsp. basil mixture; toss gently to combine.
3. Thread shrimp onto metal or soaked wooden skewers; brush with remaining basil mixture. Grill, covered, over medium heat until shrimp turn pink, 2-4 minutes per side. Remove shrimp from skewers; serve with corn mixture.
1 serving: 371 cal., 22g fat (3g sat. fat), 138mg chol., 450mg sod., 25g carb. (8g sugars, 5g fiber), 23g pro.

MY FAVORITE AVOCADO SALAD

MY FAVORITE AVOCADO SALAD

Tangy lime dressing is the perfect topper for avocado salad. Toasted walnuts add great crunch, but feel free to substitute any kind of nuts you like.
—Ilia Kaku, North Richland Hills, TX

....

Takes: 25 min. • **Makes:** 9 servings

- 1 Tbsp. lemon juice
- 2 medium avocados, peeled and cubed
- 1 pkg. (5 oz.) spring mix salad greens
- 5 plum tomatoes, chopped
- ½ cup chopped red onion
- ¼ cup chopped walnuts, toasted

LIME DRESSING
- 3 Tbsp. olive oil
- 1 Tbsp. minced fresh parsley
- 1 Tbsp. minced fresh cilantro
- 1 Tbsp. sour cream
- 1 Tbsp. lime juice
- 1 tsp. yellow mustard
- ⅛ tsp. salt
- ⅛ tsp. pepper
  Dash sugar

Drizzle lemon juice over avocados. In a serving bowl, combine salad greens, tomatoes, onion, walnuts and avocados. Whisk together dressing ingredients; pour over salad. Toss to coat.

Note: To toast nuts, bake in a shallow pan in a 350° oven for 5-10 minutes or cook in a skillet over low heat until lightly browned, stirring occasionally.

1 cup: 130 cal., 12g fat (2g sat. fat), 1mg chol., 57mg sod., 7g carb. (2g sugars, 3g fiber), 2g pro.
Diabetic exchanges: 2 fat, 1 vegetable.

MANGO & JICAMA SALAD
(PICTURED ON P. 68)

This pretty salad has become part of my regular summertime rotation because of its freshness and versatility—it's great with everything from grilled chicken to seafood! Try it with coconut-flavored vinegar for a fun tropical twist.
—Carla Mendres, Winnipeg, MB

....

Takes: 25 min. • **Makes:** 8 servings

- ½ cup white wine vinegar
- ¼ cup canola oil
- ¼ cup honey
- 1 tsp. minced fresh gingerroot
- ¼ tsp. salt
- ⅛ tsp. pepper
- 1 medium jicama (about 1½ lbs.), peeled
- 1 medium mango, peeled
- 1 medium sweet red pepper
- 2 Tbsp. lime juice
- ½ cup chopped fresh cilantro
- ⅓ cup minced fresh chives

1. For dressing, whisk together the first six ingredients.
2. Cut jicama, mango and red pepper into matchsticks; place in a large bowl. Toss with lime juice. Add herbs and dressing; toss to combine. Refrigerate, covered, until serving.

1 cup: 143 cal., 7g fat (1g sat. fat), 0 chol., 78mg sod., 20g carb. (16g sugars, 3g fiber), 1g pro.
Diabetic exchanges: 1½ fat, 1 vegetable, ½ starch.

MELON-BERRY SALAD

The best way to cool down on a warm day is to serve up a chilled fruit salad featuring the best of summer's bounty! The dressing gives this salad a creamy and rich texture, and the coconut milk makes it even more decadent. This can be served at breakfast, brunch or as a dessert! Wait until just before serving to garnish the salad. Otherwise the toasted coconut will get soggy.
—Carrie Hirsch, Hilton Head Island, SC

Takes: 20 min.
Makes: 12 servings

- 1 cup fat-free vanilla Greek yogurt
- ½ cup coconut milk
- ½ cup orange juice
- 4 cups cubed cantaloupe (½ in.)
- 4 cups cubed watermelon (½ in.)
- 2 medium navel oranges, sectioned
- 1 cup fresh raspberries
- 1 cup fresh blueberries
- ½ cup sweetened shredded coconut, toasted

1. For dressing, whisk together yogurt, coconut milk and orange juice. Refrigerate until serving.

2. To serve, place fruit in a large bowl; toss gently with dressing. Sprinkle with coconut.

Note: To toast coconut, bake in a shallow pan in a 350° oven for 5-10 minutes or cook in a skillet over low heat until golden brown, stirring occasionally.

¾ cup: 105 cal., 3g fat (3g sat. fat), 0 chol., 30mg sod., 19g carb. (16g sugars, 2g fiber), 3g pro.

Diabetic exchanges: 1 fruit, ½ fat.

MELON-BERRY SALAD

SHRIMP & SPINACH SALAD WITH HOT BACON DRESSING
(PICTURED ON P. 69)

When I meet former co-workers for lunch we always order this salad. I wanted my husband to try it, so I made it my mission to re-create it. Mission accomplished!
—Lisa L. Bynum, Brandon, MS

Takes: 30 min. • **Makes:** 6 servings

- 1½ lbs. uncooked shrimp (31-40 per lb.), peeled and deveined
- 1 tsp. Montreal steak seasoning
- 4 bacon strips, chopped
- 1 shallot, finely chopped
- ⅓ cup cider vinegar
- 1 Tbsp. olive oil
- 1 tsp. Dijon mustard
- ½ tsp. sugar
- ½ tsp. salt
- ¼ tsp. pepper
- 1 pkg. (10 oz.) fresh spinach
- ¾ cup roasted sweet red peppers
- ¼ cup sliced almonds

1. Sprinkle shrimp with steak seasoning. On four metal or soaked wooden skewers, thread the shrimp. Grill, covered, over medium heat or broil 4 in. from the heat until shrimp turn pink, 2-3 minutes on each side.

2. Meanwhile, in a large skillet, cook bacon over medium heat until crisp, stirring occasionally. Remove with a slotted spoon; drain on paper towels. Discard all but 1 Tbsp. drippings. Add shallot; cook and stir over medium heat until tender. Stir in next six ingredients; bring to a boil. Remove from heat.

3. In a large serving bowl, combine the spinach and dressing; toss to coat. Layer with shrimp and pepper slices; top with cooked bacon and almonds.

1½ cups: 212 cal., 10g fat (2g sat. fat), 145mg chol., 739mg sod., 6g carb. (2g sugars, 1g fiber), 22g pro.

Diabetic exchanges: 3 lean meat, 2 vegetable, 2 fat.

✱
TEST KITCHEN TIP
If you like wilted salads, toss spinach in the dressing before removing it from the heat. This takes only 15 to 20 seconds, so keep an eye on it and stir constantly.

BERRY-BEET SALAD

BERRY-BEET SALAD

Here's a delightfully different salad that balances the earthy flavor of beets with the natural sweetness of berries. If you prefer, substitute crumbled feta for the goat cheese.

—Amy Lyons, Mounds View, MN

Prep: 20 min. • **Bake:** 30 min. + cooling
Makes: 4 servings

- 1 each fresh red and golden beets
- ¼ cup balsamic vinegar
- 2 Tbsp. walnut oil
- 1 tsp. honey
- Dash salt
- Dash pepper
- ½ cup sliced fresh strawberries
- ½ cup fresh raspberries
- ½ cup fresh blackberries
- 3 Tbsp. chopped walnuts, toasted
- 1 shallot, thinly sliced
- 4 cups torn mixed salad greens
- 1 oz. fresh goat cheese, crumbled
- 1 Tbsp. fresh basil, thinly sliced

1. Place beets in an 8-in. square baking dish; add 1 in. of water. Cover and bake at 400° for 30-40 minutes or until tender.
2. Meanwhile, in a small bowl, whisk the vinegar, oil, honey, salt and pepper; set aside. Cool beets; peel and cut into thin slices.
3. In a large bowl, combine the beets, berries, walnuts and shallot. Pour dressing over beet mixture and toss gently to coat. Divide salad greens among four serving plates. Top with beet mixture; sprinkle with cheese and basil.

1 serving: 183 cal., 12g fat (2g sat. fat), 5mg chol., 124mg sod., 18g carb. (11g sugars, 5g fiber), 4g pro.
Diabetic exchanges: 2 fat, 1 starch.

WARM GARBANZO & TOMATO SALAD

I created this salad on a whim while on a trip with friends. We put together a bunch of ingredients we had on hand, and the result was a winner!

—Brittany DeSalvo, New Richmond, OH

Takes: 25 min.
Makes: 12 servings

EMILY'S HONEY LIME COLESLAW

- ½ cup red wine vinegar
- 3 Tbsp. olive oil, divided
- 2 Tbsp. honey
- ½ tsp. Italian seasoning
- ½ tsp. ground cinnamon
- 1 can (16 oz.) garbanzo beans or chickpeas, rinsed and drained
- 24 cherry tomatoes
- ⅛ tsp. onion salt
- ⅛ tsp. garlic salt
- 1 medium bunch romaine, torn (about 8 cups)
- 1 cup salad croutons

1. In a small bowl, whisk vinegar, 2 Tbsp. oil, honey, Italian seasoning and cinnamon.
2. In a large skillet, heat remaining oil over medium-high heat. Add beans, tomatoes, onion salt and garlic salt; cook and stir 5-7 minutes or until heated through.
3. In a large bowl, combine romaine and croutons. Add the bean mixture; drizzle with dressing and toss to coat. Serve immediately.

1 cup: 106 cal., 5g fat (1g sat. fat), 0 chol., 134mg sod., 14g carb. (5g sugars, 3g fiber), 3g pro.
Diabetic exchanges: 1 vegetable, 1 fat, ½ starch.

EMILY'S HONEY LIME COLESLAW

We like this refreshing take on slaw with a honey-lime vinaigrette rather than the traditional mayo. It's a great take-along for all those summer picnics.

—Emily Tyra, Traverse City, MI

Prep: 20 min. + chilling
Makes: 8 servings

- 1½ tsp. grated lime zest
- ¼ cup lime juice
- 2 Tbsp. honey
- 1 garlic clove, minced
- ½ tsp. salt
- ¼ tsp. pepper
- ¼ tsp. crushed red pepper flakes
- 3 Tbsp. canola oil
- 1 small head red cabbage (about ¾ lb.), shredded
- 1 cup shredded carrots (about 2 medium)
- 2 green onions, thinly sliced
- ½ cup fresh cilantro leaves

Whisk together the first seven ingredients until smooth. Gradually whisk in oil until blended. Combine cabbage, carrots and green onions; toss with lime mixture to lightly coat. Refrigerate, covered, 2 hours. Sprinkle with cilantro.

½ cup: 86 cal., 5g fat (0 sat. fat), 0 chol., 170mg sod., 10g carb. (7g sugars, 2g fiber), 1g pro.
Diabetic exchanges: 1 vegetable, 1 fat.

CRANBERRY-PECAN WHEAT BERRY SALAD

I love to experiment with different grains and wanted to give wheat berries a try. My whole family goes nuts for this salad, especially my mom.
—Kristen Heigl, Staten Island, NY

Prep: 20 min. • **Cook:** 70 min. + cooling
Makes: 8 servings

- 1 cup uncooked wheat berries, rinsed
- 2 celery ribs, finely chopped
- 1 medium tart apple, diced
- 4 green onions, sliced
- 1 cup dried cranberries
- 1 cup chopped pecans

DRESSING

- 3 Tbsp. walnut oil
- 2 Tbsp. cider vinegar
- 1 Tbsp. minced fresh sage or
  1 tsp. rubbed sage
- 2 tsp. minced fresh thyme or
  ¾ tsp. dried thyme
- 2 tsp. Worcestershire sauce
- 1 tsp. Dijon mustard
- ¾ tsp. salt
- ½ tsp. pepper

Cook wheat berries according to package directions; drain and cool. Meanwhile, combine next five ingredients; add wheat berries. Whisk together all the dressing ingredients. Pour over salad; toss to coat. Serve at room temperature or chilled.

¾ cup: 298 cal., 15g fat (1g sat. fat), 0 chol., 261mg sod., 39g carb. (17g sugars, 6g fiber), 5g pro.

CALIFORNIA BURGER BOWLS

CALIFORNIA BURGER BOWLS

Burgers are a weekly staple at our house all year round. Skip the fries, chips and bun—you won't need them with these loaded burger bowls. To spice up the mayo, add ½ teaspoon of chipotle powder.
—Courtney Stultz, Weir, KS

Takes: 25 min. • **Makes:** 4 servings

- 3 Tbsp. fat-free milk
- 2 Tbsp. quick-cooking oats
- ¾ tsp. salt
- ½ tsp. ground cumin
- ½ tsp. chili powder
- ½ tsp. pepper
- 1 lb. lean ground turkey
- 4 cups baby kale salad blend
- 1½ cups cubed fresh pineapple (½ in.)
- 1 medium mango, peeled and thinly sliced
- 1 medium ripe avocado, peeled and thinly sliced
- 1 medium sweet red pepper, cut into strips
- 4 tomatillos, husks removed, thinly sliced
- ¼ cup reduced-fat chipotle mayonnaise

1. In a large bowl, mix milk, oats and seasonings. Add turkey; mix lightly but thoroughly. Shape into four ½-in.-thick patties.
2. Place burgers on an oiled grill rack over medium heat. Grill, covered, until a thermometer reads 165°, 4-5 minutes per side. Serve over salad blend, along with remaining ingredients.

1 serving: 390 cal., 19g fat (4g sat. fat), 83mg chol., 666mg sod., 33g carb. (22g sugars, 7g fiber), 26g pro.
Diabetic exchanges: 3 lean meat, 2 vegetable, 1 fruit, 2½ fat.

* HEALTH TIP * Top these burger bowls with homemade guacamole instead of chipotle mayonnaise and they're gluten-free! Be sure to use certified gluten-free oats in the burger patties.

✱
TEST KITCHEN TIP

If you can't find tomatillos, try substituting green tomatoes or canned green chiles.

CHILI-RUBBED STEAK WITH BLACK BEAN SALAD

Busy weeknights don't stop my husband from firing up the grill. This meal-in-one recipe comes together fast. Try it with chimichurri sauce and cotija cheese.
—Naylet LaRochelle, Miami, FL

Takes: 30 min. • **Makes:** 4 servings

- 1 beef flank steak (1 lb.)
- 4 tsp. chili powder
- ½ tsp. salt
- 1 pkg. (8.8 oz.) ready-to-serve brown rice
- 1 can (15 oz.) black beans, rinsed and drained
- ½ cup salsa verde
  Minced fresh cilantro, optional

1. Rub steak with chili powder and salt. Grill, covered, over medium heat or broil 4 in. from heat 6-8 minutes on each side or until meat reaches desired doneness (for medium-rare, a thermometer should read 135°; medium, 140°).
2. Heat the rice according to package directions. Transfer rice to a small bowl; stir in beans and salsa. Slice steak thinly across the grain; serve with bean salad. If desired, sprinkle with cilantro.

3 oz. cooked beef with ¾ cup salad: 367 cal., 10g fat (4g sat. fat), 54mg chol., 762mg sod., 35g carb. (2g sugars, 6g fiber), 29g pro.
Diabetic exchanges: 3 lean meat, 2 starch.

HEIRLOOM TOMATO SALAD

This is a simple yet elegant dish that always pleases my guests. Not only is it tasty, but it is healthy, too. The more varied the colors of the tomatoes you choose, the prettier the salad will be.
—Jessie Apfel, Berkeley, CA

Prep: 20 min. + chilling
Makes: 6 servings

- 2 cups cut-up heirloom tomatoes
- 1 cup multicolored cherry tomatoes, halved
- 2 cups fresh baby spinach
- ½ cup sliced red onion

DRESSING
- 3 Tbsp. olive oil
- 2 Tbsp. white balsamic vinegar
- 1 garlic clove, minced
- ½ tsp. salt
- ¼ tsp. dried basil
- ¼ tsp. dried oregano
- ¼ tsp. dried rosemary, crushed
- ¼ tsp. dried thyme
- ¼ tsp. pepper
- ⅛ tsp. rubbed sage

Place tomatoes, spinach and onion in a large bowl. Whisk together dressing ingredients; toss with salad. Refrigerate, covered, for 2 hours. Serve salad with a slotted spoon.

⅔ cup: 75 cal., 5g fat (1g sat. fat), 0 chol., 161mg sod., 7g carb. (4g sugars, 2g fiber), 1g pro.
Diabetic exchanges: 1 vegetable, 1 fat.

CHILI-RUBBED STEAK WITH BLACK BEAN SALAD

PEAR & CHICKEN SALAD WITH GORGONZOLA

This is one salad that actually has me looking forward to my daily lunch break! The dressing is amazingly delicious, even with just three ingredients!
—Gina Fensler, Cincinnati, OH

Takes: 20 min. • **Makes:** 6 servings

- 1 pkg. (22 oz.) fully cooked frozen grilled chicken breast strips
- ¼ cup seedless raspberry or blackberry jam
- ¼ cup balsamic vinegar
- ¼ tsp. pepper
- 4 cups fresh baby spinach
- 4 cups torn romaine
- 1 small cucumber, halved and thinly sliced

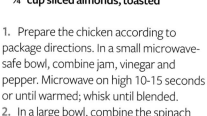

- 1 medium pear, thinly sliced
- ¼ cup crumbled Gorgonzola cheese
- ¼ cup sliced almonds, toasted

1. Prepare the chicken according to package directions. In a small microwave-safe bowl, combine jam, vinegar and pepper. Microwave on high 10-15 seconds or until warmed; whisk until blended.

2. In a large bowl, combine the spinach and romaine. Drizzle with dressing; toss to coat. Transfer to a large platter; top with chicken, cucumber and pear. Sprinkle with the cheese and almonds. Serve salad immediately.

Note: To toast nuts, spread in a dry nonstick skillet and heat over low heat until lightly browned, stirring occasionally.
2 cups: 234 cal., 7g fat (2g sat. fat), 97mg chol., 605mg sod., 19g carb. (13g sugars, 3g fiber), 27g pro.
Diabetic exchanges: 3 lean meat, 2 vegetable, ½ starch, ½ fat.

PEAR & CHICKEN SALAD WITH GORGONZOLA

MEDITERRANEAN BULGUR BOWL

You can also transform this tasty bowl into an Italian version with mozzarella, pesto, tomatoes, spinach and basil.
—Renata Smith, Brookline, MA

Takes: 30 min. • **Makes:** 4 servings

- 1 cup bulgur
- ½ tsp. ground cumin
- ¼ tsp. salt
- 2 cups water
- 1 can (15 oz.) garbanzo beans or chickpeas, rinsed and drained
- 6 oz. fresh baby spinach (about 8 cups)
- 2 cups cherry tomatoes, halved
- 1 small red onion, halved and thinly sliced
- ½ cup crumbled feta cheese
- ¼ cup hummus
- 2 Tbsp. chopped fresh mint
- 2 Tbsp. lemon juice

1. In a 6-qt. stockpot, combine the first four ingredients; bring to a boil. Reduce heat; simmer, covered, until bulgur is tender, 10-12 minutes. Stir in chickpeas; heat through.

2. Remove from heat; stir in spinach. Let stand, covered, until spinach is wilted, about 5 minutes. Stir in the remaining ingredients. Serve warm or refrigerate and serve cold.

2 cups: 311 cal., 7g fat (2g sat. fat), 8mg chol., 521mg sod., 52g carb. (6g sugars, 12g fiber), 14g pro.
* HEALTH TIP * With the spinach, tomatoes and feta cheese, this dish supplies all the vitamin A you need in a day.

SALADS

MEDITERRANEAN
BULGUR BOWL

BRUSSELS SPROUTS SALAD

My husband and I like Brussels sprouts, so I'm always looking for new ways to use them. I most often serve this colorful salad with roast pork or duck.
—Nancy Korondan, Yorkville, IL

Takes: 20 min. • **Makes:** 8 servings

- 1½ lbs. fresh Brussels sprouts, trimmed and halved
- 2 green onions, chopped
- ½ cup olive oil
- 2 Tbsp. lemon juice
- 1 to 1½ tsp. Dijon mustard
- ½ tsp. salt
- ½ tsp. dried thyme
- ¼ tsp. pepper
- 1 bunch red leaf lettuce or radicchio, torn
- 2 Tbsp. slivered almonds, toasted

1. Place Brussels sprouts in a large saucepan; add 1 in. of water. Bring to a boil. Reduce heat; simmer, covered, until tender, 8-10 minutes. Drain; rinse with cold water and pat dry. Combine with green onions.

2. Meanwhile, whisk together next six ingredients. Toss 2 Tbsp. of dressing with lettuce; transfer to a serving bowl. Pour remaining dressing over Brussels sprouts and onions; toss to coat. Mound on lettuce. Sprinkle with almonds.

Note: To toast nuts, bake in a shallow pan in a 350° oven for 5-10 minutes or cook in a skillet over low heat until lightly browned, stirring occasionally.

1 cup: 171 cal., 15g fat (2g sat. fat), 0 chol., 192mg sod., 9g carb. (2g sugars, 4g fiber), 4g pro.

Diabetic exchanges: 3 fat, 2 vegetable.

EDAMAME SALAD WITH SESAME GINGER DRESSING

EDAMAME SALAD WITH SESAME GINGER DRESSING

This bright salad has a little bit of everything: hearty greens, nutty crunch, a zip of citrusy goodness and a big protein punch. For me, it's pure bliss in a bowl.
—Darla Andrews, Schertz, TX

Takes: 15 min. • **Makes:** 6 servings

- 6 cups baby kale salad blend (about 5 oz.)
- 1 can (15 oz.) garbanzo beans or chickpeas, rinsed and drained
- 2 cups frozen shelled edamame (about 10 oz.), thawed
- 3 clementines, peeled and segmented
- 1 cup fresh bean sprouts
- ½ cup salted peanuts
- 2 green onions, diagonally sliced
- ½ cup sesame ginger salad dressing

Divide salad blend among six bowls. Top with all remaining ingredients except salad dressing. Serve with dressing.

1 serving: 317 cal., 17g fat (2g sat. fat), 0 chol., 355mg sod., 32g carb. (14g sugars, 8g fiber), 13g pro.

* HEALTH TIP * Vitamin C-rich clementines help your body absorb iron from plant sources like the kale and edamame in this salad.

TEST KITCHEN TIP
Edamame is the Japanese name for immature or green soybeans that are then steamed or boiled. They're available shelled or still in their pods in the frozen vegetable section.

CLASSIC COBB SALAD

Making this salad is a lot like putting in a garden. I plant everything in nice, neat sections, just as I do with my seedlings.
—Patricia Kile, Elizabethtown, PA

Takes: 20 min. • **Makes:** 4 servings

- 6 cups torn iceberg lettuce
- 2 medium tomatoes, chopped
- 1 medium ripe avocado, peeled and chopped
- ¾ cup diced fully cooked ham
- 2 hard-boiled large eggs, chopped
- ¾ cup diced cooked turkey
- 1¼ cups sliced fresh mushrooms
- ½ cup crumbled blue cheese
  Salad dressing of choice
  Sliced ripe olives and lemon wedges, optional

Place lettuce on a platter or in a large serving bowl. Arrange remaining ingredients in rows or sections as desired. Serve with dressing of choice; if desired, serve salad with sliced ripe olives and lemon wedges.

1 serving: 260 cal., 15g fat (5g sat. fat), 148mg chol., 586mg sod., 10g carb. (5g sugars, 4g fiber), 23g pro. **Diabetic exchanges:** 3 lean meat, 2 vegetable, 2 fat.

HOLIDAY RICE SALAD
(PICTURED ON PG. 68)

It's nice to make a cold salad like this for entertaining. You can make it ahead, and it won't take up valuable oven space.
—Debra Walter, Huntington Woods, MI

Prep: 10 min. + chilling
Makes: 14 servings

- 7 cups cooked wild rice, cooled
- 1 cup chopped pecans, toasted
- 1 cup thinly sliced green onions
- ½ cup dried cranberries
- ½ cup dried cherries or additional dried cranberries
- ½ cup golden raisins
- ½ cup minced fresh parsley
- ¼ cup slivered almonds, toasted
- 1 Tbsp. chopped fresh mint or 1 tsp. dried mint flakes

DRESSING
- ½ cup orange juice
- ⅓ cup cider vinegar
- ¼ cup olive oil
- 1 Tbsp. lime juice
- 2 tsp. sugar
- 1 tsp. salt
- ⅛ tsp. pepper

Combine the first nine ingredients. In a jar with a tight-fitting lid, combine dressing ingredients; shake well. Pour over rice mixture and toss to coat. Refrigerate, covered, for 2 hours or until serving.
Note: To toast nuts, bake in a shallow pan in a 350° oven for 5-10 minutes or cook in a skillet over low heat until lightly browned, stirring occasionally.

¾ cup: 245 cal., 11g fat (1g sat. fat), 0 chol., 175mg sod., 35g carb. (14g sugars, 3g fiber), 5g pro.
Diabetic exchanges: 2 starch, 2 fat.

CLASSIC COBB SALAD

GRILLED ASIAN CHICKEN
PASTA SALAD

GRILLED ASIAN CHICKEN PASTA SALAD

This cool noodle salad makes a great casual one-bowl dinner or a perfect dish for a potluck or buffet.
—Sharon Tipton, Casselberry, FL

Prep: 25 min. + marinating • **Grill:** 10 min.
Makes: 6 servings

- ¾ cup lime juice
- 3 Tbsp. olive oil
- 3 Tbsp. sesame oil
- 3 Tbsp. reduced-sodium soy sauce
- 2 Tbsp. minced fresh gingerroot
- 3 garlic cloves, minced
- 1 Tbsp. sugar
- 1½ lbs. boneless skinless chicken breasts
- 12 oz. uncooked angel hair pasta, broken
- 1 large sweet yellow pepper, chopped
- 1 large sweet red pepper, chopped
- 1 medium cucumber, peeled and chopped
- ¼ cup minced fresh parsley
- 2 green onions, sliced
- ¼ tsp. crushed red pepper flakes

1. Combine the first seven ingredients. Pour ¼ cup of marinade into a shallow dish, reserving remainder. Add chicken and turn to coat. Refrigerate 30 minutes.
2. Drain chicken; discard marinade. Grill chicken, covered, on an oiled grill rack over medium heat (or broil 4 in. from heat) 5-7 minutes on each side, until a thermometer reads 165°.
3. Meanwhile, cook the angel hair pasta according to package directions; drain and rinse in cold water. Combine remaining ingredients with reserved marinade. Cut chicken into 1-in. slices. Add the pasta and chicken to vegetable mixture; toss to coat. Refrigerate until serving.

1⅓ cups: 478 cal., 16g fat (3g sat. fat), 63mg chol., 321mg sod., 51g carb. (6g sugars, 3g fiber), 32g pro.

GRILLED PEACH, RICE & ARUGULA SALAD

GRILLED PEACH, RICE & ARUGULA SALAD

I created this hearty salad when I needed to clear out some leftovers in the fridge, and it became an instant hit! Grilling the peaches is the ultimate taste-of-summer flavor boost.
—Lauren Wyler, Dripping Springs, TX

Takes: 30 min. • **Makes:** 6 servings

- 3 Tbsp. cider vinegar
- 2 Tbsp. Dijon mustard
- 2 Tbsp. canola oil
- 2 Tbsp. maple syrup
- 1 Tbsp. finely chopped shallot
- ¼ tsp. cayenne pepper

SALAD

- 1 pkg. (8.8 oz.) ready-to-serve long grain and wild rice
- 2 medium peaches, quartered
- 6 cups fresh arugula (about 4 oz.)
- 6 bacon strips, cooked and crumbled
- ½ cup crumbled goat cheese

1. For dressing, whisk together first six ingredients.
2. Prepare rice according to package directions; cool slightly. Place peaches on an oiled grill rack over medium heat. Grill, covered, until lightly browned, 6-8 minutes, turning occasionally.
3. To serve, add bacon and ¼ cup dressing to rice. Line a platter with arugula; top with rice mixture and peaches. Drizzle with the remaining dressing; top with cheese.

1 serving: 218 cal., 11g fat (3g sat. fat), 20mg chol., 530mg sod., 23g carb. (9g sugars, 2g fiber), 7g pro.
Diabetic exchanges: 1 starch, 1 vegetable, 2 fat.

HOT SPINACH APPLE SALAD

HOT SPINACH APPLE SALAD

With a light sweet-tangy dressing, the spinach doesn't wilt and the apples retain their crunch. We serve this salad with homemade bread.
—Denise Albers, Freeburg, IL

Takes: 20 min. • **Makes:** 10 servings

- 6 bacon strips, diced
- ¼ cup cider vinegar
- 3 Tbsp. brown sugar
- 9 cups fresh baby spinach
- 2 unpeeled large red apples, thinly sliced
- 1 medium red onion, chopped (about ¾ cup)

1. In a large skillet, cook bacon until crisp. Remove to paper towels. Drain, reserving 2 Tbsp. drippings.

2. In same skillet, combine vinegar, brown sugar and reserved drippings. Bring to a boil; cook and stir until sugar is dissolved. Cool slightly.

3. Meanwhile, in a serving bowl, combine spinach, apples, onion and bacon. Drizzle with warm dressing; toss to coat. Serve immediately.

1 serving: 117 cal., 7g fat (2g sat. fat), 11mg chol., 135mg sod., 11g carb. (9g sugars, 2g fiber), 3g pro.

Diabetic exchanges: 1 vegetable, 1 fat, ½ starch.

LEMON VINAIGRETTE POTATO SALAD

(PICTURED ON P. 69)

I developed this recipe for a friend who was looking for a potato salad that could withstand Fourth of July weather. The vinaigrette was a safe, delicious alternative to traditional mayonnaise-based potato salads. I've also substituted fresh thyme for the basil. Any fresh herbs you like would be great!
—Melanie Cloyd, Mullica Hill, NJ

Prep: 25 min. • **Cook:** 15 min.
Makes: 12 servings

- 3 lbs. red potatoes, cut into 1-in. cubes
- ½ cup olive oil
- 3 Tbsp. lemon juice
- 2 Tbsp. minced fresh basil
- 2 Tbsp. minced fresh parsley
- 1 Tbsp. red wine vinegar
- 1 tsp. grated lemon zest
- ¾ tsp. salt
- ½ tsp. pepper
- 1 small onion, finely chopped

1. Place potatoes in a large saucepan and cover with water. Bring to a boil. Reduce heat; cover and simmer for 10-15 minutes or until tender. Meanwhile, in a small bowl, whisk the oil, lemon juice, herbs, vinegar, lemon zest, salt and pepper.

2. Drain potatoes. Place in a large bowl; add onion. Drizzle with vinaigrette; toss to coat. Serve warm or chill until serving.

¾ cup: 165 cal., 9g fat (1g sat. fat), 0 chol., 155mg sod., 19g carb. (1g sugars, 2g fiber), 2g pro.

Diabetic exchanges: 2 fat, 1 starch.

TURKEY & PASTA RANCH SALAD

This easy pasta salad is loaded with plenty of fresh vegetables, and the classic ranch dressing makes it appealing to kids.
—Julie Peterson, Crofton, MD

Takes: 25 min. • **Makes:** 6 servings

- 2 cups uncooked whole wheat spiral pasta (about 5 oz.)
- 2 medium sweet peppers, chopped
- 1 medium zucchini, thinly sliced
- 1 yellow summer squash, thinly sliced
- ½ cup finely chopped red onion
- 2 cups cubed cooked turkey or chicken
- 3 Tbsp. chopped fresh parsley
- ½ cup peppercorn ranch salad dressing
- ¼ tsp. salt
- ¼ cup shredded Parmesan cheese

1. Cook the pasta according to package directions. Drain and rinse with cold water; drain well.
2. Place pasta, vegetables, turkey and parsley in a large bowl; toss with dressing and salt. Sprinkle with cheese.

1⅔ cups: 256 cal., 11g fat (2g sat. fat), 50mg chol., 383mg sod., 20g carb. (4g sugars, 4g fiber), 19g pro.
Diabetic exchanges: 3 lean meat, 1½ fat, 1 starch, 1 vegetable.

MANDARIN BROCCOLI SALAD

Sweet, crunchy and colorful, this salad has a fresh mix of textures and flavors. It tastes even better when you chill it overnight, if you can wait that long.
—Margaret Allen, Abingdon, VA

Prep: 25 min. + chilling
Makes: 9 servings

- ¾ cup mayonnaise
- ¼ cup sugar
- 4 tsp. cider vinegar
- 4 cups fresh broccoli florets
- 1 small red onion, halved and sliced
- ½ cup raisins
- ½ cup pecan halves, toasted
- 1 can (11 oz.) mandarin oranges, drained

Whisk mayonnaise, sugar and vinegar; set aside. In a salad bowl, combine broccoli, onion, raisins and pecans. Drizzle with dressing; toss to coat. Gently stir in the oranges. Refrigerate, covered, at least 3 hours before serving.
¾ cup: 229 cal., 17g fat (2g sat. fat), 1mg chol., 105mg sod., 18g carb. (14g sugars, 2g fiber), 2g pro.

TURKEY & PASTA RANCH SALAD

SIDES

"*I recommend serving these wedges alongside a salad for a light lunch or serving them as a side dish with a chicken or beef entree.*"
—Beth Ask, Ulster, PA

Lemony Green Beans (p. 103) **Grilled Brussels Sprouts** (p. 109) **Rosemary Beets** (p. 109)
Fiesta Corn & Beans (p. 112) **Parmesan Potato Wedges** (p. 104) **Bok Choy & Radishes** (p. 101)

SPINACH RICE

I like to serve this Greek-style rice dish alongside steaks with mushrooms. It makes an elegant meal that can be doubled for guests.
—Jeanette Cakouros, Brunswick, ME

Takes: 20 min. • **Makes:** 2 servings

- 2 Tbsp. olive oil
- ½ cup chopped onion
- ¾ cup water
- 1 Tbsp. dried parsley flakes
- ¼ to ½ tsp. salt
- ⅛ tsp. pepper
- ½ cup uncooked instant rice
- 2 cups fresh baby spinach

1. In a saucepan, heat oil over medium-high heat; saute onion until tender. Stir in water, parsley, salt and pepper; bring to a boil. Stir in rice; top with spinach.
2. Cover; remove from heat. Let stand until the rice is tender, 7-10 minutes. Stir to combine.

¾ cup: 235 cal., 14g fat (2g sat. fat), 0 chol., 326mg sod., 25g carb. (2g sugars, 2g fiber), 3g pro.
Diabetic exchanges: 3 fat, 1½ starch, 1 vegetable.

FINGERLING POTATOES WITH FRESH PARSLEY & CHIVES

FINGERLING POTATOES WITH FRESH PARSLEY & CHIVES

We use seasonings like adobo, Sazon, fresh parsley and minced chives when we grill potatoes. We have even smoked the fingerling potatoes in our portable smoker before grilling.
—Teri Rasey, Cadillac, MI

Prep: 30 min. + marinating • **Grill:** 10 min.
Makes: 6 servings

- 2 lbs. fingerling potatoes
- ¼ cup olive oil
- ½ tsp. Goya Sazon without annatto
- ½ tsp. adobo seasoning
- 2 Tbsp. minced fresh parsley
- 2 Tbsp. minced chives

1. Place potatoes in a 6-qt. stockpot; add water to cover. Bring to a boil. Reduce heat; cook, uncovered, 15-20 minutes or until tender. Drain.
2. In a large bowl, combine olive oil and seasonings; reserve 1 tablespoon. Add potatoes; toss to coat. Let stand for 15 minutes. Thread potatoes onto 4 metal or soaked wooden skewers. Grill, covered, over medium heat 8-10 minutes or until browned, turning once. Cool slightly.
3. Remove the potatoes from skewers. Transfer to a large bowl. Add reserved marinade and herbs; toss to coat.

1 serving: 215 cal., 9g fat (1g sat. fat), 0 chol., 172mg sod., 30g carb. (2g sugars, 3g fiber), 4g pro.
Diabetic exchanges: 2 starch, 2 fat.

CRANBERRY WILD RICE PILAF

This lovely side dish is perfect for the holidays or anytime you want to add a special touch. Dried cranberries, currants and almonds serve up color and texture. Many of my co-workers now make this rice pilaf for their families.
—Pat Gardetta, Osage Beach, MO

Prep: 25 min. • **Bake:** 50 min.
Makes: 8 servings

- ¾ cup uncooked wild rice
- 3 cups chicken broth
- ½ cup medium pearl barley
- ¼ cup dried currants
- 1 Tbsp. butter
- ⅓ cup sliced almonds, toasted
- ¼ cup dried cranberries, chopped

1. Preheat oven to 325°. In a saucepan, combine wild rice and broth; bring to a boil. Reduce heat; simmer, covered, for 10 minutes. Remove from heat; stir in barley, currants and butter. Transfer to a greased 1½-qt. baking dish.
2. Bake, covered, until wild rice and barley are tender, 50-60 minutes. Stir in almonds and cranberries.

¾ cup: 166 cal., 4g fat (1g sat. fat), 6mg chol., 382mg sod., 30g carb. (8g sugars, 4g fiber), 5g pro.
Diabetic exchanges: 2 starch, 1 fat.

CRANBERRY WILD RICE PILAF

APRICOT-GINGER ACORN SQUASH

Sweet and savory flavors come together in this dish that will make a squash lover out of anyone. It's a treat—but has hardly any butter, and it's low in sodium. For less sugar, we use all-fruit apricot preserves.
—Trisha Kruse, Eagle, ID

Prep: 10 min. • **Bake:** 1 hour
Makes: 2 servings

- 1 small acorn squash
- 2 Tbsp. apricot preserves
- 4 tsp. butter, melted
- 1½ tsp. reduced-sodium soy sauce
- ¼ tsp. ground ginger
- ¼ tsp. pepper

1. Preheat oven to 350°. Cut squash lengthwise in half; remove seeds. Cut a thin slice from bottoms to level if desired. Place in a greased 11x7-in. baking dish, cut side up.
2. Mix the remaining ingredients; spoon over squash. Bake, covered, 45 minutes. Uncover; bake until tender, 15-20 minutes.

½ squash: 234 cal., 8g fat (5g sat. fat), 20mg chol., 221mg sod., 43g carb. (15g sugars, 4g fiber), 3g pro.

BROWN SUGAR OAT MUFFINS

BROWN SUGAR OAT MUFFINS

Since Kansas is one of the top wheat-producing states, it seems only fitting to share a recipe containing whole wheat flour. These are great muffins to have for breakfast or a late-night snack with a cup of hot cocoa.
—Regina Stock, Topeka, KS

Takes: 35 min. • **Makes:** 1 dozen

- 1 cup old-fashioned oats
- 1 cup whole wheat flour
- ¾ cup packed brown sugar
- ½ cup all-purpose flour
- 2 tsp. baking powder
- ½ tsp. salt
- 2 large eggs
- ¾ cup 2% milk
- ¼ cup canola oil
- 1 tsp. vanilla extract
  Peanut butter and honey, optional

1. Preheat oven to 400°. Mix first six ingredients. In another bowl, whisk together eggs, milk, oil and vanilla. Add to oat mixture; stir just until moistened.
2. Fill greased or paper-lined muffin cups two-thirds full. Bake until a toothpick inserted in center comes out clean, 15-17 minutes.
3. Cool muffins 5 minutes before removing to a wire rack. Serve warm. If desired, spread with peanut butter and honey.

1 muffin: 192 cal., 7g fat (1g sat. fat), 32mg chol., 202mg sod., 30g carb. (14g sugars, 2g fiber), 4g pro.
Diabetic exchanges: 2 starch, 1½ fat.

BOK CHOY & RADISHES

(PICTURED ON P. 97)

This is such a great-tasting, good-for-you recipe. With bok choy and radishes, the simple dish capitalizes on the fresh flavors of spring.
—Ann Baker, Texarkana, TX

Takes: 25 min. • **Makes:** 8 servings

- 1 head bok choy
- 2 Tbsp. butter
- 1 Tbsp. olive oil
- 12 radishes, thinly sliced
- 1 shallot, sliced

HONEY GARLIC GREEN BEANS

- 1 tsp. lemon-pepper seasoning
- ¾ tsp. salt

1. Cut off and discard root end of bok choy, leaving stalks with leaves. Cut green leaves from stalks. Cut leaves into 1-in. slices; set aside. Cut the white stalks into 1-in. pieces.
2. In a large skillet, cook bok choy stalks in butter and oil for 3-5 minutes or until crisp-tender. Add the radishes, shallot, lemon pepper, salt and reserved bok choy leaves; cook and stir for 3 minutes or until heated through.

¾ cup: 59 cal., 5g fat (2g sat. fat), 8mg chol., 371mg sod., 3g carb. (2g sugars, 1g fiber), 2g pro.
Diabetic exchanges: 1 vegetable, 1 fat.

HONEY GARLIC GREEN BEANS

Green beans are great, but they can seem ordinary on their own. Just a couple extra ingredients give them a sweet and salty attitude. This is definitely my family's favorite way to enjoy them.
—Shannon Dobos, Calgary, AB

Takes: 20 min. • **Makes:** 8 servings

- 4 Tbsp. honey
- 2 Tbsp. reduced-sodium soy sauce
- 4 garlic cloves, minced
- ¼ tsp. salt
- ¼ tsp. crushed red pepper flakes
- 2 lbs. fresh green beans, trimmed

1. Whisk together first five ingredients; set aside. In a 6-qt. stockpot, bring 10 cups water to a boil. Add beans in batches; cook, uncovered, just until crisp-tender, 2-3 minutes. Remove the beans and immediately drop into ice water. Drain and pat dry.
2. Coat stockpot with cooking spray. Add beans; cook, stirring constantly, over high heat until slightly blistered, 2-3 minutes. Add sauce; continue stirring until beans are coated and sauce starts to evaporate slightly, 2-3 minutes. Remove from heat.

¾ cup: 72 cal., 0 fat (0 sat. fat), 0 chol., 225mg sod., 18g carb. (12g sugars, 4g fiber), 2g pro.
Diabetic exchanges: 1 vegetable, ½ starch.

VEGETABLE & BARLEY PILAF

Hearty, colorful, easy and fast were the reviews we gave this good-for-you dish. Barley has a healthy amount of soluble fiber. Besides helping you feel full, it can help to lower cholesterol, too! You can easily substitute other fresh veggies you have on hand.
—Jesse Klausmeier, Burbank, CA

Takes: 30 min. • **Makes:** 4 servings

- 1 large zucchini, quartered and sliced
- 1 large carrot, chopped
- 1 Tbsp. butter
- 2 cups reduced-sodium chicken broth
- 1 cup quick-cooking barley
- 2 green onions, chopped
- ½ tsp. dried marjoram
- ¼ tsp. salt
- ⅛ tsp. pepper

1. In a large saucepan, saute zucchini and carrot in butter until crisp-tender. Add the broth; bring to a boil. Stir in barley. Reduce heat; cover and simmer until barley is tender, 10-12 minutes.
2. Stir in the onions, marjoram, salt and pepper. Remove from the heat; cover and let stand for 5 minutes.
¾ cup: 219 cal., 4g fat (2g sat. fat), 8mg chol., 480mg sod., 39g carb. (3g sugars, 10g fiber), 9g pro.

KALE & FENNEL SKILLET

KALE & FENNEL SKILLET

I love to mix different vegetables together and use different herbs and spices to change things up. If you can't find apple sausage for this skillet, a good mild Italian sausage would substitute just fine.
—Patricia Levenson, Santa Ana, CA

Prep: 10 min. • **Cook:** 25 min.
Makes: 6 servings

- 2 Tbsp. extra virgin olive oil
- 1 small onion, thinly sliced
- 1 small fennel bulb, thinly sliced
- ½ lb. fully cooked apple chicken sausage links or cooked Italian sausage links, halved lengthwise and sliced into half-moons
- 2 garlic cloves, minced
- 3 Tbsp. dry sherry or dry white wine
- 1 Tbsp. herbes de Provence
- ⅛ tsp. salt
- ⅛ tsp. pepper
- 1 bunch kale, and torn into bite-sized pieces

1. In a large skillet, heat olive oil over medium-high heat. Add onion and fennel; cook and stir until onion begins to brown, 6-8 minutes. Add sausage, garlic, sherry and seasonings; cook until sausage starts to caramelize, 4-6 minutes.
2. Add kale; cook, covered, stirring occasionally, until tender, 15-17 minutes.
Note: Look for herbes de Provence in the spice aisle.
¾ cup: 167 cal., 8g fat (2g sat. fat), 27mg chol., 398mg sod., 16g carb. (6g sugars, 3g fiber), 9g pro.
Diabetic exchanges: 2 vegetable, 1 lean meat, 1 fat.

SLOW-COOKED RATATOUILLE

I get my son to eat eggplant and other vegetables by cooking this classic French dish low and slow. It's a perfect way to use abundant summer vegetables and herbs. I like to serve it over rice with garlic cheese bread.
—Diane Goedde, Red Lodge, MT

Prep: 25 min. + standing • **Cook:** 5 hours
Makes: 10 servings

- 1 medium eggplant, peeled and cut into 1-in. cubes
- 1 Tbsp. plus 1 tsp. salt, divided
- 2 medium onions, halved and thinly sliced
- 4 medium tomatoes, chopped
- 3 medium zucchini, cut into ¾-in. slices
- 2 celery ribs, chopped
- 3 Tbsp. olive oil
- 2 tsp. dried basil or 2 Tbsp. minced fresh basil
- 4 garlic cloves, minced
- ½ tsp. pepper
- 1 can (6 oz.) tomato paste
- 1 can (2¼ oz.) sliced ripe olives, drained
- ⅓ cup coarsely chopped fresh basil

1. Place eggplant in a colander over a plate; sprinkle with 1 Tbsp. salt and toss. Let stand 45 minutes. Rinse and drain well; blot dry with paper towels.
2. Place eggplant and remaining vegetables in a 5- or 6-qt. slow cooker. Add oil, dried basil, garlic, pepper and remaining salt; toss to combine.
3. Cook, covered, on low 5-6 hours or until onions are tender. Stir in tomato paste, olives and fresh basil; heat through.

Freeze option: Cool ratatouille; freeze in freezer containers. To use, thaw partially in refrigerator overnight. Microwave, covered, on high in a microwave-safe dish until heated through, stirring gently.

¾ cup: 102 cal., 5g fat (1g sat. fat), 0 chol., 380mg sod., 13g carb. (7g sugars, 4g fiber), 3g pro.
Diabetic exchanges: 2 vegetable, 1 fat.

LEMONY GREEN BEANS
(PICTURED ON P. 96)

You can throw this dish together in just a few minutes, using ingredients you probably already have on hand. That's the beauty of it.
—Jennifer Capoano, Carlstadt, NJ

Takes: 20 min. • **Makes:** 6 servings

- ¼ cup chicken broth
- 2 Tbsp. olive oil
- 1½ lbs. fresh green beans, trimmed
- ¾ tsp. lemon-pepper seasoning
  Lemon wedges

In a large skillet, heat chicken broth and olive oil over medium-high heat. Add green beans; cook and stir until crisp-tender. Sprinkle with lemon pepper. Serve with lemon wedges.

1 serving: 76 cal., 5g fat (1g sat. fat), 0 chol., 88mg sod., 8g carb. (3g sugars, 4g fiber), 2g pro.
Diabetic exchanges: 1 vegetable, 1 fat

CAULIFLOWER MASH

This quick and easy mashed cauliflower is a great alternative to same-old mashed spuds, and it's healthier, too!
—Nick Iverson, Denver, CO

Takes: 20 min. • **Makes:** 6 servings

- 1 large head cauliflower, chopped (about 6 cups)
- ½ cup chicken broth
- 2 garlic cloves, crushed
- 1 tsp. whole peppercorns
- 1 bay leaf
- ½ tsp. salt

1. Place cauliflower in a large saucepan; add water to cover. Bring to a boil. Reduce the heat. Simmer, covered, until tender, 10-12 minutes. Drain; return to pan.
2. Meanwhile, combine the remaining ingredients in a small saucepan. Bring to a boil. Immediately remove from heat and strain; discard garlic, peppercorns and bay leaf. Add broth to cauliflower. Mash until desired consistency.

⅔ cup: 26 cal., 0 fat (0 sat. fat), 0 chol., 308mg sod., 5g carb. (2g sugars, 2g fiber), 2g pro.
Diabetic exchanges:: 1 vegetable.

SLOW-COOKED RATATOUILLE

LEMON-GARLIC LIMA BEANS

PARMESAN POTATO WEDGES

I recommend serving these wedges alongside a salad for a light lunch or serving them as a side dish with a chicken or beef entree.
—Beth Ask, Ulster, PA

Prep: 10 min. • **Bake:** 30 min.
Makes: 8 servings

- ¼ cup grated Parmesan cheese
- 1 tsp. garlic salt
- ½ tsp. garlic powder
- ½ tsp. dried oregano
- ½ tsp. paprika
- 4 medium baking potatoes (about 8 oz. each)
  Cooking spray

1. Preheat oven to 400°. Mix the first five ingredients.
2. Cut each potato lengthwise into eight wedges; place in a parchment paper-lined 15x10x1-in. pan. Spritz with cooking spray; sprinkle with cheese mixture. Bake until tender, about 30 minutes.

4 wedges: 101 cal., 1g fat (0 sat. fat), 2mg chol., 297mg sod., 20g carb. (1g sugars, 2g fiber), 3g pro.
Diabetic exchanges: 1½ starch.

SPICY GRILLED EGGPLANT

This grilled side goes well with pasta or meats also made on the grill. Thanks to the Cajun seasoning, it gets more attention than an ordinary veggie.
—Greg Fontenot, The Woodlands, TX

Takes: 20 min. • **Makes:** 8 servings

- 2 small eggplants, cut into ½-in. slices
- ¼ cup olive oil
- 2 Tbsp. lime juice
- 3 tsp. Cajun seasoning

1. Brush eggplant slices with oil. Drizzle with lime juice; sprinkle with the Cajun seasoning. Let stand 5 minutes.
2. Grill eggplant, covered, over medium heat or broil 4 in. from heat until tender, 4-5 minutes per side.

1 serving: 88 cal., 7g fat (1g sat. fat), 0 chol., 152mg sod., 7g carb. (3g sugars, 4g fiber), 1g pro.
Diabetic exchanges: 1½ fat, 1 vegetable.

LEMON-GARLIC LIMA BEANS

When I was growing up on Cyprus, my mother would often make this side dish to have with roast lamb. Although I hated lima beans when I was a kid (who didn't?), I love them now. They always remind me of home.
—Paris Paraskeva, San Francisco, CA

Prep: 15 min. + soaking • **Cook:** 1¼ hours
Makes: 6 servings

- 1 lb. dried lima beans
- 2 bay leaves
- 3 Tbsp. extra virgin olive oil, divided
- 1 medium onion, chopped
- 4 garlic cloves, thinly sliced
- ¼ cup chopped fresh parsley
- 2 Tbsp. lemon juice
- 1 Tbsp. chopped fresh oregano
- 2 tsp. grated lemon zest
- ½ tsp. salt
- ¼ tsp. pepper
  Additional chopped fresh parsley

1. Rinse and sort beans; soak according to package directions. Drain and rinse beans, discarding liquid.
2. Place beans in a large saucepan; add bay leaves and water to cover by 2 in. Bring to a boil. Reduce heat; simmer, covered, until beans are tender, 1¼-1½ hours. Drain.
3. In a large skillet, heat 1 Tbsp. oil over medium heat. Add onion; cook and stir until tender, 3-4 minutes. Add garlic; cook 1 minute longer. Add next six ingredients. Stir in the drained beans and remaining oil; toss to combine. Sprinkle with additional chopped parsley.

Electric Pressure-Cooker Option:
Rinse and sort lima beans; place in a large bowl. Add 2 qt. water and 1 Tbsp. salt; stir to combine. Soak, covered, at room temperature overnight. Drain and rinse beans, discarding liquid. Transfer to a 6-qt. electric pressure cooker. Add enough water to cover and 1 tsp. canola oil. Lock lid; close pressure-release valve. Select manual setting; adjust pressure to low, and set time to 8 minutes. When finished cooking, allow pressure to naturally release for 5 minutes, then quick-release pressure. Press cancel. Drain and proceed as directed.

½ cup: 326 cal., 8g fat (1g sat. fat), 0 chol., 209mg sod., 51g carb. (7g sugars, 16g fiber), 16g pro.

TEST KITCHEN TIP
Eat these as a warm side dish, or pulse them in a food processor for a hummus-like dip.

PARMESAN POTATO WEDGES

ROASTED RADISHES

Radishes aren't just for salads anymore. This abundant springtime veggie makes a colorful side to any meal.
—*Taste of Home* Test Kitchen

Prep: 10 min. • **Bake:** 30 min.
Makes: 6 servings

- 2¼ lbs. radishes, trimmed and quartered (about 6 cups)
- 3 Tbsp. olive oil
- 1 Tbsp. minced fresh oregano or 1 tsp. dried oregano
- ¼ tsp. salt
- ⅛ tsp. pepper

1. Preheat oven to 425°. Toss radishes with remaining ingredients. Transfer to a greased 15x10x1-in. pan.
2. Roast until crisp-tender, about 30 minutes, stirring once.

⅔ cup: 88 cal., 7g fat (1g sat. fat), 0mg chol., 165mg sod., 6g carb. (3g sugars, 3g fiber), 1g pro.
Diabetic exchanges: 1 vegetable, 1½ fat.

CHINESE CHARD
WITH ALMONDS

CHINESE CHARD WITH ALMONDS

The chard in my garden inspires all kinds of recipes. This one makes a great side dish, especially in spring and summer.
—Nancy Heishman, Las Vegas, NV

Prep: 20 min. • **Cook:** 15 min.
Makes: 4 servings

- 1 bunch Swiss chard (about 1 lb.), chopped
- 1 Tbsp. olive oil
- 1 large sweet red pepper, cut into strips
- 1 large tomato, diced
- 1 small red onion, diced
- 3 garlic cloves, minced
- 1 Tbsp. minced fresh gingerroot
- 1 Tbsp. hoisin sauce
- ¾ tsp. Chinese five-spice powder
- ¾ tsp. kosher salt
  Dash crushed red pepper flakes
- 2 Tbsp. lemon juice
- ½ cup sliced almonds, toasted

1. In a large saucepan over medium-high heat, bring 2 in. of water to a boil. Add chard; cook, covered, until crisp-tender, about 5 minutes. Drain; set aside.
2. In same saucepan, heat olive oil over medium-high heat. Add pepper, tomato and onion; saute until pepper is crisp-tender, 3-4 minutes. Add garlic; cook 1 minute more. Stir in the next five ingredients; add cooked chard. Cook and stir until pepper is tender, 3-4 minutes ; add lemon juice. Top with almonds.
Note: To toast nuts, bake in a shallow pan in a 350° oven for 5-10 minutes or cook in a skillet over low heat until lightly browned, stirring occasionally.
¾ cup: 156 cal., 10g fat (1g sat. fat), 0 chol., 611mg sod., 15g carb. (6g sugars, 5g fiber), 5g pro.
Diabetic exchanges: 2 fat, 1 starch.

COLCANNON POTATOES

Every Irish family has its own colcannon recipe, since it's a classic dish. My recipe comes from my father's family in Ireland. It's part of my St. Pat's menu, along with lamb chops, carrots and soda bread.
—Marilou Robinson, Portland, OR

Prep: 25 min. • **Cook:** 35 min.
Makes: 12 servings

- 1 medium head cabbage (about 2 lbs.), shredded
- 4 lbs. medium potatoes (about 8), peeled and quartered
- 2 cups whole milk
- 1 cup chopped green onions
- 1½ tsp. salt
- ½ tsp. pepper
- ¼ cup butter, melted
  Minced fresh parsley
  Crumbled cooked bacon

1. Place cabbage and 2 cups water in a large saucepan; bring to a boil. Reduce heat; simmer, covered, until cabbage is tender, about 10 minutes. Drain, reserving cooking liquid; keep cabbage warm in a separate dish.

2. In the same pan, combine potatoes and reserved cooking liquid. Add water to cover potatoes; bring to a boil. Reduce heat; cook, uncovered, until potatoes are tender, 15-20 minutes. Meanwhile, place milk, green onions, salt and pepper in a small saucepan; bring just to a boil and remove from heat.

3. Drain potatoes; place in a large bowl and mash. Add milk mixture; beat just until blended. Stir in cabbage. To serve, drizzle with butter; top with parsley and bacon.

1 cup: 168 cal., 5g fat (3g sat. fat), 14mg chol., 361mg sod., 27g carb. (6g sugars, 4g fiber), 4g pro.
Diabetic exchanges: 2 starch, 1 fat.

BEANS & CARAMELIZED ONIONS

Brown sugar, bacon and cider vinegar season this simple side. I often make it for family and friends, and it never fails to please!
—Jill Heatwole, Pittsville, MD

Prep: 10 min. • **Cook:** 40 min.
Makes: 8 servings

- 4 bacon strips, chopped
- 2 large onions, cut into ½-in. wedges
- 2 lbs. fresh green beans, trimmed
- 3 Tbsp. cider vinegar
- 1 to 2 Tbsp. brown sugar
- ¼ tsp. salt
- ¼ tsp. pepper

1. In a large skillet, cook chopped bacon over medium heat until crisp, stirring occasionally. Using a slotted spoon, remove bacon to paper towels, reserving 2 Tbsp. drippings in pan.

2. In drippings, saute onions over medium heat until softened. Reduce the heat to medium-low; cook onions until deep golden brown, 30-40 minutes, stirring occasionally. Stir in cider vinegar and brown sugar.

3. In a pot of boiling water, cook green beans, uncovered, until crisp-tender, 4-7 minutes; drain. Add to onions; cook 1 minute, tossing to combine. Stir in bacon; sprinkle with salt and pepper.

1 serving: 106 cal., 6g fat (2g sat. fat), 7mg chol., 146mg sod., 12g carb. (7g sugars, 4g fiber), 3g pro.
Diabetic exchanges: 1 vegetable, 1 fat, ½ starch.

COLCANNON POTATOES

GRILLED BRUSSELS SPROUTS

GRILLED BRUSSELS SPROUTS

During a beach vacation, in an effort to cook our entire meal outside on the grill, I made our not-so-simple veggie choice into a simple grilled side dish. For spicier sprouts, season with red pepper flakes .
—Tiffany Ihle, Bronx, NY

Takes: 25 min. • **Makes:** 4 servings

- 16 fresh Brussels sprouts (about
     1½-in. diameter), trimmed
- 1 medium sweet red pepper
- 1 medium onion
- ½ tsp. salt
- ½ tsp. garlic powder
- ¼ tsp. coarsely ground pepper
- 1 Tbsp. olive oil

1. In a large saucepan, place a steamer basket over 1 in. of water. Bring water to a boil. Place Brussels sprouts in basket. Reduce heat to maintain a simmer; steam, covered, until crisp-tender, 4-6 minutes. Cool slightly; cut each sprout in half.
2. Cut red pepper and onion into 1½-in. pieces. On four metal or soaked wooden skewers, alternately thread the Brussels sprouts, red pepper and onion pieces. Mix the salt, garlic powder and pepper. Brush the vegetables with oil; sprinkle with salt mixture. Grill, covered, over medium heat or broil 4 in. from the heat until vegetables are tender, 10-12 minutes, turning occasionally.
1 skewer: 84 cal., 4g fat (1g sat. fat), 0 chol., 316mg sod., 11g carb. (4g sugars, 4g fiber), 3g pro.
Diabetic exchanges: 1 vegetable, ½ fat.

ROSEMARY BEETS

(PICTURED ON P. 97)

We're a family of beet eaters. For a simple side dish, I use a slow cooker and let the beets mellow with rosemary and thyme.
—Nancy Heishman, Las Vegas, NV

Prep: 20 min. • **Cook:** 6 hours
Makes: 8 servings

- ⅓ cup honey
- ¼ cup white balsamic vinegar
- 1 Tbsp. minced fresh rosemary or
     1 tsp. dried rosemary, crushed
- 2 tsp. minced fresh thyme or
     ¾ tsp. dried thyme
- 1 Tbsp. olive oil
- 2 garlic cloves, minced
- ¾ tsp. salt
- ½ tsp. Chinese five-spice powder
- ½ tsp. coarsely ground pepper
- 5 large fresh beets (about 3½ lbs.),
     peeled and trimmed
- 1 medium red onion, chopped
- 1 medium orange, peeled and chopped
- 1 cup crumbled feta cheese

1. In a small bowl, whisk the first nine ingredients until blended. Place beets in a greased 4-qt. slow cooker. Add onion and orange. Pour honey mixture over top.
2. Cook, covered, on low 6-8 hours or until beets are tender. Remove beets; cut into wedges. Return to slow cooker. Serve warm, or refrigerate and serve cold. Serve with a slotted spoon; sprinkle with cheese.
¾ cup: 200 cal., 4g fat (2g sat. fat), 8mg chol., 511mg sod., 37g carb. (31g sugars, 5g fiber), 6g pro.
Diabetic exchanges: 2 vegetable, 1 starch, 1 fat.

CONFETTI QUINOA

CONFETTI QUINOA

If you've never tried quinoa, start with my easy side, brimming with colorful veggies. I serve it with orange-glazed chicken.
—Kim Ciepluch, Kenosha, WI

Takes: 30 min. • **Makes:** 4 servings

- 2 cups water
- 1 cup quinoa, rinsed
- ½ cup chopped fresh broccoli
- ½ cup coarsely chopped zucchini
- ¼ cup shredded carrots
- ½ tsp. salt
- 1 Tbsp. lemon juice
- 1 Tbsp. olive oil

In a large saucepan, bring water to a boil. Add next five ingredients. Reduce heat; simmer, covered, until liquid is absorbed, 12-15 minutes. Stir in lemon juice and oil; heat through. Remove from heat; fluff with a fork.
⅔ cup: 196 cal., 6g fat (1g sat. fat), 0 chol., 307mg sod., 29g carb. (1g sugars, 4g fiber), 7g pro.
Diabetic exchanges: 2 starch, ½ fat.

SLOW-COOKED LEMONY SPRING VEGGIES

These spuds do a slow simmer with onion and carrots for a comfort-food side that will buck up any entree. Finish with a sprinkle of chives.
—*Taste of Home* Test Kitchen

Prep: 10 min. • **Cook:** 4¼ hours
Makes: 8 servings

4 medium carrots, halved lengthwise and cut into 1-in. pieces
1 large sweet onion, coarsely chopped
1½ lbs. baby red potatoes, quartered
3 Tbsp. butter, melted
¾ tsp. salt
¼ tsp. pepper
1 cup frozen peas, thawed
1 tsp. grated lemon zest
¼ cup minced fresh chives

1. Place carrots and onion in a 4-qt. slow cooker; top with potatoes. Drizzle with melted butter; sprinkle vegetables with salt and pepper. Cook, covered, on low until tender, 4-5 hours.
2. Add peas to slow cooker. Cook, covered, on high until heated through, 10-15 minutes. Stir in lemon zest. Sprinkle with chives.

¾ cup: 141 cal., 5g fat (3g sat. fat), 11mg chol., 298mg sod., 23g carb. (5g sugars, 3g fiber), 3g pro.
Diabetic exchanges: 1½ starch, 1 fat.

SMOKY CAULIFLOWER BITES

These healthy little treats work well as a side or as a fun appetizer. Roasting the cauliflower adds a deeper flavor and gives it an irresistible crunch.
—Courtney Stultz, Weir, KS

Takes: 20 min. • **Makes:** 4 servings

3 Tbsp. olive oil
¾ tsp. sea salt
1 tsp. paprika
½ tsp. ground cumin
¼ tsp. ground turmeric
⅛ tsp. chili powder
1 medium head cauliflower, broken into florets

Preheat oven to 450°. Mix the first six ingredients. Add cauliflower florets; toss to coat. Transfer to a 15x10x1-in. baking pan. Roast until tender, 15-20 minutes, stirring halfway.

1 cup: 129 cal., 11g fat (2g sat. fat), 0 chol., 408mg sod., 8g carb. (3g sugars, 3g fiber), 3g pro.
Diabetic exchanges: 2 fat, 1 vegetable.

✱
TEST KITCHEN TIP
Squirt a little Sriracha or hot pepper sauce on these bites as soon as they come out of the oven. And if you really like smoky flavor, amp it up by using smoked Spanish-style paprika.

SLOW-COOKED LEMONY SPRING VEGGIES

SIDES

**ROASTED ITALIAN GREEN
BEANS & TOMATOES**

ROSEMARY ROASTED
BABY CARROTS

*Baby carrots go over big when seasoned
with the subtle taste of rosemary. I like to
sprinkle raisins on top for a combination
of sweet and savory.*
—Aysha Schurman, Ammon, ID

Prep: 10 min. • **Bake:** 25 min.
Makes: 8 servings

- 2 lbs. fresh baby carrots
- 2 Tbsp. olive oil
- 4 tsp. brown sugar
- 2 garlic cloves, minced
- 2 tsp. minced fresh rosemary or
  ½ tsp. dried rosemary, crushed
- ½ tsp. salt
- ½ tsp. onion powder
- ½ tsp. ground cumin
- ½ tsp. pepper
- 2 green onions, thinly sliced

1. Preheat oven to 425°. Place carrots in
a large bowl. In a small bowl, mix oil, brown
sugar, garlic and seasonings; add to carrots
and toss to coat.
2. Transfer to two 15x10x1-in. baking
pans coated with cooking spray. Roast
25-30 minutes or until tender, stirring
once. Sprinkle with green onions.
¾ cup: 82 cal., 4g fat (0 sat. fat), 0 chol.,
238mg sod., 12g carb. (8g sugars, 2g fiber),
1g pro.
Diabetic exchanges: 2 vegetable, ½ fat.

ROASTED ITALIAN GREEN
BEANS & TOMATOES

*When you roast green
beans and grape tomatoes,
their flavors really shine
through. I love seeing
the vibrant colors of this
healthy dish light up our dinner table.*
—Brittany Allyn, Mesa, AZ

Takes: 25 min. • **Makes:** 8 servings

- 1½ lbs. fresh green beans, trimmed and
  halved
- 1 Tbsp. olive oil
- 1 tsp. Italian seasoning
- ½ tsp. salt
- 2 cups grape tomatoes, halved
- ½ cup grated Parmesan cheese

1. Preheat oven to 425°. Place green
beans in a 15x10x1-in. baking pan coated
with cooking spray. Mix olive oil, Italian
seasoning and salt; drizzle over beans. Toss
to coat. Roast 10 minutes, stirring once.
2. Add tomatoes to pan. Roast until
beans are crisp-tender and tomatoes are
softened, 4-6 minutes longer. Sprinkle
with cheese.
¾ cup: 70 cal., 3g fat (1g sat. fat), 4mg chol.,
231mg sod., 8g carb. (3g sugars, 3g fiber),
4g pro.
Diabetic exchanges: 1 vegetable, ½ fat.

GARLIC PARMESAN ASPARAGUS

the garlic, ginger, vinegar, soy sauce, sesame oil and cayenne; saute 1 minute longer. Add the basil; toss to combine. Sprinkle with sesame seeds.

½ cup: 60 cal., 3g fat (0 sat. fat), 0 chol., 59mg sod., 6g carb. (3g sugars, 2g fiber), 3g pro. **Diabetic exchanges:** 1 vegetable, ½ fat.

FIESTA CORN & BEANS

Bursting with southwestern flavors, the zesty veggie medley here can be served as a side dish or a meatless entree. The dollop of yogurt provides a cool, creamy finishing touch.
—Gerald Hetrick, Erie, PA

Prep: 25 min. • **Cook:** 3 hours
Makes: 10 servings

- 1 large onion, chopped
- 1 medium green pepper, cut into 1-in. pieces
- 1 to 2 jalapeno peppers, seeded and sliced
- 1 Tbsp. olive oil
- 1 garlic clove, minced
- 2 cans (16 oz. each) kidney beans, rinsed and drained
- 1 pkg. (16 oz.) frozen corn
- 1 can (14½ oz.) diced tomatoes, undrained
- 1 tsp. chili powder
- ¾ tsp. salt
- ½ tsp. ground cumin
- ½ tsp. pepper
  Optional toppings: plain yogurt and sliced ripe olives

1. In a large skillet, saute chopped onion and peppers in oil until tender. Add garlic; cook 1 minute longer. Transfer to a 4-qt. slow cooker. Stir in the beans, corn, tomatoes and seasonings.

2. Cover and cook on low for 3-4 hours or until heated through. Serve with yogurt and olives if desired.

Note: Wear disposable gloves when cutting hot peppers; the oils can burn skin. Avoid touching your face.

¾ cup: 149 cal., 2g fat (0 sat. fat), 0 chol., 380mg sod., 28g carb. (5g sugars, 7g fiber), 8g pro. **Diabetic exchanges:** 1 starch, 1 lean meat, 1 vegetable.

GARLIC PARMESAN ASPARAGUS

Pair any entree with this fresh side dish for a truly succulent meal. With subtle garlic, melted butter and a hint of Parmesan cheese, what's not to love?
—Tara Ernspiker, Falling Waters, WV

Takes: 15 min. • **Makes:** 4 servings

- 1 lb. fresh asparagus, trimmed
- 1 garlic clove, minced
- 2 Tbsp. butter, melted
- 1 Tbsp. grated Parmesan cheese

In a large skillet, bring ½ in. of water to a boil. Add asparagus and garlic; cook, covered, until asparagus is crisp-tender, 3-5 minutes; drain. Toss asparagus with butter and cheese.

1 serving: 71 cal., 6g fat (4g sat. fat), 16mg chol., 74mg sod., 3g carb. (1g sugars, 1g fiber), 2g pro.
Diabetic exchanges: 1½ fat, 1 vegetable.

SUGAR SNAP PEA STIR-FRY

Fresh ginger, soy sauce and sesame oil provide a nice blend of flavors in this Asian-inspired recipe for fresh sugar snap peas. This quick recipe will complement many spring entrees, including ham, lamb, chicken and fish.
—Taste of Home Test Kitchen

Takes: 20 min. • **Makes:** 6 servings

- 1 lb. fresh sugar snap peas
- 2 tsp. canola oil
- 1 garlic clove, minced
- 2 tsp. minced fresh gingerroot
- 1½ tsp. balsamic vinegar
- 1½ tsp. reduced-sodium soy sauce
- 1 tsp. sesame oil
  Dash cayenne pepper
- 1 Tbsp. minced fresh basil or 1 tsp. dried basil
- 2 tsp. sesame seeds, toasted

In a large nonstick skillet or wok, saute the peas in canola oil until crisp-tender. Add

SIDES

FIESTA CORN & BEANS

GRILLED LIME-BALSAMIC SWEET POTATOES

This is one of my go-to dishes when we're tailgating at sporting events. Tailgating is all about camaraderie and preparing food that's good to grill, and that's just what these sweet potato wedges are!
—Raquel Perazzo, West New York, NJ

Prep: 15 min. • **Grill:** 10 min./batch
• **Makes:** 8 servings

- 5 medium sweet potatoes (about 3 lbs.)
- 2 Tbsp. olive oil
- 1 tsp. salt
- ¼ tsp. pepper
- ¼ cup chopped fresh cilantro
- ¼ cup packed brown sugar
- ¼ cup lime juice
- 3 Tbsp. white or regular balsamic glaze

1. Peel and cut each sweet potato lengthwise into eight wedges; place in a large bowl. Toss with oil, salt and pepper.
2. In batches, cook potatoes on a greased grill rack, covered, over medium heat until tender, 8-10 minutes, turning occasionally.
3. In a large bowl, mix all the remaining ingredients; add potatoes and toss to coat.

5 potato wedges: 197 cal., 4g fat (1g sat. fat), 0 chol., 309mg sod., 41g carb. (23g sugars, 4g fiber), 2g pro.

VEGETABLE MEDLEY

This is a wonderful side dish to make in summer when garden vegetables are plentiful. If you have fresh corn, use that instead of frozen.
—Terry Maly, Olathe, KS

Prep: 15 min. • **Cook:** 5 hours
Makes: 8 servings

- 4 cups diced peeled potatoes
- 1½ cups frozen whole kernel corn
- 4 medium tomatoes, seeded and diced
- 1 cup sliced carrots
- ½ cup chopped onion
- ¾ tsp. salt
- ½ tsp. sugar
- ½ tsp. dill weed
- ⅛ tsp. pepper

In a 3-qt. slow cooker, combine all ingredients. Cover and cook on low for 5-6 hours or until vegetables are tender.

GARLIC ASIAGO CAULIFLOWER RICE

1 cup: 116 cal., 1g fat (1g sat. fat), 0 chol., 243mg sod., 27g carb. (0 sugars, 4g fiber), 3g pro.
Diabetic exchanges: 1½ starch.

GARLIC ASIAGO CAULIFLOWER RICE

The garlic seasoning and Asiago really pack a punch, making this five-ingredient low-carb side dish a real weeknight winner.
—Colleen Delawder, Herndon, VA

Takes: 20 min. • **Makes:** 6 servings

- 1 medium head cauliflower
- 2 Tbsp. unsalted butter
- 1 Tbsp. extra virgin olive oil
- 1½ tsp. garlic-herb seasoning blend
- ½ cup finely grated Asiago cheese

Using a food processor fitted with the steel blade, or a box grater, finely shred cauliflower (there should be about 6 cups). In a large cast-iron or other heavy skillet, heat butter, oil and seasoning blend over medium-high heat. When butter is melted, stir in cauliflower, working in batches if necessary. Cook, uncovered, until tender, 10-15 minutes, stirring occasionally (there should be about 4 cups cauliflower rice). Add cheese; stir until well combined.

⅔ cup: 112 cal., 9g fat (4g sat. fat), 18mg chol., 103mg sod., 5g carb. (2g sugars, 2g fiber), 4g pro.
Diabetic exchanges: 2 fat, 1 vegetable.

WAFFLE IRON ACORN SQUASH

I love to get the kids involved in cooking, and this squash is so simple even a small child can cook it with minimal adult supervision. The recipe is fun, fast and no-fuss, and doesn't use valuable oven space before big family meals.
—Donna Kelly, Draper, UT

Prep: 10 min. • **Bake:** 5 min./batch
Makes: 4 servings

- 3 Tbsp. maple syrup
- ¾ tsp. ground chipotle pepper
- ½ tsp. salt
- 1 small acorn squash

1. Preheat a greased waffle maker. Mix syrup, chipotle pepper and salt.

2. Cut squash crosswise into ½-in.-thick slices. Using round cookie cutters, cut out centers to remove squash strings and seeds. If necessary, halve the slices to fit waffle maker.

3. Bake slices in waffle maker just until tender and lightly browned, 3-4 minutes. Serve with syrup mixture.

1 serving: 98 cal., 0 fat (0 sat. fat), 0 chol., 463mg sod., 25g carb. (12g sugars, 2g fiber), 1g pro.

Diabetic exchanges: 1½ starch.

TEST KITCHEN TIP

Cut slices just ½ in. thick. If slices are thicker, the waffle iron won't close all the way. A panini press also works to make this squash.

WAFFLE IRON ACORN SQUASH

MUSHROOM & SPINACH SAUTE

Mushrooms and spinach make a super-fast combination that's perfect for two. It's easy to double or triple for a crowd.
—Pauline Howard, Lago Vista, TX

Takes: 10 min. • **Makes:** 2 servings

- 2 tsp. olive oil
- 2 cups sliced fresh mushrooms
- 2 garlic cloves, minced
- 1 pkg. (5 to 6 oz.) fresh baby spinach
- ⅛ tsp. salt
- ⅛ tsp. pepper

In a large skillet, heat oil over medium-high heat. Add sliced mushrooms; saute until tender, about 2 minutes. Add the garlic; cook 1 minute longer. Add spinach in batches; cook and stir until wilted, about 1 minute. Season with salt and pepper. Serve immediately.

¾ cup: 76 cal., 5g fat (1g sat. fat), 0mg chol., 208mg sod., 6g carb. (2g sugars, 2g fiber), 4g pro.

Diabetic exchanges: 1 vegetable, 1 fat.

SPRING ASPARAGUS

This fresh, colorful side dish is delicious served warm or cold. I always get lots of compliments on the homemade dressing.
—Millie Vickery, Lena, IL

Takes: 25 min. • **Makes:** 8 servings

1½ lbs. fresh asparagus, trimmed and cut into 2-in. pieces
2 small tomatoes, cut into wedges
3 Tbsp. cider vinegar
¾ tsp. Worcestershire sauce
⅓ cup sugar
1 Tbsp. grated onion
½ tsp. salt
½ tsp. paprika
⅓ cup canola oil
⅓ cup sliced almonds, toasted
⅓ cup crumbled blue cheese, optional

1. In a large saucepan, bring 1 cup water to a boil. Add asparagus; cook, covered, until crisp-tender, 3-5 minutes. Drain; place in a large bowl. Add tomatoes; cover and keep warm.
2. Place vinegar, Worcestershire sauce, sugar, onion, salt and paprika in a blender; cover and process until smooth. While processing, gradually add oil in a steady stream. Toss with asparagus mixture. Top with almonds and, if desired, cheese.
Note: To toast nuts, bake in a shallow pan in a 350° oven for 5-10 minutes or cook in a skillet over low heat until lightly browned, stirring occasionally.
¾ cup: 154 cal., 11g fat (1g sat. fat), 0 chol., 159mg sod., 12g carb. (10g sugars, 1g fiber), 2g pro.
Diabetic exchanges: 2 fat, 1 vegetable, ½ starch.

LEMON GARLIC MUSHROOMS

I baste whole mushrooms with a lemony sauce to prepare this simple side dish, which everyone enjoys. Using skewers or a basket makes it easy to turn them as they grill to perfection.
—Diane Hixon, Niceville, FL

Takes: 15 min. • **Makes:** 4 servings

¼ cup lemon juice
3 Tbsp. minced fresh parsley
2 Tbsp. olive oil
3 garlic cloves, minced

BRUSSELS SPROUTS WITH GARLIC & GOAT CHEESE

Pepper to taste
1 lb. large fresh mushrooms

1. For dressing, whisk together the first five ingredients. Toss the mushrooms with 2 Tbsp. dressing.
2. Grill the mushrooms, covered, over medium-high heat until tender, 5-7 minutes per side. Toss with remaining dressing before serving.
1 serving: 94 cal., 7g fat (1g sat. fat), 0mg chol., 2mg sod., 6g carb. (0g sugars, 0g fiber), 3g pro.
Diabetic exchanges: 1 vegetable, 1½ fat.

BRUSSELS SPROUTS WITH GARLIC & GOAT CHEESE

I wanted to up my veggie game, so I smothered fresh Brussels sprouts with garlic and goat cheese. Although it's really a side dish, I love to eat a larger portion of it for lunch!
—Brenda Williams, Santa Maria, CA

Prep: 20 min. • **Bake:** 20 min.
Makes: 16 servings

3 lbs. Brussels sprouts, trimmed and halved
¼ cup olive oil
8 garlic cloves, minced
1 tsp. salt
½ tsp. pepper
1 pkg. (5.3 oz.) fresh goat cheese, crumbled

Preheat oven to 425°. Toss the first five ingredients; spread in a greased 15x10x1-in. pan. Roast until tender, 20-25 minutes, stirring occasionally. Transfer to a bowl; toss with cheese.
⅔ cup: 81 cal., 5g fat (1g sat. fat), 6mg chol., 205mg sod., 8g carb. (2g sugars, 3g fiber), 4g pro.
Diabetic exchanges: 1 vegetable, 1 fat.
* HEALTH TIP * Brussels sprouts are loaded with fat-soluble vitamin K. We need to serve it up with a little fat to absorb the nutrients—thank you, goat cheese and olive oil!

ONE-PAN WONDERS

"I substituted turkey for pork in this classic Chinese recipe. It was a hit at our church potluck, and my husband and two children love it, too."
—Leigh Lundy, York, NE

Pork & Asparagus Sheet-Pan Dinner (p. 125) **Sweet Potato Stew** (p. 122) **Spanish Rice with Chicken & Peas** (p. 127)
Chicken with Pear & Sweet Potato (p. 126) **Turkey Lo Mein** (p.128) **Lemon-Dijon Pork Sheet-Pan Supper** (p. 122)

APPLE CHICKEN QUESADILLAS

TEQUILA LIME SHRIMP ZOODLES

This tangy shrimp is a great way to cut carbs without sacrificing flavor. If you don't have a spiralizer, use thinly julienned zucchini to get a similar effect.
—Brigette Schroeder, Yorkville, IL

Takes: 30 min. • **Makes:** 4 servings

- 3 Tbsp. butter, divided
- 1 shallot, minced
- 2 garlic cloves, minced
- ¼ cup tequila
- 1½ tsp. grated lime zest
- 2 Tbsp. lime juice
- 1 Tbsp. olive oil
- 1 lb. uncooked shrimp (31-40 per lb.), peeled and deveined
- 2 medium zucchini, spiralized (about 6 cups)
- ½ tsp. salt
- ¼ tsp. pepper
- ¼ cup minced fresh parsley
  Additional grated lime zest

1. In a large skillet, heat 2 Tbsp. butter over medium heat. Add shallot and garlic; cook 1-2 minutes. Remove from heat; stir in tequila, lime zest and lime juice. Cook over medium heat until liquid is almost evaporated, 2-3 minutes.
2. Add olive oil and remaining butter; stir in shrimp and zucchini. Sprinkle with salt and pepper. Cook and stir until shrimp begin to turn pink and zucchini is crisp-tender, 4-5 minutes. Sprinkle with parsley and additional lime zest.

1¼ cups: 246 cal., 14g fat (6g sat. fat), 161mg chol., 510mg sod., 7g carb. (3g sugars, 1g fiber), 20g pro.
Diabetic exchanges: 3 lean meat, 3 fat, 1 vegetable.
* HEALTH TIP * Shrimp are naturally high in cholesterol, but not to worry. The greatest impact on blood cholesterol comes from saturated and trans fats, and shrimp has little saturated and no trans fat.

APPLE CHICKEN QUESADILLAS

My sister came up with an easy recipe that can be served as a main course or an appetizer. People are surprised by the combination of chicken, apples, tomatoes and corn inside the crispy tortillas, but they love it.
—Stacia Slagle, Maysville, MO

Takes: 25 min. • **Makes:** 6 servings

- 2 medium tart apples, sliced
- 1 cup diced cooked chicken breast
- ½ cup shredded cheddar cheese
- ½ cup shredded part-skim mozzarella cheese
- ½ cup fresh or frozen corn, thawed
- ½ cup chopped fresh tomatoes
- ½ cup chopped onion
- ¼ tsp. salt
- 6 flour tortillas (8 in.), warmed
  Optional toppings: shredded lettuce, salsa and sour cream

1. Preheat oven to 400°. Toss together first eight ingredients. Place ¾ cup mixture on one half of each tortilla. Fold tortillas to close; secure with toothpicks.
2. Place on a baking sheet coated with cooking spray. Bake until golden brown, 13-18 minutes, turning halfway through cooking. Discard toothpicks. Serve with toppings as desired.

1 quesadilla: 300 cal., 10g fat (4g sat. fat), 33mg chol., 475mg sod., 38g carb. (6g sugars, 3g fiber), 16g pro.
Diabetic exchanges: 2½ starch, 2 medium-fat meat.

TEQUILA LIME
SHRIMP ZOODLES

LEMON-DIJON PORK SHEET-PAN SUPPER

LEMON-DIJON PORK SHEET-PAN SUPPER

Most nights, I need a meal that I can get on the table with minimal effort and delicious results. This sheet-pan supper has become an all-time favorite, not only because of its bright flavors, but its speedy cleanup time, too!
—Elisabeth Larsen, Pleasant Grove, UT

Prep: 20 min. • **Bake:** 20 min.
Makes: 4 servings

- 4 tsp. Dijon mustard
- 2 tsp. grated lemon zest
- 1 garlic clove, minced
- ½ tsp. salt
- 2 Tbsp. canola oil
- 1½ lbs. sweet potatoes (about 3 medium), cut into ½-in. cubes
- 1 lb. fresh Brussels sprouts (about 4 cups), quartered
- 4 boneless pork loin chops (6 oz. each)
  Coarsely ground pepper, optional

1. Preheat oven to 425°. In a large bowl, mix first four ingredients; gradually whisk in the oil. Remove 1 Tbsp. mixture for brushing pork chops. Add the vegetables to remaining mixture; toss to coat.

2. Place pork chops and vegetables in a 15x10x1-in. pan coated with cooking spray. Brush chops with reserved mustard mixture. Roast 10 minutes.

3. Turn the chops and stir vegetables; roast until a thermometer inserted in pork chops reads 145° and the vegetables are tender, 10-15 minutes. If desired, sprinkle with pepper. Let stand for 5 minutes before serving.

1 pork chop with 1¼ cups vegetables:
516 cal., 17g fat (4g sat. fat), 82mg chol., 505mg sod., 51g carb. (19g sugars, 9g fiber), 39g pro.

Diabetic exchanges: 5 lean meat, 3 starch, 1½ fat, 1 vegetable.

* HEALTH TIP * The bright colors in this dish ensure you're getting a variety of nutrients. Sweet potatoes are an excellent source of vitamin A, and Brussels sprouts are loaded with vitamin K.

TEST KITCHEN TIP
Cutting the Brussels sprouts and potatoes fairly small means they'll be perfectly tender by the time the pork is cooked.

SWEET POTATO STEW
(PICTURED ON P. 118)

Beef broth and herbs complement the sweet potatoes' subtle sweetness in this hearty stew that's perfect for fall.
—Helen Vail, Glenside, PA

Prep: 20 min. • **Cook:** 20 min.
Makes: 4 servings

- 2 cans (14½ oz. each) reduced-sodium beef broth
- ¾ lb. lean ground beef (90% lean)
- 2 medium sweet potatoes, peeled and cut into ½-in. cubes
- 1 small onion, finely chopped
- ½ cup V8 juice
- 1 Tbsp. golden raisins
- 1 garlic clove, minced
- ½ tsp. dried thyme
  Dash cayenne pepper

In a large saucepan, bring broth to a boil. Crumble beef into broth. Cook, covered, for 3 minutes, stirring occasionally. Add remaining ingredients; return to a boil. Reduce heat; simmer, uncovered, until meat is no longer pink and potatoes are tender, about 15 minutes.

1¼ cups: 265 cal., 7g fat (3g sat. fat), 58mg chol., 532mg sod., 29g carb. (13g sugars, 4g fiber), 20g pro.

Diabetic exchanges: 2 starch, 2 lean meat.

SUMMER BOUNTY RATATOUILLE

The name says it all! Make use of your garden's surplus with this comforting dish. Pronounced ra-tuh-TOO-ee and originating from France's Nice, ratatouille is a vegetable dish traditionally made with eggplant, tomatoes, onions, zucchini, garlic, bell peppers and various herbs. I highly recommend accompanying it with some freshly baked bread.
—Phyllis Jacques, Venice, FL

Prep: 20 min. + standing • **Cook:** 1 hour
Makes: 12 servings

- 1 large eggplant, peeled and cut into 1-in. cubes
- 1½ tsp. kosher salt, divided
- 3 Tbsp. olive oil
- 2 medium sweet red peppers, cut into ½-in. strips
- 2 medium onions, peeled and chopped
- 4 garlic cloves, minced
- ¼ cup tomato paste
- 1 Tbsp. herbes de Provence
- ½ tsp. pepper
- 3 cans (14½ oz. each) diced tomatoes, undrained
- 1½ cups water
- 4 medium zucchini, quartered lengthwise and sliced ½-in. thick
- ¼ cup chopped fresh basil
- 2 Tbsp. minced fresh rosemary
- 2 Tbsp. minced fresh parsley
- 2 French bread baguettes (10½ oz. each), cubed and toasted

1. Place eggplant in a colander over a plate; toss with 1 tsp. kosher salt. Let stand 30 minutes. Rinse and drain well.
2. In a Dutch oven, heat oil over medium-high heat; saute peppers and onions until tender, 8-10 minutes. Add garlic; cook and stir 1 minute. Stir in tomato paste, herbs de Provence, pepper, remaining salt, tomatoes and water. Add zucchini and eggplant; bring to a boil. Reduce heat; simmer, uncovered, until the flavors are blended, 40-45 minutes, stirring occasionally.
3. Stir in fresh herbs. Serve over French bread baguette cubes.

Note: Look for herbes de Provence in the spice aisle.

1 cup ratatouille with 1 cup bread cubes: 205 cal., 4g fat (1g sat. fat), 0 chol., 542mg sod., 38g carb. (8g sugars, 6g fiber), 7g pro.

HAMBURGER CASSEROLE

This recipe is such a hit it's traveled all over the country! My mother originated the recipe in Pennsylvania, I brought it to Texas when I married, I'm still making it in California, and my daughter treats her friends to this oldie in Colorado. It's hearty, yet simple to prepare.
—Helen Carmichall, Santee, CA

Prep: 20 min. • **Cook:** 45 min.
Makes: 10 servings

- 2 lbs. lean ground beef (90% lean)
- 4 lbs. potatoes, peeled and sliced ¼ in. thick
- 1 large onion, sliced
- 1 tsp. salt
- ½ tsp. pepper
- 1 tsp. beef bouillon granules
- 1 cup boiling water
- 1 can (28 oz.) diced tomatoes, undrained
  Minced fresh parsley, optional

In a Dutch oven, layer half of the meat, potatoes and onion. Sprinkle with half of the salt and pepper. Repeat layers. Dissolve bouillon in water; pour over all. Top with tomatoes. Cover and cook over medium heat until potatoes are tender, 45-50 minutes. Garnish with parsley if desired.

1 cup: 270 cal., 8g fat (3g sat. fat), 57mg chol., 493mg sod., 30g carb. (5g sugars, 3g fiber), 21g pro.
Diabetic exchanges: 3 lean meat, 2 starch.

SUMMER BOUNTY RATATOUILLE

PORK & ASPARAGUS SHEET-PAN DINNER

When time is of the essence, it's nice to have a quick and easy meal idea in your back pocket. Not only is it delicious, but you can clean it up in a flash.
—Joan Hallford, North Richland Hills, TX

Prep: 20 min. • **Bake:** 20 min.
Makes: 4 servings

- ¼ cup olive oil, divided
- 3 cups diced new potatoes
- 3 cups cut fresh asparagus (1-in. pieces)
- ¼ tsp. salt
- ¼ tsp. pepper
- 1 large gala or Honeycrisp apple, peeled and cut into ½-in. slices
- 2 tsp. brown sugar
- 1 tsp. ground cinnamon
- ¼ tsp. ground ginger
- 4 boneless pork loin chops (1 in. thick and about 6 oz. each)
- 2 tsp. southwest seasoning

1. Preheat oven to 425°. Line a 15x10x1-in. baking pan with foil; brush with 2 tsp. olive oil.
2. In a large bowl, toss potatoes with 1 Tbsp. olive oil. Place in one section of prepared baking pan. In same bowl, toss asparagus with 1 Tbsp. olive oil; place in another section of pan. Sprinkle salt and pepper over potatoes and asparagus.
3. In same bowl, toss apple with 1 tsp. olive oil. In a small bowl, mix brown sugar, cinnamon and ginger; sprinkle over apples and toss to coat. Transfer to a different section of pan.
4. Brush pork chops with remaining olive oil; sprinkle both sides with southwest seasoning. Place the chops in remaining section of pan. Bake until a thermometer inserted in pork reads 145° and potatoes and apples are tender, 20-25 minutes. Let stand 5 minutes before serving.

1 serving: 486 cal., 23g fat (5g sat. fat), 82mg chol., 447mg sod., 32g carb. (10g sugars, 5g fiber), 37g pro.

CASABLANCA CHICKEN COUSCOUS

CASABLANCA CHICKEN COUSCOUS

To give risotto—that favorite Italian comfort food—an update, I used couscous and lively North African-inspired flavors to deliver all the satisfaction of the creamy classic.
—Roxanne Chan, Albany, CA

Prep: 20 min. • **Cook:** 15 min. + standing
Makes: 6 servings

- 1 Tbsp. olive oil
- 1 medium onion, chopped
- 1 lb. boneless skinless chicken thighs, cut into 1-in. pieces
- 1 pkg. (8.8 oz.) uncooked Israeli couscous
- ½ tsp. salt
- ¼ tsp. pepper
- ¼ tsp. crushed red pepper flakes
- 2 cans (14½ oz. each) reduced-sodium chicken broth
- ⅔ cup dried tropical fruit
- 1 can (15 to 15½ oz.) garbanzo beans or chickpeas, rinsed and drained
- ½ cup plain yogurt
- 1 small carrot, grated
- ¼ cup minced fresh parsley
- 1 medium lemon

1. In a large skillet, heat the olive oil over medium-high heat. Add onion; saute until softened, 3-4 minutes. Add the chicken, couscous, salt, pepper and pepper flakes; cook and stir until the chicken begins to brown, 3-5 minutes. Add broth and dried fruit; cook, uncovered, until chicken and couscous are tender and fruit is moist, 8-10 minutes.
2. Stir in remaining ingredients; heat through. Remove from heat. Let stand, covered, 10 minutes. Meanwhile, zest lemon peel into strips; cut lemon into six wedges. Top couscous with zest strips and serve with lemon wedges.

1⅓ cups: 448 cal., 11g fat (3g sat. fat), 53mg chol., 715mg sod., 63g carb. (17g sugars, 4g fiber), 25g pro.

TEST KITCHEN TIP

Israeli couscous is much larger than regular couscous and takes longer to cook, so don't be tempted to substitute one for the other. Israeli couscous may be labeled pearl couscous or ptitim in Middle Eastern markets.

CHICKEN WITH PEAR & SWEET POTATO

(PICTURED ON P. 118)

When my husband was deployed to Iraq, one of my girlfriends shared this yummy chicken. When he returned home, I made it a tradition at our house.
—Cathryn Eckley, Fort Meade, MD

Takes: 30 min. • **Makes:** 4 servings

- 4 **boneless skinless chicken breast halves (5 oz. each)**
- ¼ **tsp. pepper**
- ¾ **tsp. salt, divided**
- 1 **Tbsp. canola oil**
- 1 **medium sweet potato (about ¾ lb.), peeled and cut into ½-in. pieces**
- ½ **cup plus 3 Tbsp. water, divided**
- 1 **medium ripe pear, cut into ½-in. pieces**
- 1 **Tbsp. red wine vinegar**
- 1 **Tbsp. Dijon mustard**
- 1 **tsp. minced fresh tarragon or ¼ tsp. dried tarragon**

1. Pound chicken breasts with a meat mallet to ½-in. thickness; sprinkle with pepper and ½ tsp. salt.

2. In a large nonstick skillet, heat oil over medium heat. Add the chicken; cook until no longer pink, 3-4 minutes on each side. Remove from pan; keep warm.

3. In same pan, combine sweet potato and ½ cup water; bring to a boil. Reduce heat; simmer, covered, 5 minutes. Stir in pear; cook, covered, until potato is tender, 4-5 minutes longer. Add vinegar, mustard and tarragon; stir in the remaining water and heat through. Serve with chicken.

4 oz. cooked chicken with ¾ cup potato mixture: 301 cal., 7g fat (1g sat. fat), 78mg chol., 610mg sod., 28g carb. (13g sugars, 4g fiber), 30g pro.
Diabetic exchanges: 4 lean meat, 1½ starch, ½ fat.

TAKEOUT BEEF FRIED RICE

TAKEOUT BEEF FRIED RICE

Transform leftover beef into a fabulous dinner for six. Hoisin-flavored beef works great in this recipe, but you can use flank steak or roast beef as well.
—*Taste of Home* Test Kitchen

Takes: 30 min. • **Makes:** 6 servings

- 1 **Tbsp. plus 1 tsp. canola oil, divided**
- 3 **large eggs**
- 1 **can (11 oz.) mandarin oranges**
- 2 **medium sweet red peppers, chopped**
- 1 **cup fresh sugar snap peas, trimmed**
- 1 **small onion, thinly sliced**
- 3 **garlic cloves, minced**
- ½ **tsp. crushed red pepper flakes**
- 4 **cups cold cooked rice**
- 2 **cups cooked beef, sliced across grain into bite-sized pieces**
- 1 **cup beef broth**
- ¼ **cup reduced-sodium soy sauce**
- ½ **tsp. salt**
- ¼ **tsp. ground ginger**

1. In a large skillet, heat 1 Tbsp. oil over medium-high heat. Whisk the eggs until blended; pour into skillet. Mixture should set immediately at edge. As eggs set, push cooked portions toward center, letting uncooked portions flow underneath. When eggs are thickened and no liquid egg remains, remove to a cutting board and chop. Meanwhile, drain oranges, reserving 2 Tbsp. juice.

2. In same skillet, heat remaining oil over medium-high heat. Add peppers, sugar snap peas and onion; cook and stir until crisp-tender, 1-2 minutes. Add garlic and pepper flakes; cook 1 minute longer. Add remaining ingredients and reserved juice; heat through. Gently stir in the eggs and drained oranges.

1⅓ cups: 367 cal., 9g fat (2g sat. fat), 136mg chol., 793mg sod., 45g carb. (11g sugars, 3g fiber), 26g pro.
Diabetic exchanges: 3 starch, 3 lean meat, 1 fat.

ONE-POT STUFFED PEPPER DINNER

Thick like a chili and rich with stuffed-pepper flavor, this dish will warm you up on chilly days.
—Charlotte Smith, McDonald, PA

....

Takes: 30 min. • **Makes:** 4 servings

- 1 lb. lean ground beef (90% lean)
- 3 medium green peppers, chopped (about 3 cups)
- 3 garlic cloves, minced
- 2 cans (14½ oz. each) Italian diced tomatoes, undrained
- 2 cups water
- 1 can (6 oz.) tomato paste
- 2 Tbsp. shredded Parmesan cheese
- ¼ tsp. pepper
- 1 cup uncooked instant rice
  Additional Parmesan cheese, optional

1. In a Dutch oven, cook and crumble beef with green peppers and garlic over medium-high heat until no longer pink and peppers are tender, 5-7 minutes; drain.
2. Stir in tomatoes, water, tomato paste, 2 Tbsp. cheese and pepper; bring to a boil. Stir in rice; remove from heat. Let stand, covered, 5 minutes. If desired, sprinkle with additional cheese.

2 cups: 415 cal., 10g fat (4g sat. fat), 72mg chol., 790mg sod., 51g carb. (20g sugars, 5g fiber), 30g pro.

SPANISH RICE WITH CHICKEN & PEAS

(PICTURED ON P. 119)

My mom made this juicy chicken and rice for us every Wednesday. I still make it for my hubby. It reminds me of family dinners growing up.
—Josee Lanzi, New Port Richey, FL

....

Prep: 15 min. • **Cook:** 30 min.
Makes: 6 servings

- 1 lb. boneless skinless chicken breasts, cut into 1½-in. pieces
- 1 Tbsp. all-purpose flour
- ½ tsp. pepper
- ½ tsp. salt, divided
- 4 tsp. plus 1 Tbsp. olive oil, divided
- 1 small sweet red pepper, chopped
- 1 small onion, chopped
- 1 celery rib, chopped
- 1½ cups uncooked long grain rice
- 1 tsp. ground cumin
- 1 tsp. chili powder
- 2¼ cups chicken broth
- 1 can (14½ oz.) diced tomatoes, undrained
- 1 cup frozen peas, thawed

1. In a small bowl, toss chicken with flour, pepper and ¼ tsp. salt. In a Dutch oven, heat 4 tsp. oil over medium-high heat. Brown chicken, stirring occasionally; remove from pan.
2. In same pan, heat remaining oil over medium heat. Add pepper, onion and celery; cook and stir until onion is tender, 2-4 minutes. Add the rice, cumin, chili powder and remaining salt; stir to coat rice. Stir in remaining ingredients; bring to a boil. Reduce heat; simmer, covered, 10 minutes.
3. Place browned chicken over rice (do not stir in). Cook, covered, until rice is tender and chicken is cooked through, about 5 minutes longer.

1½ cups: 367 cal., 8g fat (1g sat. fat), 44mg chol., 755mg sod., 50g carb. (5g sugars, 4g fiber), 22g pro.
Diabetic exchanges: 3 starch, 2 lean meat, 1 vegetable, 1 fat.

ONE-POT STUFFED PEPPER DINNER

MEXICAN TURKEY SKILLET

TURKEY LO MEIN

I substituted turkey for pork in this classic Chinese recipe. It was a hit at our church potluck, and my husband and two children love it, too.
—Leigh Lundy, York, NE

Takes: 30 min. • **Makes:** 6 servings

- 1 lb. lean ground turkey
- 2 medium carrots, thinly sliced
- 1 medium onion, chopped
- ½ tsp. garlic powder
- 2 pkg. (3 oz. each) ramen noodles
- 1½ cups water
- 6 cups shredded cabbage
- 1 cup frozen peas, thawed
- ¼ cup reduced-sodium soy sauce

1. In a large skillet, cook and crumble turkey with carrots, onion and garlic powder over medium-high heat until no longer pink, 5-7 minutes.

2. Break up noodles and add to skillet; stir in contents of seasoning packets and water. Bring to a boil. Reduce heat; simmer, covered, 3-5 minutes. Add the remaining ingredients; cook and stir until cabbage is crisp-tender, 1-3 minutes.

1⅓ cups: 297 cal., 11g fat (4g sat. fat), 52mg chol., 580mg sod., 29g carb. (3g sugars, 4g fiber), 21g pro.
Diabetic exchanges: 2 starch, 2 lean meat.

> **DID YOU KNOW?**
>
> Lean ground turkey (93% lean) contains 53% less fat and 38% less saturated fat than regular ground turkey (85% lean). It works great in casseroles, tacos and other dishes that use crumbled meat. Higher-fat meat works better for burgers or meat loaf.

MEXICAN TURKEY SKILLET

This family-friendly main dish with turkey, black beans and vegetables has a rich Mexican flavor that may seem indulgent, but it's delightfully light. It cooks in one skillet, so it's a snap to clean up for a weeknight supper.
—Taste of Home Test Kitchen

Prep: 20 min. • **Bake:** 30 min.
Makes: 8 servings

- 1 lb. lean ground turkey
- 1 cup chopped zucchini
- ½ cup chopped sweet red pepper
- 2 tsp. canola oil
- 2 cups cooked rice
- 1 can (15 oz.) black beans, rinsed and drained
- 1 can (14½ oz.) Mexican stewed tomatoes
- 1 can (8 oz.) tomato sauce
- ½ tsp. ground cumin
- ¼ tsp. salt
- ¼ tsp. pepper
- 1 cup shredded reduced-fat Mexican cheese blend
- Chopped avocado, optional

1. In a large nonstick ovenproof skillet, cook turkey over medium heat until no longer pink; drain. Set turkey aside. In the same skillet, saute the zucchini and red pepper in oil until crisp-tender, about 2 minutes.

2. Stir in turkey, rice, beans, tomatoes, tomato sauce, cumin, salt and pepper. Cover and bake at 350° for 30 minutes. Sprinkle with cheese blend. Let stand for 5 minutes before serving. Garnish with avocado if desired.

1 cup: 254 cal., 9g fat (3g sat. fat), 55mg chol., 616mg sod., 25g carb. (4g sugars, 4g fiber), 19g pro.
Diabetic exchanges: 2 lean meat, 1 starch, 1 vegetable, ½ fat.

STOVETOP MAINS

"This wonderfully tender steak is a treat even for folks not watching their diet. When my mother-in-law shared the recipe, she said it cooks up in no time...and she was right!"
—Susan Adair, Somerset, KY

Poached Chicken (p. 149) Quick Shrimp Creole (p. 163) Glazed Rosemary Pork (p.164)
Broccoli-Pork Stir-Fry with Noodles (p.153) Gingered Pepper Steak (p. 133) Quinoa Unstuffed Peppers (p. 136)

PORK CHOPS WITH HONEY-GARLIC SAUCE

The honey and garlic sauce on this pork is so good, I sometimes double it so there's extra for dipping whatever veggie we have on the side.

—Michelle Smith, Eldersburg, MD

Takes: 25 min. • **Makes:** 4 servings

- 4 bone-in pork loin chops (6 oz. each)
- ¼ cup lemon juice
- ¼ cup honey
- 2 Tbsp. reduced-sodium soy sauce
- 1 garlic clove, minced

In a large skillet coated with cooking spray, cook pork chops over medium heat until a thermometer reads 145°, 5-6 minutes on each side. Remove pork chops; let stand for 5 minutes. Combine remaining ingredients; add to skillet. Cook over medium heat for 3-4 minutes, stirring occasionally. Serve with chops.

1 pork chop with 2 Tbsp. sauce: 249 cal., 7g fat (3g sat. fat), 74mg chol., 342mg sod., 19g carb. (18g sugars, 0 fiber), 27g pro.
Diabetic exchanges: 4 lean meat, 1 starch.

CHEESY CHICKEN & BROCCOLI ORZO

CHEESY CHICKEN & BROCCOLI ORZO

Broccoli and rice casserole tops my family's comfort food list, but when we need something fast, this is the stuff. Chicken and veggie orzo cooked on the stovetop speeds everything up.

—Mary Shivers, Ada, OK

Takes: 30 min. • **Makes:** 6 servings

- 1¼ cups uncooked orzo pasta
- 2 pkg. (10 oz. each) frozen broccoli with cheese sauce
- 2 Tbsp. butter
- 1½ lbs. boneless skinless chicken breasts, cut into ½-in. cubes
- 1 medium onion, chopped
- ¾ tsp. salt
- ½ tsp. pepper

1. Cook orzo according to package directions. Meanwhile, heat broccoli with cheese sauce according to the package directions.

2. In a large skillet, heat butter over medium heat. Add chicken, onion, salt and pepper; cook and stir 6-8 minutes or until chicken is no longer pink and onion is tender. Drain orzo. Stir the orzo and broccoli with cheese sauce into skillet; heat through.

1 cup: 359 cal., 9g fat (4g sat. fat), 77mg chol., 655mg sod., 38g carb. (4g sugars, 3g fiber), 30g pro.
Diabetic exchanges: 3 lean meat, 2 starch, 1 vegetable, 1 fat.

ITALIAN TURKEY CUTLETS

Served with a lovely herbed tomato sauce, these cutlets taste so good that my son often requests them for his birthday dinner. But they're easy enough to make anytime, even when there's not a special occasion to celebrate.

—Janet Bumb, Beallsville, MD

Takes: 30 min. • **Makes:** 4 servings

- 2 tsp. plus 1 Tbsp. olive oil, divided
- 1 small onion, finely chopped
- 2 garlic cloves, minced
- 1 can (14½ oz.) Italian stewed tomatoes, undrained
- 1 Tbsp. minced fresh basil or 1 tsp. dried basil
- 1 tsp. dried oregano
- ½ tsp. dried rosemary, crushed
- 1 pkg. (17.6 oz.) turkey breast cutlets
- ½ tsp. salt
- ⅛ tsp. pepper
- 2 Tbsp. shredded Parmesan cheese

1. In a large saucepan, heat 2 tsp. oil; saute onion until tender. Add garlic; cook and stir 1 minute. Stir in tomatoes and herbs; bring to a boil. Reduce heat; cook, uncovered, over medium heat until sauce is thickened, about 10 minutes.

2. Meanwhile, sprinkle both sides of turkey with salt and pepper. In a large nonstick skillet, heat remaining oil over medium-high heat. In batches, cook turkey until no longer pink, turning once. Serve with sauce. Sprinkle with cheese.

1 serving: 242 cal., 8g fat (2g sat. fat), 73mg chol., 700mg sod., 9g carb. (4g sugars, 1g fiber), 32g pro.
Diabetic exchanges: 4 lean meat, 1 vegetable, 1 fat.

GINGERED PEPPER STEAK

(PICTURED ON P. 131)

This wonderfully tender steak is a treat even for folks not watching their diet. When my mother-in-law shared the recipe, she said it cooks up in no time... and she was right!

—Susan Adair, Somerset, KY

Takes: 20 min. • **Makes:** 4 servings

- 2 tsp. cornstarch
- 2 tsp. sugar
- ¼ tsp. ground ginger
- ¼ cup reduced-sodium soy sauce
- 1 Tbsp. cider or white wine vinegar
- 1 lb. beef flank steak, cut into ¼-in.-thick strips
- 2 tsp. canola oil, divided
- 2 medium green peppers, julienned
  Hot cooked rice, optional

1. Mix first five ingredients until smooth. Add beef; toss to coat.

2. In a large skillet, heat 1 tsp. oil over medium-high heat; stir-fry peppers until crisp-tender, 2-3 minutes. Remove from pan.

3. In same pan, heat remaining oil over medium-high heat; stir-fry beef until browned, 2-3 minutes. Stir in peppers. If desired, serve over rice.

1 cup stir-fry: 224 cal., 11g fat (4g sat. fat), 54mg chol., 644mg sod., 7g carb. (4g sugars, 1g fiber), 23g pro.
Diabetic exchanges: 3 lean meat, 1 vegetable, ½ fat.

ITALIAN TURKEY CUTLETS

HOISIN TURKEY LETTUCE WRAPS

I'm married to a marathon runner, which means dinners need to be healthy but flavor-packed. These low-carb wraps are quick and easy. He loves the health aspect, and I love the taste!
—Melissa Pelkey Hass, Waleska, GA

Takes: 30 min. • **Makes:** 4 servings

- 1 lb. lean ground turkey
- ½ lb. sliced fresh mushrooms
- 1 medium sweet red pepper, diced
- 1 medium onion, finely chopped
- 1 medium carrot, shredded
- 1 Tbsp. sesame oil
- ¼ cup hoisin sauce
- 2 Tbsp. balsamic vinegar
- 2 Tbsp. reduced-sodium soy sauce
- 1 Tbsp. minced fresh gingerroot
- 2 garlic cloves, minced
- 8 Bibb or Boston lettuce leaves

In a large skillet, cook and crumble turkey with vegetables in sesame oil over medium-high heat until turkey is no longer pink, 8-10 minutes, breaking up turkey into crumbles. Stir in hoisin sauce, vinegar, soy sauce, ginger and garlic; cook and stir over medium heat until sauce is slightly thickened, about 5 minutes. Serve in lettuce leaves.

2 wraps: 292 cal., 13g fat (3g sat. fat), 79mg chol., 629mg sod., 19g carb. (11g sugars, 3g fiber), 26g pro.
Diabetic exchanges: 3 lean meat, 1 starch, 1 vegetable, 1 fat.

QUICKPEA CURRY

QUICKPEA CURRY

This colorful curry is a nice change of pace for a weeknight. I like to substitute fresh peas for frozen when they're in season.
—Beth Fleming, Downers Grove, IL

Prep: 15 min. • **Cook:** 35 min.
Makes: 6 servings

- 1 Tbsp. canola oil
- 1 medium onion, finely chopped
- 2 garlic cloves, minced
- 1 Tbsp. curry powder
- 2 cans (14½ oz. each) diced tomatoes, undrained
- 2 cans (15 oz. each) chickpeas or garbanzo beans, rinsed and drained
- 2 cups cubed peeled sweet potato (about 1 medium)
- 1 cup light coconut milk
- 2 tsp. sugar
- ¼ tsp. crushed red pepper flakes
- 1 cup uncooked whole wheat pearl (Israeli) couscous
- 1½ cups frozen peas (about 6 oz.)
- ¼ tsp. salt
- Chopped fresh parsley
- Plain yogurt, optional

1. In a large skillet, heat oil over medium heat; saute onion and garlic with curry powder until tender, 3-4 minutes. Stir in tomatoes, chickpeas, sweet potato, coconut milk, sugar and pepper flakes; bring to a boil. Reduce heat; simmer, uncovered, until mixture is thickened and potatoes are tender, 25-30 minutes, stirring occasionally.

2. Meanwhile, prepare couscous and peas separately according to package directions. Stir salt into peas.

3. To serve, divide couscous among six bowls. Top with chickpea mixture, peas, parsley and, if desired, yogurt.

1 serving: 390 cal., 8g fat (2g sat. fat), 0 chol., 561mg sod., 68g carb. (14g sugars, 13g fiber), 13g pro.

TEST KITCHEN TIP

Leftover coconut milk can be frozen or stirred into oatmeal or herbal tea, or even added to whisked eggs before scrambling them for a soft, fluffy version.

QUINOA UNSTUFFED PEPPERS

(PICTURED ON P. 131)

This deconstructed stuffed pepper dish packs a wallop of flavor. I make it all the time, and I make sure my freezer's stocked with single-serve portions to take to work.
—Rebecca Ende, Phoenix, NY

Takes: 30 min. • **Makes:** 4 servings

- 1½ cups vegetable stock
- ¾ cup quinoa, rinsed
- 1 lb. Italian turkey sausage links, casings removed
- 1 medium sweet red pepper, chopped
- 1 medium green pepper, chopped
- ¾ cup chopped sweet onion
- 1 garlic clove, minced
- ¼ tsp. garam masala
- ¼ tsp. pepper
- ⅛ tsp. salt

1. In a small saucepan, bring stock to a boil. Add quinoa. Reduce heat; simmer, covered, until liquid is absorbed, 12-15 minutes. Remove from heat.

2. In a large skillet, cook and crumble sausage with peppers and onion over medium-high heat until no longer pink, 8-10 minutes. Add garlic and seasonings; cook and stir 1 minute. Stir in quinoa.

Freeze option: Place cooled quinoa mixture in freezer containers. To use, partially thaw in refrigerator overnight. Microwave, covered, on high in a microwave-safe dish until heated through, stirring occasionally.

1 cup: 261 cal., 9g fat (2g sat. fat), 42mg chol., 760mg sod., 28g carb. (3g sugars, 4g fiber), 17g pro.

Diabetic exchanges: 2 starch, 2 medium-fat meat.

TEST KITCHEN TIP

This dish really is a fusion of flavors. The garam masala and Italian flavors in the sausage don't fight each other. They work together with the hint of cinnamon for a unique blend of balanced flavors.

QUICK CHICKEN PARMESAN

QUICK CHICKEN PARMESAN

My mother inspired me to develop my first pasta sauce. It's tangy, simple and really satisfying. The longer it simmers, the better it gets, so keep that in mind if you have time to spare.
—Danielle Grochowski, Milwaukee, WI

Prep: 10 min. • **Cook:** 25 min.
Makes: 4 servings

- 12 oz. frozen grilled chicken breast strips (about 3 cups)
- 1 can (14½ oz.) diced tomatoes, undrained
- 1 can (6 oz.) tomato paste
- 2 Tbsp. dry red wine or chicken broth
- 1 Tbsp. olive oil
- 1½ tsp. Italian seasoning
- 1 garlic clove, minced
- ½ tsp. sugar
- ⅓ cup shredded Parmesan cheese
- ⅓ cup shredded part-skim mozzarella cheese
  Hot cooked pasta

1. Heat a large skillet over medium heat. Add chicken strips; cook and stir 5-8 minutes or until heated through. Remove from pan.

2. In same skillet, combine tomatoes, tomato paste, wine, oil, Italian seasoning, garlic and sugar; bring to a boil, stirring occasionally. Reduce heat; simmer, uncovered, 10-15 minutes to allow flavors to blend, stirring occasionally.

3. Stir in chicken. Sprinkle with cheeses; cook, covered, 1-2 minutes longer or until cheese is melted. Serve with pasta.

1 cup: 248 cal., 9g fat (3g sat. fat), 86mg chol., 739mg sod., 15g carb. (8g sugars, 3g fiber), 28g pro.

Diabetic exchanges: 3 lean meat, 2 vegetable, 2 fat.

★ ★ ★ ★ ★ **READER REVIEW**

"I love this sauce! It is very tasty and light. I made this with leftover turkey instead of the grilled chicken. I doubled the sauce to use some on the pasta. Definitely a keeper. Thank you!"

ANNRMS TASTEOFHOME.COM

SAUTEED PORK CHOPS WITH GARLIC SPINACH

My family enjoys cooking up easy and delicious meals. This pork chop recipe is also inexpensive, which makes cooking easier for everyone. Keep an eye on the spinach—it cooks fast!
—Joe Valerio, Whitinsville, MA

Takes: 20 min. • **Makes:** 4 servings

- 1 Tbsp. olive oil
- 4 bone-in pork loin chops (8 oz. each)
- ¼ tsp. salt
- ¼ tsp. pepper
- 1 medium lemon

GARLIC SPINACH

- 1 Tbsp. olive oil
- 3 garlic cloves, thinly sliced
- 2 pkg. (5 oz. each) fresh spinach, stems removed
- ½ tsp. salt
- ¼ tsp. coarsely ground pepper
- 1 tsp. lemon juice

1. In a large skillet, heat oil over medium-high heat. Sprinkle pork chops with salt and pepper; add to skillet. Saute until a thermometer reads 145°, about 5 minutes per side. Remove to a serving platter; squeeze juice from lemon over chops. Tent with foil; let stand at least 5 minutes before serving.

2. For garlic spinach, heat oil over medium-high heat in same skillet. Add garlic; cook until it just begins to brown, about 45 seconds. Add spinach; cook and stir just until wilted, 2-3 minutes. Sprinkle with salt and pepper. Remove from heat; add lemon juice. Transfer to serving platter. Remove foil from pork; serve spinach with chops.

1 pork chop with ½ cup spinach: 310 cal., 17g fat (5g sat. fat), 98mg chol., 607mg sod., 4g carb. (1g sugars, 1g fiber), 36g pro.
Diabetic exchanges: 4 lean meat, 1½ fat, 1 vegetable.

TILAPIA WITH LEMON CAPER SAUCE

My husband and I are always trying to increase the amount of fish in our diet. This recipe is fast, easy, and enjoyable, even for non-fish lovers.
—Catherine Jensen, Blytheville, AR

Takes: 25 min. • **Makes:** 4 servings

- 4 tilapia fillets (6 oz. each)
- ½ tsp. salt
- ¼ tsp. pepper
- 1 Tbsp. all-purpose flour
- 1 Tbsp. olive oil
- ½ cup reduced-sodium chicken broth
- 2 Tbsp. lemon juice
- 1 Tbsp. butter
- 1 Tbsp. drained capers
  Lemon wedges, optional
  Hot cooked pasta, optional

1. Sprinkle tilapia with salt and pepper. Dust lightly with flour.

2. In a large skillet, heat oil over medium heat. Add tilapia; cook until lightly browned and fish just begins to flake easily with a fork, 3-5 minutes per side. Remove from pan; keep warm.

3. Add broth, lemon juice, butter and capers to same skillet; cook and stir until the mixture is reduced by half, about 5 minutes. Spoon over tilapia. If desired, serve with pasta and lemon wedges.

1 fillet with 1 Tbsp. sauce: 207 cal., 8g fat (3g sat. fat), 90mg chol., 500mg sod., 2g carb. (0 sugars, 0 fiber), 32g pro.
Diabetic exchanges: 5 lean meat, ½ fat.

SAUTEED PORK CHOPS WITH GARLIC SPINACH

THAI CHICKEN LINGUINE

MOM'S ROAST BEEF

Everyone loves slices of this fork-tender beef and its savory gravy. This well-seasoned roast is Mom's specialty. People always ask what her secret ingredients are. Now you have the delicious recipe for our favorite meat dish!
—Linda Gaido, New Brighton, PA

Prep: 20 min. • **Cook:** 2½ hours + standing
Makes: 8 servings

- 1 Tbsp. canola oil
- 1 beef eye round roast (about 2½ lbs.)
- 1 garlic clove, minced
- 2 tsp. dried basil
- 1 tsp. salt
- 1 tsp. dried rosemary, crushed
- ½ tsp. pepper
- 1 medium onion, chopped
- 1 tsp. beef bouillon granules
- 1 cup brewed coffee
- ¾ cup water

GRAVY
- ¼ cup all-purpose flour
- ¼ cup cold water

1. In a Dutch oven, heat oil over medium heat; brown roast on all sides. Remove from pan. Mix garlic and seasonings; sprinkle over roast.
2. Add onion to same pan; cook and stir over medium heat until tender; stir in bouillon, coffee and ¾ cup water. Add roast; bring to a boil. Reduce heat; simmer, covered, until meat is tender, about 2½ hours.
3. Remove roast from pan, reserving cooking juices. Tent with foil; let stand 10 minutes before slicing.
4. Mix flour and cold water until smooth; stir into cooking juices. Bring to a boil, stirring constantly. Cook and stir until thickened, 1-2 minutes. Serve with roast.
1 serving: 210 cal., 6g fat (2g sat. fat), 58mg chol., 435mg sod., 5g carb. (1g sugars, 1g fiber), 32g pro.
Diabetic exchanges: 4 lean meat, ½ fat.

THAI CHICKEN LINGUINE

When I'm feeding a crowd, I multiply this Thai-inspired chicken with pasta and snow peas. The merrymaking begins when everybody digs in, even the kids.
—Teri Rumble, Jensen Beach, FL

Takes: 30 min. • **Makes:** 6 servings

- 8 oz. uncooked whole wheat linguine
- ⅓ cup reduced-sodium soy sauce
- ¼ cup lime juice
- 3 Tbsp. brown sugar
- 2 Tbsp. rice vinegar
- 1 Tbsp. Thai chili sauce
- 2 Tbsp. peanut oil, divided
- 1 lb. boneless skinless chicken breasts, cubed
- 1 cup fresh snow peas
- 1 medium sweet red pepper, julienned
- 4 garlic cloves, minced
- 2 large eggs, beaten
- ⅓ cup chopped unsalted peanuts

1. Cook linguine according to package directions. Meanwhile, in a small bowl, mix soy sauce, lime juice, brown sugar, vinegar and chili sauce until blended.
2. In a large nonstick skillet, heat 1 Tbsp. oil over medium-high heat. Add chicken; stir-fry 5-7 minutes or until no longer pink. Remove from pan. Stir-fry snow peas and pepper in remaining oil until crisp-tender. Add garlic; cook 1 minute longer. Add eggs; cook and stir until set.
3. Drain linguine; add to vegetable mixture. Stir soy sauce mixture and add to pan. Bring to a boil. Add chicken; heat through. Sprinkle with peanuts.
1⅓ cups: 377 cal., 13g fat (2g sat. fat), 104mg chol., 697mg sod., 44g carb. (12g sugars, 5g fiber), 25g pro.
Diabetic exchanges: 3 starch, 3 lean meat, 2 fat.

FISH TACOS WITH GUACAMOLE

FISH TACOS WITH GUACAMOLE

Fish tacos are my new favorite thing—lighter and healthier than beef tacos smothered in cheese. Try adding tomatoes, green onions and chopped jalapeno on top.
—Deb Perry, Traverse City, MI

Prep: 25 min. • **Cook:** 10 min.
Makes: 4 servings

- 2 cups angel hair coleslaw mix
- 1½ tsp. canola oil
- 1½ tsp. lime juice

GUACAMOLE
- 1 medium ripe avocado, peeled and quartered
- 2 Tbsp. fat-free sour cream
- 1 Tbsp. finely chopped onion
- 1 Tbsp. minced fresh cilantro
- ⅛ tsp. salt
  Dash pepper

TACOS
- 1 lb. tilapia fillets, cut into 1-in. pieces
- ¼ tsp. salt
- ⅛ tsp. pepper
- 2 tsp. canola oil
- 8 corn tortillas (6 in.), warmed

Optional toppings: hot pepper sauce, chopped tomatoes, green onions and jalapeno pepper

1. In a small bowl, toss coleslaw mix with oil and lime juice; refrigerate until serving. In another bowl, mash avocado with a fork; stir in sour cream, onion, cilantro, salt and pepper.
2. Sprinkle tilapia with salt and pepper. In a large nonstick skillet, heat oil over medium-high heat. Add tilapia; cook until fish just begins to flake easily with a fork, 3-4 minutes on each side. Serve in tortillas with coleslaw, guacamole and desired toppings.

2 tacos: 308 cal., 12g fat (2g sat. fat), 56mg chol., 299mg sod., 28g carb. (2g sugars, 6g fiber), 25g pro.
Diabetic exchanges: 3 lean meat, 2 starch, 2 fat.

PEPPER RICOTTA PRIMAVERA

Garlic, peppers and herbs top creamy ricotta cheese in this meatless skillet meal you can make in just 20 minutes.
—Janet Boulger, Botwood, NL

Takes: 20 min. • **Makes:** 6 servings

- 1 cup part-skim ricotta cheese
- ½ cup fat-free milk
- 4 tsp. olive oil
- 1 garlic clove, minced
- ½ tsp. crushed red pepper flakes
- 1 medium green pepper, julienned
- 1 medium sweet red pepper, julienned
- 1 medium sweet yellow pepper, julienned
- 1 medium zucchini, sliced
- 1 cup frozen peas, thawed
- ¼ tsp. dried oregano
- ¼ tsp. dried basil
- 6 oz. fettuccine, cooked and drained

Whisk together ricotta cheese and milk; set aside. In a large skillet, heat oil over medium heat. Add garlic and pepper flakes; saute 1 minute. Add next seven ingredients. Cook and stir over medium heat until vegetables are crisp-tender, about 5 minutes. Add cheese mixture to fettuccine; top with vegetables. Toss to coat. Serve immediately.

1 cup: 229 cal., 7g fat (3g sat. fat), 13mg chol., 88mg sod., 31g carb. (6g sugars, 4g fiber), 11g pro.
Diabetic exchanges: 2 starch, 1 medium-fat meat, ½ fat.

PEPPER STEAK WITH SQUASH

My family loves it when I fix this colorful stir-fry with savory flank steak and plenty of veggies. We serve it over rice for a satisfying supper that's on the table fast.
—Gayle Lewis, Yucaipa, CA

Takes: 30 min. • **Makes:** 6 servings

- 1 can (14½ oz.) reduced-sodium beef broth
- 2 Tbsp. reduced-sodium soy sauce
- 3 Tbsp. cornstarch
- 2 Tbsp. canola oil, divided
- 1 beef flank steak (1 lb.), cut into thin strips
- 1 medium green pepper, cut into thin strips
- 1 medium sweet red pepper, cut into thin strips
- 2 medium zucchini, cut into thin strips
- 1 small onion, cut into thin strips
- 3 garlic cloves, minced
- 1 cup fresh snow peas
- 1 cup sliced fresh mushrooms
- 1 can (8 oz.) sliced water chestnuts, drained
  Hot cooked rice

1. Mix broth and soy sauce with cornstarch until smooth. Set aside.
2. In a large skillet, heat 1 Tbsp. oil over medium-high heat. Add beef; stir-fry until no longer pink, 2-3 minutes. Remove from the pan.
3. In same skillet, heat remaining oil. Stir-fry peppers about 2 minutes. Add zucchini, onion and garlic; cook and stir 2 minutes longer. Add snow peas, mushrooms and water chestnuts. Stir-fry until crisp-tender, about 2 minutes more.
4. Stir cornstarch mixture and add to pan. Bring to a boil; cook and stir until sauce is thickened, 1-2 minutes. Return beef to skillet; heat through. Serve with hot cooked rice.

1½ cups stir-fry: 229 cal., 11g fat (3g sat. fat), 37mg chol., 381mg sod., 16g carb. (5g sugars, 3g fiber), 18g pro.
Diabetic exchanges: 2 lean meat, 1 vegetable, ½ starch.

✱
TEST KITCHEN TIP
Spice this recipe up a bit by adding ginger, sesame oil or a touch of hoisin sauce.

PEACH SALSA CHICKEN

Peachy sweetness mellows out the jalapeno kick in this homemade salsa. The whole meal is done in a half hour!
—Kristi Silk, Ferndale, WA

Takes: 30 min. • **Makes:** 2 servings

- 1 large peach, peeled and chopped
- ½ cup chopped sweet onion
- ¼ cup salsa
- 1 small jalapeno pepper, seeded and minced
- 2 Tbsp. finely chopped fresh cilantro
- 2 Tbsp. lime juice
- 1 cup chicken broth
- ½ cup uncooked long grain rice
- 2 boneless skinless chicken breast halves (5 oz. each)
- ¼ tsp. salt
- ¼ tsp. pepper
- 1 Tbsp. olive oil

1. Mix first six ingredients. In a small saucepan, bring broth and ¼ cup peach mixture to a boil. Stir in rice; return to a boil. Reduce heat; simmer, covered, until liquid is absorbed and the rice is tender, 15-18 minutes.
2. Meanwhile, sprinkle chicken with salt and pepper. In a skillet, heat oil over medium heat; brown chicken on both sides. Add remaining peach mixture; bring to a boil. Reduce heat; simmer, covered, until a thermometer inserted in chicken reads 165°, 7-9 minutes. Serve with rice.

1 serving: 467 cal., 11g fat (2g sat. fat), 78mg chol., 772mg sod., 56g carb. (10g sugars, 3g fiber), 35g pro.

PEPPER STEAK WITH SQUASH

TUNA STEAK ON FETTUCCINE

TUNA STEAK ON FETTUCCINE

For something new to do with tuna, I suggest this tangy dish. Although I prefer the marinade on tuna or mahi mahi, it's great on any fish, grilled, baked or broiled.
—Caren Stearns, Austin, TX

Prep: 10 min. + marinating
Cook: 20 min. • **Makes:** 2 servings

- 8 Tbsp. white wine or chicken broth, divided
- 3 Tbsp. olive oil, divided
- 1 tsp. dried basil, divided
- 1 tsp. dried oregano, divided
- ¼ tsp. salt, divided
- ⅛ tsp. pepper, divided
- 1 tuna, swordfish or halibut steak (about 10 oz.), cut in half
- ½ cup thinly sliced sweet onion
- 1 cup canned diced tomatoes, undrained
- ¼ tsp. brown sugar
- 3 oz. uncooked fettuccine

1. In a resealable plastic bag, combine 2 Tbsp. wine, 2 Tbsp. oil, ¼ tsp. basil, ¼ tsp. oregano, and half the salt and pepper; add tuna. Seal bag and turn to coat; refrigerate 1 hour.
2. In a large skillet, saute onion in remaining oil until tender. Add tomatoes, brown sugar and remaining wine, basil, oregano, salt and pepper. Bring to a boil. Reduce heat; simmer, uncovered, until bubbly and slightly thickened, 4-6 minutes. Meanwhile, cook fettuccine according to package directions.
3. Drain tuna, discarding marinade. Place tuna over tomato mixture; return to a boil. Reduce heat; simmer, covered, until fish just begins to flake easily with a fork, about 6 minutes. Remove tuna and keep warm. Drain fettuccine; add to tomato mixture and toss to coat. Divide between two plates; top with tuna.

1 serving: 505 cal., 17g fat (3g sat. fat), 55mg chol., 518mg sod., 41g carb. (8g sugars, 5g fiber), 42g pro.

APPLE CIDER PORK CHOPS

APPLE CIDER PORK CHOPS

With cider gravy, these pork chops are a must for fall family dinners. I serve them with buttered egg noodles to soak up more of that delicious sauce.
—Debiana Casterline
Egg Harbor Township, NJ

Takes: 25 min. • **Makes:** 6 servings

- 2 Tbsp. olive oil
- 6 boneless pork loin chops (6 to 8 oz. each), about ¾ in. thick
- 1 garlic clove, minced
- 1 Tbsp. Dijon mustard
- 1 tsp. honey
- ½ tsp. apple pie spice
- ½ tsp. coarsely ground pepper
- ¼ tsp. dried thyme
- ¼ tsp. salt
- 1 cup apple cider
- 1 Tbsp. plus 1 tsp. cornstarch
- 2 Tbsp. water
  Minced fresh parsley

1. In a large skillet, heat olive oil over medium heat. Brown pork chops on both sides.
2. Meanwhile, in a small bowl, combine next seven ingredients; stir in apple cider. Pour over pork chops. Reduce heat to medium-low; cook, covered, until a thermometer inserted into chops reads 145°, about 4-5 minutes. Remove chops from skillet; let stand for 5 minutes.
3. In a small bowl, mix cornstarch and water until smooth; stir into cider mixture in skillet. Return to a boil, stirring constantly; cook and stir until thickened, 1-2 minutes. Pour over chops; sprinkle with parsley.

1 pork chop: 301 cal., 14g fat (4g sat. fat), 82mg chol., 210mg sod., 8g carb. (5g sugars, 0 fiber), 33g pro.
Diabetic exchanges: 4 lean meat, 1 fat, ½ starch.

TEST KITCHEN TIP

Make a couple of crosswise slices just barely through the outer layer of fat, and your pork chops will be less likely to curl when cooking.

ASPARAGUS HAM DINNER

CHORIZO SPAGHETTI SQUASH SKILLET

Get your noodle fix minus the pasta with this spiced-up meal that comes together in one skillet. It's a fill-you-up dinner that's low in calories—a weeknight winner!
—Sherrill Oake, Springfield, MA

Takes: 30 min. • **Makes:** 4 servings

- 1 small spaghetti squash (about 2 lbs.)
- 1 Tbsp. canola oil
- 1 pkg. (12 oz.) fully cooked chorizo chicken sausage links or flavor of choice, sliced
- 1 medium sweet yellow pepper, chopped
- 1 medium sweet onion, halved and sliced
- 1 cup sliced fresh mushrooms
- 1 can (14½ oz.) no-salt-added diced tomatoes, undrained
- 1 Tbsp. reduced-sodium taco seasoning
- ¼ tsp. pepper
  Chopped green onions, optional

1. Halve squash lengthwise; discard seeds. Place squash on a microwave-safe plate, cut side down; microwave on high until tender, about 15 minutes. Cool slightly.
2. Meanwhile, in a large skillet, heat 1 Tbsp. oil over medium-high heat; saute sausage, yellow pepper, onion and mushrooms until onion is tender, about 5 minutes.
3. Separate strands of squash with a fork; add to skillet. Stir in tomatoes and seasonings; bring to a boil. Reduce heat; simmer, uncovered, until flavors are blended, about 5 minutes. If desired, top with green onions.

1½ cups: 299 cal., 12g fat (3g sat. fat), 65mg chol., 725mg sod., 34g carb. (12g sugars, 6g fiber), 18g pro.
Diabetic exchanges: 2 starch, 2 lean meat, 1 vegetable, 1 fat.

TEST KITCHEN TIP

If you don't have taco seasoning on hand, feel free to substitute your own blend of chili powder, onion powder, garlic powder, oregano, cayenne pepper and salt to taste.

ASPARAGUS HAM DINNER

I've been making this low-fat meal for my family for years, and we always look forward to it. With asparagus, tomato, pasta and chunks of ham, it's a tempting blend of tastes and textures.
—Rhonda Zavodny, David City, NE

Takes: 25 min. • **Makes:** 6 servings

- 2 cups uncooked corkscrew or spiral pasta
- ¾ lb. fresh asparagus, cut into 1-in. pieces
- 1 medium sweet yellow pepper, julienned
- 1 Tbsp. olive oil
- 6 medium tomatoes, diced
- 6 oz. boneless fully cooked ham, cubed
- ¼ cup minced fresh parsley
- ½ tsp. salt
- ½ tsp. dried oregano
- ½ tsp. dried basil
- ⅛ to ¼ tsp. cayenne pepper
- ¼ cup shredded Parmesan cheese

Cook pasta according to package directions. Meanwhile, in a large cast-iron or other heavy skillet, saute asparagus and yellow pepper in oil until crisp-tender. Add tomatoes and ham; heat through. Drain pasta; add to vegetable mixture. Stir in parsley and seasonings. Sprinkle with Parmesan cheese.

1⅓ cups: 204 cal., 5g fat (1g sat. fat), 17mg chol., 561mg sod., 29g carb. (5g sugars, 3g fiber), 12g pro.
Diabetic exchanges: 1½ starch, 1 lean meat, 1 vegetable, ½ fat.

CHICKEN & BROCCOLI STIR-FRY

This Asian stir-fry is a household best bet. The spicy sauce works with chicken, seafood, pork or beef. Add whatever veggies you have on hand.
—Kristin Rimkus, Snohomish, WA

Takes: 25 min. • **Makes:** 4 servings

- 2 Tbsp. rice vinegar
- 2 Tbsp. mirin (sweet rice wine)
- 2 Tbsp. chili garlic sauce
- 1 Tbsp. cornstarch
- 1 Tbsp. reduced-sodium soy sauce
- 2 tsp. fish sauce or additional soy sauce
- ½ cup reduced-sodium chicken broth, divided
- 2 cups instant brown rice
- 2 tsp. sesame oil
- 4 cups fresh broccoli florets
- 2 cups cubed cooked chicken
- 2 green onions, sliced

1. In a small bowl, mix the first six ingredients and ¼ cup chicken broth until smooth. Cook rice according to package directions.
2. Meanwhile, in a large skillet, heat oil over medium-high heat. Add broccoli; stir-fry 2 minutes. Add remaining broth; cook 1-2 minutes or until broccoli is crisp-tender. Stir sauce mixture and add to the pan. Bring to a boil; cook and stir 1-2 minutes or until sauce is thickened.
3. Stir in chicken and green onions; heat through. Serve with rice.

1 cup chicken mixture with ⅔ cup rice: 387 cal., 9g fat (2g sat. fat), 62mg chol., 765mg sod., 45g carb. (6g sugars, 4g fiber), 28g pro.
Diabetic exchanges: 3 lean meat, 2½ starch, 1 vegetable, ½ fat.

TURKEY CUTLETS WITH PAN GRAVY

Using turkey cutlets means you can sit down quickly to dinner because they cook so fast. You can use thin boneless, skinless chicken breasts as well.
—Margaret Wilson, San Bernardino, CA

Takes: 20 min. • **Makes:** 4 servings

- 1 tsp. poultry seasoning
- ¼ tsp. seasoned salt
- ¼ tsp. pepper, divided
- 1 pkg. (17.6 oz.) turkey breast cutlets
- 2 Tbsp. canola oil
- 2 Tbsp. butter
- ¼ cup all-purpose flour
- 2 cups chicken broth

1. Mix poultry seasoning, seasoned salt and ⅛ tsp. pepper; sprinkle over turkey. In a large skillet, heat oil over medium-high heat. Add cutlets in batches; cook until no longer pink, 2-3 minutes per side. Remove from pan; keep warm.
2. In same pan, melt butter over medium heat; stir in flour until smooth. Gradually stir in broth. Bring to a boil; cook and stir until thickened, about 2 minutes. Sprinkle with remaining pepper. Serve with turkey.

1 serving: 292 cal., 15g fat (5g sat. fat), 89mg chol., 772mg sod., 7g carb. (1g sugars, 0 fiber), 31g pro.
Diabetic exchanges: 4 lean meat, 3 fat, ½ starch.

CHICKEN & BROCCOLI STIR-FRY

HEALTHIER-THAN-EGG ROLLS

VEGETARIAN LINGUINE

Looking for a tasty alternative to meat-and-potatoes meals? Try this colorful pasta dish. My oldest son came up with the stick-to-the-ribs dinner that's loaded with fresh mushrooms, zucchini and other vegetables, plus basil and cheeses.
—Jane Bone, Cape Coral, FL

Takes: 30 min. • **Makes:** 6 servings

- 6 oz. uncooked linguine
- 2 Tbsp. butter
- 1 Tbsp. olive oil
- 2 medium zucchini, thinly sliced
- ½ lb. fresh mushrooms, sliced
- 1 large tomato, chopped
- 2 green onions, chopped
- 1 garlic clove, minced
- ½ tsp. salt
- ¼ tsp. pepper
- 1 cup shredded provolone cheese
- 3 Tbsp. shredded Parmesan cheese
- 2 tsp. minced fresh basil

Cook linguine according to package directions. Meanwhile, in a large skillet, heat butter and oil over medium heat. Add zucchini and mushrooms; saute for 3-5 minutes. Add tomato, onions, garlic and seasonings. Reduce heat; simmer, covered, about 3 minutes. Drain linguine; add to vegetable mixture. Sprinkle with cheeses and basil. Toss to coat.

1½ cupss: 260 cal., 13g fat (7g sat. fat), 25mg chol., 444mg sod., 26g carb. (3g sugars, 2g fiber), 12g pro.
Diabetic exchanges: 1½ starch, 1½ fat, 1 medium-fat meat, 1 vegetable.

HEALTHIER-THAN-EGG ROLLS

Frying anything at home is a little intimidating for me, but I love eggrolls. With this recipe, I've figured out a way to get the best part of the eggroll—without the mess. This can be used to stuff eggroll wrappers, but we love it on its own, too.
—Sue Mitchell, Kerrville, TX

Takes: 25 min. • **Makes:** 4 servings

- 1 lb. lean ground chicken
- 1½ cups sliced fresh mushrooms
- 1 medium onion, chopped
- 2 garlic cloves, minced
- 1 tsp. minced fresh gingerroot
- 2 Tbsp. reduced-sodium soy sauce
- 1 pkg. (14 oz.) coleslaw mix
- 1 Tbsp. sesame oil
- 3 cups hot cooked brown rice
- ½ cup sweet-and-sour sauce
- Wonton strips, optional

1. In a large skillet, cook and crumble chicken with mushrooms, onion, garlic and ginger over medium-high heat until no longer pink, 6-8 minutes; drain. Stir in soy sauce.
2. Add coleslaw mix; cook and stir until wilted, 3-4 minutes. Stir in sesame oil. Serve with rice and sweet-and-sour sauce. If desired, top with wonton strips.

1¼ cups chicken mixture with ¾ cup rice: 451 cal., 11g fat (3g sat. fat), 81mg chol., 591mg sod., 58g carb. (13g sugars, 6g fiber), 30g pro.

TEST KITCHEN TIP

Use instant brown rice to get this dish to the table fast. Or make it even faster with ready-to-eat brown rice, which just needs to be heated in the microwave.

VEGETARIAN LINGUINE

PORK CHOPS WITH CRANBERRY PAN SAUCE

Moist and tender pork chops get a sweet, light cranberry glaze in this weeknight-friendly entree. It's one of my husband's favorite recipes, and it's quite suitable for company, too.
—Stephanie Homme, Baton Rouge, LA

Takes: 30 min. • **Makes:** 6 servings

- 6 boneless pork loin chops (4 oz. each)
- ¾ tsp. salt
- ¼ tsp. coarsely ground pepper
- 2 tsp. cornstarch
- 1 cup cranberry-apple juice
- 2 tsp. honey
- ¾ cup dried cranberries
- 1 Tbsp. minced fresh tarragon
- 1 Tbsp. minced fresh parsley
- 3 cups hot cooked brown rice

1. Sprinkle chops with salt and pepper. In a large skillet coated with cooking spray, brown the chops over medium heat, 3-5 minutes per side. Remove from pan.
2. In same pan, mix cornstarch, juice and honey until smooth; stir in cranberries and herbs. Bring to a boil, stirring to loosen browned bits from the pan; cook until thickened and bubbly, about 2 minutes.
3. Add pork chops. Reduce heat; simmer, covered, until a thermometer inserted in pork reads 145°, 4-5 minutes. Let pork stand for 5 minutes before serving. Serve with rice.

1 pork chop with ½ cup rice: 374 cal., 8g fat (3g sat. fat) 55mg chol., 333mg sod., 52g carb. (23g sugars, 3g fiber), 25g pro.

HARVEST BOW TIES

HARVEST BOW TIES

Spaghetti squash and bow ties make this meatless dish hearty and filling. Add a can of black beans if you'd like more protein. For variety, you can switch up the type of tomatoes. Try Italian-seasoned ones, or diced tomatoes with mild green chiles.
—Anne Lynch, Beacon, NY

Prep: 25 min. • **Cook:** 15 min.
Makes: 8 servings

- 1 small spaghetti squash (about 1½ lbs.)
- 12 oz. uncooked bow tie pasta (about 4½ cups)
- 2 Tbsp. olive oil
- 1 lb. sliced fresh mushrooms
- 1 cup chopped sweet onion
- 2 garlic cloves, minced
- 1 can (14½ oz.) diced tomatoes, undrained
- 6 oz. fresh baby spinach (about 8 cups)
- ¾ tsp. salt
- ½ tsp. pepper
- 2 Tbsp. butter
- 2 Tbsp. sour cream

1. Halve squash lengthwise; discard seeds. Place squash on a microwave-safe plate, cut side down. Microwave, uncovered, on high until tender, 9-11 minutes. Cool slightly. Meanwhile, in a 6-qt. stockpot, cook pasta according to package directions. Drain; return to pot.
2. In a large skillet, heat oil over medium-high heat; saute mushrooms and onion until tender. Add garlic; cook and stir 1 minute. Separate strands of squash with a fork; add to skillet. Stir in tomatoes, spinach, salt and pepper; cook until spinach is wilted, stirring occasionally. Stir in butter and sour cream until blended.
3. Add mixture to pasta. Heat through, tossing to coat.

1½ cups: 279 cal., 9g fat (3g sat. fat), 9mg chol., 364mg sod., 44g carb. (5g sugars, 5g fiber), 9g pro.

SCALLOPS WITH LINGUINE

A buttery garlic sauce spices up a bowlful of linguine, bay scallops and vegetables. Celebrate something special or toast the end of another workday with this dish that's perfectly sized for two.
—Paula Jones, Brooksville, FL

Takes: 25 min. • **Makes:** 2 servings

2 oz. uncooked linguine
1 Tbsp. cornstarch
1 cup chicken broth
2 Tbsp. white wine or additional chicken broth
1½ tsp. butter
1 garlic clove, minced
¾ cup sliced fresh mushrooms
2 green onions, sliced
¼ cup grated carrot
½ lb. bay scallops
1½ tsp. minced fresh parsley
Lemon wedges, optional

1. Cook linguine according to package directions; drain. Meanwhile, in a small bowl, mix cornstarch, broth and wine until smooth. In a nonstick skillet, heat butter over medium heat. Add garlic; cook and stir 1 minute. Add mushrooms, green onions and carrot; stir-fry 2-3 minutes or until vegetables are crisp-tender.

2. Stir cornstarch mixture and add to pan. Bring to a boil; cook and stir 1-2 minutes or until sauce is thickened. Reduce heat. Add the scallops and parsley; cook until scallops are firm and opaque. Serve with linguine and, if desired, lemon wedges.

½ cup scallop mixture with ½ cup linguine: 281 cal., 5g fat (2g sat. fat), 47mg chol., 709mg sod., 32g carb. (3g sugars, 2g fiber), 25g pro.
Diabetic exchanges: 3 lean meat, 2 starch, ½ fat.

POACHED CHICKEN

(PICTURED ON P. 130)

You can't beat poaching for chicken breasts that are moist and tender. Once they're cooled, store extras in the freezer for quick meals.
—James Schend, Pleasant Prairie, WI

Takes: 25 min. • **Makes:** 4 servings

4 boneless skinless chicken breast halves (6 oz. each)
½ cup white wine
Aromatic ingredients: 6 whole peppercorns, 3 thyme sprigs, 1 rosemary sprig, 1 smashed garlic clove and 1 bay leaf
1 tsp. salt

In a skillet or saucepan just large enough to hold chicken in one layer, combine chicken, wine, aromatics and salt; add cold water to cover by 1 in. Bring to a boil. Reduce heat to low; simmer, covered, until a thermometer inserted in chicken reads 170°, 15-20 minutes. Serve warm, or cool completely before refrigerating.

1 chicken breast half: 192 cal., 4g fat (1g sat. fat), 94mg chol., 141mg sod., 0 carb. (0 sugars, 0 fiber), 34g pro.
Diabetic exchanges: 5 lean meat.

SCALLOPS WITH LINGUINE

CHIVE CRAB CAKES

CHIVE CRAB CAKES

These tasty crab cakes are perfect for appetizers, or with a salad for a light meal.
—Cindy Worth, Lapwai, ID

Prep: 20 min. + chilling
Cook: 10 min./batch
Makes: 12 crab cakes

- 4 large egg whites
- 1 large egg
- 2 cups panko (Japanese) bread crumbs, divided
- 6 Tbsp. minced fresh chives
- 3 Tbsp. all-purpose flour
- 1 to 2 tsp. hot pepper sauce
- 1 tsp. baking powder
- ½ tsp. salt
- ¼ tsp. pepper
- 4 cans (6 oz. each) crabmeat, drained, flaked and cartilage removed
- 2 Tbsp. canola oil
  Lemon wedges, optional

1. In a large bowl, lightly beat the egg whites and egg. Add ¾ cup of the bread crumbs, chives, flour, pepper sauce, baking powder, salt and pepper; mix well. Fold in crab. Cover and refrigerate for at least 2 hours.

2. Place remaining bread crumbs in a shallow bowl. Drop crab mixture by scant ¼ cupfuls into crumbs. Gently coat and shape into ½-in.-thick patties.

3. In a large nonstick skillet, cook crab cakes in oil in batches over medium-high heat for 3-4 minutes on each side or until golden brown. If desired, serve with lemon wedges.

1 crab cake: 119 cal., 3g fat (0 sat. fat), 71mg chol., 509mg sod., 8g carb. (0 sugars, 0 fiber), 13g pro.

SWEET POTATO & TURKEY COUSCOUS

SWEET POTATO & TURKEY COUSCOUS

After our Thanksgiving feast, we always have leftover turkey and sweet potatoes. I put them together in this quick, easy and nutritious main dish and serve it with a simple green salad.
—Roxanne Chan, Albany, CA

Takes: 30 min. • **Makes:** 6 servings

- 1 lb. sweet potatoes (about 2 medium), peeled and cut into ¾-in. cubes
- 1 Tbsp. canola oil
- 1 pkg. (8.8 oz.) uncooked pearl (Israeli) couscous
- ¼ cup chopped onion
- ¼ cup chopped celery
- ½ tsp. poultry seasoning
- ½ tsp. salt
- ½ tsp. pepper
- 2 cans (14½ oz. each) chicken broth
- 2 cups chopped cooked turkey
- ¼ cup dried cranberries
- 1 tsp. grated orange zest
  Chopped fresh parsley

1. Place sweet potatoes in a saucepan; add water to cover. Bring to a boil. Reduce the heat; cook, uncovered, until tender, 8-10 minutes. Drain.

2. Meanwhile, in a large cast-iron or other heavy skillet, heat oil over medium-high heat; saute couscous, onion and celery until couscous is lightly browned. Stir in seasonings and broth; bring to a boil. Reduce heat; simmer, uncovered, until couscous is tender, about 10 minutes.

3. Stir in turkey, cranberries, orange zest and potatoes. Cook, covered, over low heat until heated through. Sprinkle with chopped parsley.

1 cup: 365 cal., 5g fat (1g sat. fat), 50mg chol., 848mg sod., 59g carb. (13g sugars, 3g fiber), 21g pro.

STOVETOP BEEF & SHELLS

I fix this supper when I'm pressed for time. It's as tasty as it is fast. Team it with salad, bread and fruit for a comforting meal.

—Donna Roberts, Manhattan, KS

Takes: 30 min. • **Makes:** 4 servings

1½ cups uncooked medium pasta shells (about 4 oz.)
1 lb. lean ground beef (90% lean)
1 medium onion, chopped
1 garlic clove, minced
1 can (15 oz.) crushed tomatoes
1 can (8 oz.) tomato sauce
1 tsp. sugar
½ tsp. salt
½ tsp. pepper

1. Cook pasta according to package directions; drain.
2. Meanwhile, in a large skillet, cook and crumble beef with onion and garlic over medium-high heat until no longer pink, 5-7 minutes. Stir in remaining ingredients; bring to a boil. Reduce heat; simmer, uncovered, until flavors are blended, 10-15 minutes.
3. Stir in pasta; heat through.

1¼ cups: 344 cal., 11g fat (4g sat. fat), 71mg chol., 815mg sod., 35g carb. (9g sugars, 4g fiber), 29g pro.
Diabetic exchanges: 3 lean meat, 2 starch, 1 vegetable.

RICOTTA, TOMATO & CORN PASTA

RICOTTA, TOMATO & CORN PASTA

I love to make healthy meals with produce from my latest farmers market trip. This pasta takes just 30 minutes from pantry to dinner table. You can easily make it a meat entree by adding shredded cooked chicken.

—Jerilyn Korver, Bellflower, CA

Takes: 30 min. • **Makes:** 8 servings

3 cups uncooked whole wheat elbow macaroni (about 12 oz.)
1 can (15 oz.) cannellini beans, rinsed and drained
2 cups cherry tomatoes, halved
1 cup fresh or frozen corn, thawed
½ cup finely chopped red onion
½ cup part-skim ricotta cheese
¼ cup grated Parmesan cheese
2 Tbsp. minced fresh basil or 2 tsp. dried basil
1 Tbsp. olive oil
3 garlic cloves, minced
1 tsp. salt
1 tsp. minced fresh rosemary or ½ tsp. dried rosemary, crushed
½ tsp. pepper
3 cups arugula or baby spinach
   Chopped fresh parsley, optional

1. Cook pasta according to package directions. Drain and rinse with cold water; drain well.
2. In a large bowl, combine beans, tomatoes, corn, onion, ricotta and Parmesan cheeses, basil, oil, garlic, salt, rosemary and pepper. Stir in pasta. Add arugula; toss gently to combine. If desired, sprinkle with parsley. Serve immediately.

1½ cups: 275 cal., 5g fat (1g sat. fat), 7mg chol., 429mg sod., 46g carb. (4g sugars, 8g fiber), 13g pro.
Diabetic exchanges: 3 starch, 1 lean meat.

MEAT & POTATO PATTIES

During World War II, when meat was rationed and had to be purchased with tokens, this recipe went a long way in feeding a family. To this day, I still reach for it whenever I want something different from regular hamburgers. By the way, children really like these (just as I did when I was a child!).
—Gladys Klein, Burlington, WI

Prep: 10 min. • **Cook:** 25 min.
Makes: 4 servings

- ¾ lb. lean ground beef (90% lean)
- ¾ cup finely shredded potatoes
- ¼ cup finely chopped onion
- 2 Tbsp. chopped green pepper
- 1 large egg, beaten
- ¼ tsp. salt
- 1 Tbsp. canola oil
- 1 cup tomato juice
- 1 Tbsp. all-purpose flour
- ¼ cup water

1. Combine the first six ingredients. Shape into four patties; press to flatten slightly. In a large skillet, heat oil over medium-high heat. Brown patties on both sides; drain. Add tomato juice. Simmer, covered, until a thermometer inserted into meat reads 160°, 20-25 minutes. Remove patties to a serving platter; keep warm.

2. Whisk flour into water; gradually add to skillet. Reduce heat to medium-low; cook, stirring constantly, until thickened. Spoon over patties. Serve immediately.

1 patty: 237 cal., 12g fat (4g sat. fat), 99mg chol., 373mg sod., 12g carb. (2g sugars, 1g fiber), 20g pro.

How To Make Perfectly Tender Meat Patties

The secret to tender meat loaves and patties is to not overwork the meat. After mixing the other ingredients, gently crumble the ground meat over the top (this makes it faster to mix without overhandling). Mix the ingredients just until blended.

BROCCOLI-PORK STIR-FRY WITH NOODLES

(PICTURED ON P. 130)

I combined several recipes to come up with this one that my family loves. It is not only quick and delicious but healthy. I sometimes substitute boneless, skinless chicken breasts for the pork.
—Joan Hallford, North Richland Hills, TX

Takes: 30 min. • **Makes:** 4 servings

- 6 oz. uncooked whole wheat linguine
- 2 Tbsp. cornstarch
- 3 Tbsp. reduced-sodium soy sauce
- 1½ cups reduced-sodium chicken broth
- 3 green onions, chopped
- 1½ tsp. canola oil
- 1 pork tenderloin (1 lb.), cut into bite-sized pieces
- 1 Tbsp. minced fresh gingerroot
- 3 garlic cloves, minced
- 1½ lbs. fresh broccoli florets (about 10 cups)
- 1 Tbsp. sesame seeds, toasted

1. Cook linguine according to package directions; drain and keep warm. Whisk cornstarch into soy sauce and broth until smooth; stir in green onions.

2. In a large nonstick skillet, heat oil over medium-high heat; stir-fry pork 3 minutes. Add ginger and garlic; cook and stir until pork is browned, 2 minutes. Remove from the pan.

3. Add broth mixture to skillet; bring to a boil. Cook and stir until thickened, 1-2 minutes. Add broccoli; reduce heat. Simmer, covered, until broccoli is crisp-tender, 5-8 minutes. Stir in pork; heat through, 2-3 minutes.

4. Serve over linguine; sprinkle with sesame seeds.

1 serving: 376 cal., 8g fat (2g sat. fat), 64mg chol., 595mg sod., 47g carb. (4g sugars, 9g fiber), 35g pro.

Diabetic exchanges: 3 lean meat, 2 starch, 2 vegetable, ½ fat.

TEST KITCHEN TIP
Don't limit yourself with veggies. Carrots, snap peas and sprouts would all be great in this!

MEAT & POTATO PATTIES

COD WITH SWEET PEPPERS

STEAKS WITH MUSHROOM SAUCE

These rich steaks are smothered in a rich mushroom-wine sauce to create a wonderfully savory entree.
—Stephanie Allee, Chambersburg, PA

Prep: 15 min. • **Cook:** 20 min.
Makes: 4 servings

- 1 cup boiling water
- ½ cup sun-dried tomatoes (not packed in oil), julienned
- 2 tsp. butter
- 2 cups whole fresh mushrooms, quartered
- 1 shallot, chopped
- 2 garlic cloves, minced
- 1 beef top sirloin steak (1½ lbs.), cut into 4 pieces
- ½ tsp. pepper
- ¼ tsp. salt
- 1 Tbsp. olive oil
- ½ cup dry red wine or reduced-sodium beef broth
- ¼ tsp. dried thyme
- 1 to 2 Tbsp. all-purpose flour
- 1¼ cups reduced-sodium beef broth

1. In a small bowl, pour boiling water over the sun-dried tomatoes; let stand for 5 minutes. Drain.
2. In a large skillet coated with cooking spray, heat butter over medium-high heat; saute the mushrooms and shallots until tender, 3-4 minutes. Add garlic; cook and stir 1 minute. Remove from pan.
3. Sprinkle steaks with pepper and salt. In same skillet, heat oil over medium heat; cook steaks until desired doneness (for medium-rare, a thermometer should read 135°; medium, 140°), 5-7 minutes per side. Remove from pan; keep warm.
4. Add wine and thyme to skillet; bring to a boil, stirring to loosen any browned bits from pan. Cook, uncovered, until liquid is reduced by half. In a bowl, mix flour and broth until smooth; gradually add to wine mixture. Stir in sun-dried tomatoes and the mushroom mixture; bring to a boil. Cook and stir until thickened, about 2 minutes. Spoon over the steaks.

1 serving: 353 cal., 12g fat (4g sat. fat), 76mg chol., 402mg sod., 13g carb. (6g sugars, 3g fiber), 39g pro.
Diabetic exchanges: 5 lean meat, 1 starch.

COD WITH SWEET PEPPERS

This quick and delicious dish is a family favorite. I like to use three or four different colors of peppers.
—Judy Grebetz, Racine, WI

Takes: 25 min. • **Makes:** 4 servings

- 1 medium onion, halved and sliced
- 1 cup reduced-sodium chicken broth
- 1 Tbsp. lemon juice
- 3 garlic cloves, minced
- 1½ tsp. dried oregano
- ½ tsp. grated lemon zest
- ¼ tsp. salt
- 4 cod fillets (6 oz. each)
- ¾ cup julienned green pepper
- ¾ cup julienned sweet red pepper
- 2½ tsp. cornstarch
- 1 Tbsp. cold water
- 1 medium lemon, halved and sliced

1. In a large nonstick skillet, combine the first seven ingredients. Bring to a boil. Reduce heat; cover and simmer until onion is tender, 6-8 minutes.
2. Arrange fish and peppers over onion mixture. Cover and simmer until fish flakes easily with a fork and peppers are tender, 6-9 minutes. Remove fish and vegetables and keep warm.
3. Combine cornstarch and water until smooth; gradually stir into pan juices. Bring to a boil; cook and stir until thickened, about 2 minutes. Spoon over fish and vegetables. Serve with lemon.

1 serving: 168 cal., 1g fat (0 sat. fat), 65mg chol., 398mg sod., 10g carb. (4g sugars, 2g fiber), 29g pro.
Diabetic exchanges: 4 lean meat, 1 vegetable.

STEAKS WITH
MUSHROOM SAUCE

TURKEY ASPARAGUS STIR-FRY

TURKEY ASPARAGUS STIR-FRY

Twenty minutes is all you'll need to make this quick stir-fry. Lean turkey, asparagus and mushrooms make the dish super nutritious, too.

—Darlene Kennedy, Galion, OH

Takes: 20 min. • **Makes:** 5 servings

- 1 Tbsp. olive oil
- 1 lb. boneless skinless turkey breast halves, cut into strips
- 1 lb. fresh asparagus, cut into 1-in. pieces
- 4 oz. fresh mushrooms, sliced
- 2 medium carrots, quartered lengthwise and cut into 1-in. pieces
- 4 green onions, cut into 1-in. pieces
- 2 garlic cloves, minced
- ½ tsp. ground ginger
- ⅔ cup cold water
- 2 Tbsp. reduced-sodium soy sauce
- 4 tsp. cornstarch
- 1 can (8 oz.) sliced water chestnuts, drained
- 3½ cups hot cooked white or brown rice
- 1 medium tomato, cut into wedges

1. In a large skillet or wok, heat oil over medium-high heat. Add turkey; stir-fry until no longer pink, about 5 minutes. Remove and keep warm.

2. Add next six ingredients to pan; stir-fry until vegetables are crisp-tender, about 5 minutes. Combine water, soy sauce and cornstarch; add to skillet with water chestnuts. Bring to a boil; cook and stir 1-2 minutes or until sauce is thickened. Return turkey to skillet and heat through. Serve with rice and tomato wedges.

1 cup with ¾ cup rice: 343 cal., 5g fat (1g sat. fat), 52mg chol., 363mg sod., 47g carb. (4g sugars, 4g fiber), 28g pro.

Diabetic exchanges: 3 starch, 3 lean meat, 1 vegetable, ½ fat.

APPLE CHICKEN CURRY

When she was in college, my daughter introduced me to curry dishes. Now we love the aroma of apples simmering with chicken, curry powder, healthy vegetables and coconut milk.

—Dawn Elliott, Greenville, MI

Takes: 30 min. • **Makes:** 4 servings

- 4 boneless skinless chicken thighs (about 1 lb.)
- ¾ tsp. salt, divided
- ¼ tsp. pepper
- 1 Tbsp. olive oil
- 1 medium sweet red pepper, julienned
- 1 small onion, halved and thinly sliced
- 3 tsp. curry powder
- 2 garlic cloves, minced
- 2 medium Granny Smith apples, cut into ¾-in. pieces
- 1 cup frozen peas
- 1 cup light coconut milk
- 2 cups hot cooked brown rice

1. Sprinkle chicken with ½ tsp. salt and the pepper. In a large skillet, heat oil over medium-high heat. Brown chicken on both sides; remove from pan.

2. Add red pepper and onion to skillet; cook and stir 5 minutes. Stir in the curry powder and garlic; cook 1 minute longer. Stir in the apples, peas, coconut milk and remaining salt.

3. Return chicken to pan; bring to a boil. Reduce heat; simmer, covered, until a thermometer inserted in chicken reads 170°, 8-10 minutes. Serve with rice.

1 serving: 435 cal., 17g fat (6g sat. fat), 76mg chol., 550mg sod., 43g carb. (13g sugars, 7g fiber), 26g pro.

Diabetic exchanges:: 3 lean meat, 2½ starch, 2 fat, ½ fruit.

* HEALTH TIP * Regular and instant brown rice are very similar nutritionally, so feel free to take a shortcut.

SUMMER GARDEN CHICKEN STIR-FRY

I tend to substitute the vegetables in this dish depending on what is in season, so a summer version of this stir-fry might include baby green beans, too.
—Wendy Chiapparo, Mena, AR

....

Takes: 30 min. • **Makes:** 4 servings

- 2 Tbsp. cornstarch
- 1⅓ cups chicken broth
- 3 Tbsp. cider vinegar
- 2 Tbsp. brown sugar
- 2 Tbsp. soy sauce
- ¼ tsp. crushed red pepper flakes
- 2 Tbsp. olive oil, divided
- 1 lb. boneless skinless chicken breasts, cut into ¾-in. cubes
- 2 medium carrots, thinly sliced diagonally
- 1 medium zucchini, halved lengthwise and sliced
- 1 medium yellow summer squash, halved lengthwise and sliced
- 1 medium sweet red pepper, julienned
- 2 garlic cloves, minced
- 1 tsp. minced fresh gingerroot
- 6 green onions, sliced diagonally
  Hot cooked rice

1. Mix first six ingredients until blended. In a large skillet, heat 1 Tbsp. olive oil over medium-high heat; stir-fry chicken until no longer pink, 4-5 minutes. Remove from pan.
2. In same pan, heat remaining oil over medium-high heat. Stir-fry carrots, zucchini and yellow squash 2 minutes. Add pepper, garlic and ginger; stir-fry until pepper is crisp-tender, 1-2 minutes.
3. Mix cornstarch mixture and stir into vegetables. Bring to a boil; cook and stir until sauce is thickened, 2-3 minutes. Stir in green onions and chicken; heat through. Serve with rice.

1¼ cups stir-fry: 284 cal., 10g fat (2g sat. fat), 64mg chol., 878mg sod., 21g carb. (12g sugars, 3g fiber), 27g pro.
Diabetic exchanges: 3 lean meat, 2 fat, 1 starch, 1 vegetable.

NAKED FISH TACOS

This is one of my husband's all-time-favorite meals. I've even converted some friends to fish lovers after they tried this. I serve the tacos with fresh melon when it's in season to balance the subtle heat of the cabbage mixture.
—Elizabeth Bramkamp, Gig Harbor, WA

....

Takes: 25 min. • **Makes:** 2 servings

- 1 cup coleslaw mix
- ¼ cup chopped fresh cilantro
- 1 green onion, sliced
- 1 tsp. chopped seeded jalapeno pepper
- 4 tsp. canola oil, divided
- 2 tsp. lime juice
- ½ tsp. ground cumin
- ½ tsp. salt, divided
- ¼ tsp. pepper, divided
- 2 tilapia fillets (6 oz. each)
- ½ medium ripe avocado, peeled and sliced

1. Place first four ingredients in a bowl; toss with 2 tsp. oil, lime juice, cumin, ¼ tsp. salt and ⅛ tsp. pepper. Refrigerate until serving.
2. Pat fillets dry with paper towels; sprinkle with the remaining salt and pepper. In a large nonstick skillet, heat remaining oil over medium-high heat; cook tilapia until fish just begins to flake easily with a fork, 3-4 minutes per side. Top with slaw and avocado.

1 serving: 293 cal., 16g fat (2g sat. fat), 83mg chol., 663mg sod., 6g carb. (1g sugars, 3g fiber), 33g pro.
Diabetic exchanges: 5 lean meat, 3 fat, 1 vegetable.

* HEALTH TIP * If you're following a low-carb diet, this dish is for you! If not, pair it up with a whole grain side like brown rice pilaf or corn and pepper saute.

SUMMER GARDEN CHICKEN STIR-FRY

**TENDERLOIN WITH
HERB SAUCE**

TENDERLOIN WITH HERB SAUCE

Treat yourself to pork tenderloin in a rich and creamy sauce with a slightly spicy kick. This is very simple to prepare and always tasty.

—Monica Shipley, Tulare, CA

Takes: 25 min. • **Makes:** 6 servings

- 2 pork tenderloins (1 lb. each)
- ½ tsp. salt
- 4 tsp. butter
- ⅔ cup half-and-half cream
- 2 Tbsp. minced fresh parsley
- 2 tsp. herbes de Provence
- 2 tsp. reduced-sodium soy sauce
- 1 tsp. beef bouillon granules
- ½ to ¾ tsp. crushed red pepper flakes

1. Cut each tenderloin into 12 slices; sprinkle with salt. In a large nonstick skillet, heat butter over medium heat; brown pork in batches, 3-4 minutes per side. Return all pork to pan.

2. Mix remaining ingredients; pour over pork. Cook, uncovered, over low heat until sauce is thickened and a thermometer inserted in pork reads 145°, 2-3 minutes, stirring occasionally. Let stand 5 minutes before serving.

Note: Look for herbes de Provence in the spice aisle.

SKILLET FISH DINNER

This healthy recipe takes very little time. We enjoy it with a spinach salad and whole wheat rolls.

—Janet Cooper Claggett, Olney, MD

Takes: 20 min. • **Makes:** 2 servings

- 1 celery rib, chopped
- ½ cup chopped green pepper
- ½ cup chopped onion
- 1 tsp. olive oil
- 2 to 3 plum tomatoes, chopped
- ¼ tsp. salt
  Dash pepper
- ½ lb. cod, haddock or orange roughy fillets
- ¼ to ½ tsp. seafood seasoning
  Hot cooked rice
  Hot pepper sauce, optional

SCALLOPS WITH SNOW PEAS

In a skillet, saute the celery, green pepper and onion in oil until almost tender. Add tomatoes; cook and stir for 1-2 minutes. Sprinkle with salt and pepper. Top with the fish fillets and sprinkle with seafood seasoning. Reduce heat; cover and simmer for 6 minutes. Break the fish into chunks. Cook about 3 minutes longer or until fish flakes easily with a fork. Serve over rice. Serve with hot pepper sauce if desired.

1 serving: 142 cal., 3g fat (1g sat. fat), 43mg chol., 461mg sod., 9g carb. (4g sugars, 3g fiber), 19g pro.

Diabetic exchanges: 3 lean meat, 1 vegetable, ½ fat.

SCALLOPS WITH SNOW PEAS

The vibrant, crisp pea pods in this dish are a nice contrast to the tender, buttery scallops. This dish is bright and fresh.

—Barb Carlucci, Orange Park, FL

Takes: 30 min. • **Makes:** 4 servings

- 2 Tbsp. cornstarch
- 2 Tbsp. reduced-sodium soy sauce
- ⅔ cup water
- 4 tsp. canola oil, divided
- 1 lb. bay scallops
- ½ lb. fresh snow peas, halved diagonally
- 2 medium leeks (white portion only), cut into 3x½-in. strips
- 1½ tsp. minced fresh gingerroot
- 3 cups hot cooked brown rice

1. Mix cornstarch, soy sauce and water. In a large nonstick skillet, heat 2 tsp. oil over medium-high heat; stir-fry scallops until firm and opaque, 1-2 minutes. Remove from pan.

2. In same pan, heat remaining oil over medium-high heat; stir-fry snow peas, leeks and ginger until the peas are just crisp-tender, 4-6 minutes. Stir cornstarch mixture; add to pan. Cook and stir until sauce is thickened, about 1 minute. Add scallops; heat through. Serve with rice.

1 cup stir-fry with ¾ cup rice: 378 cal., 7g fat (1g sat. fat), 27mg chol., 750mg sod., 57g carb. (4g sugars, 5g fiber), 21g pro.

TEST KITCHEN TIP

Bay scallops are the smallest of the scallops and are usually available in a 70/120 size, meaning there are about 70 to 120 scallops per pound.

PORK CHOPS WITH NECTARINE SAUCE

As a dietitian, I'm always looking for ways to make meals healthy and delicious. These juicy chops are fast, too.
—Suellen Pineda, Victor, NY

Takes: 30 min. • **Makes:** 4 servings

- 4 boneless pork loin chops (6 oz. each)
- ½ tsp. salt
- ½ tsp. dried thyme
- ¼ tsp. pepper
- 3 Tbsp. all-purpose flour
- 1 Tbsp. canola oil
- 1 small onion, finely chopped
- 1 garlic clove, minced
- 3 medium nectarines or peeled peaches, cut into ½-in. slices
- ½ cup reduced-sodium chicken broth
- 1 Tbsp. honey, optional

1. Sprinkle pork chops with seasonings. Dredge lightly with flour. In a large skillet, heat oil over medium heat; cook chops until a thermometer reads 145°, 4-5 minutes per side. Remove from pan; keep warm.

2. Add onion to same pan; cook and stir over medium heat 2 minutes. Add garlic; cook and stir 1 minute. Add nectarines; cook until lightly browned on both sides. Stir in broth and, if desired, honey; bring to a boil. Reduce heat; simmer, uncovered, until nectarines are softened and sauce is slightly thickened, about 5 minutes. Serve with chops.

1 pork chop with ½ cup sauce: 330 cal., 14g fat (4g sat. fat), 82mg chol., 414mg sod., 16g carb. (9g sugars, 2g fiber), 35g pro.
Diabetic exchanges: 5 lean meat, 1 fruit, 1 fat.

TOMATO & PEPPER
SIRLOIN STEAK

TOMATO & PEPPER SIRLOIN STEAK

The beefy sauce and zippy peppers in this dish offer an amazing amount of flavor for under 300 calories.
—Gayle Tarkowski, Traverse City, MI

Prep: 15 min. • **Cook:** 35 min.
Makes: 6 servings

- ½ cup all-purpose flour
- ¾ tsp. salt
- ½ tsp. pepper
- 1½ lbs. beef top sirloin steak, thinly sliced
- 3 Tbsp. canola oil
- 1 small onion, chopped
- 1 garlic clove, minced
- 1 can (28 oz.) diced tomatoes, undrained
- 2 large green peppers, cut into strips
- 2 to 3 Tbsp. beef broth
- 1½ tsp. Worcestershire sauce
  Hot cooked rice

1. In a large bowl or shallow dish, combine flour, salt and pepper. Add beef slices, a few pieces at a time. Toss gently to coat.
2. In a Dutch oven, heat oil over medium-high heat. Brown beef in batches. Add the onion; cook and stir until tender, 3-4 minutes. Add garlic; cook 1 minute longer. Add tomatoes; bring to a boil. Reduce heat. Simmer, covered, stirring occasionally, until the meat is tender, 10-15 minutes.
3. Stir in green peppers, broth and Worcestershire sauce; simmer, covered, until peppers are tender, 10-15 minutes. Serve with rice.

1 cup pepper steak mixture: 284 cal., 12g fat (2g sat. fat), 46mg chol., 552mg sod., 17g carb. (6g sugars, 4g fiber), 27g pro.
Diabetic exchanges: 3 lean meat, 2 starch, 1½ fat.

TEST KITCHEN TIP

Replace the sirloin with chicken or turkey for a leaner (but still super flavorful) option.

LIGHT & LEMONY SCAMPI

A touch more lemon helped me trim the calories in our favorite shrimp scampi recipe. For those who want to indulge, pass around the Parmesan.

—Ann Sheehy, Lawrence, MA

Prep: 20 min. • **Cook:** 15 min.
Makes: 4 servings

- 1 lb. uncooked shrimp (26-30 per lb.)
- 8 oz. uncooked multigrain angel hair pasta
- 1 Tbsp. butter
- 1 Tbsp. olive oil
- 2 green onions, thinly sliced
- 4 garlic cloves, minced
- ½ cup reduced-sodium chicken broth
- 2 tsp. grated lemon zest
- 3 Tbsp. lemon juice
- ½ tsp. freshly ground pepper
- ¼ tsp. salt
- ¼ tsp. crushed red pepper flakes
- ¼ cup minced fresh parsley
    Grated Parmesan cheese, optional

1. Peel and devein shrimp, removing tails. Cut each shrimp lengthwise in half. Cook pasta according to package directions.
2. In a large nonstick skillet, heat butter and oil over medium-high heat. Add shrimp, green onions and garlic; cook and stir until shrimp turn pink, 2-3 minutes. Remove from pan with a slotted spoon.
3. Add broth, lemon zest, lemon juice, pepper, salt and pepper flakes to same pan. Bring to a boil; cook until liquid is slightly reduced, about 1 minute. Return shrimp to pan; heat through. Remove from heat.
4. Drain pasta; divide among four bowls. Top with shrimp mixture; sprinkle with parsley. If desired, serve with cheese.

1 serving: 378 cal., 10g fat (3g sat. fat), 146mg chol., 405mg sod., 42g carb. (3g sugars, 5g fiber), 29g pro.
Diabetic exchanges: 3 very lean meat, 2½ starch, 1½ fat.

PINTO BEAN STEW

This thick, hearty stew is chock-full of beans and vegetables and makes a wonderful supper on cold winter days. It also freezes well.

—Gina Passantino, Amherst, NY

Prep: 15 min. + soaking
Cook: 1½ hours • **Makes:** 6 servings

- 1 cup dried pinto beans
- 2 cups cold water
- ½ cup chopped carrot
- 2 garlic cloves, minced
- ¾ tsp. chili powder
- ½ tsp. salt
    Dash cayenne pepper
- 1 pkg. (16 oz.) frozen corn, thawed
- 1 large onion, chopped
- 1 medium green pepper, chopped
- 1 can (14½ oz.) diced tomatoes, undrained
- 2 to 3 tsp. balsamic vinegar
- ¼ tsp. sugar

1. Sort beans and rinse with cold water. Place the beans in a large saucepan; add water to cover by 2 in. Bring to a boil; boil for 2 minutes. Remove from the heat; cover and let stand for 1 hour.
2. Drain and rinse beans, discarding liquid. Return beans to the pan; add the cold water, carrot, garlic, chili powder, salt and cayenne. Bring to a boil. Reduce heat; cover and simmer for 45 minutes or until beans are almost tender.
3. In a nonstick skillet coated with cooking spray, saute the corn, onion and green pepper until tender. Add to the bean mixture. Cover and cook for 45 minutes.
4. Stir in the tomatoes, vinegar and sugar. Cook 5 minutes longer or until heated through.

1 cup: 214 cal., 1g fat (0 sat. fat), 0 chol., 303mg sod., 44g carb. (7g sugars, 9g fiber), 10g pro.
Diabetic exchanges: 2 starch, 1 lean meat, 1 vegetable.

LIGHT & LEMONY SCAMPI

**CREAMY LENTILS WITH
KALE ARTICHOKE SAUTE**

LEMON-BASIL CHICKEN ROTINI

*My husband and sons like to have meat
with their meals, but I prefer more
veggies. This combo is colorful and
healthy, and it keeps everyone happy.*
—Anna-Marie Williams, League City, TX

Prep: 25 min. • **Cook:** 20 min.
Makes: 6 servings

- 3 cups uncooked white fiber rotini or
  whole wheat rotini
- 2 tsp. olive oil
- 1 lb. boneless skinless chicken breasts,
  cut into ¾-in. strips
- 1½ cups sliced fresh mushrooms
- 1½ cups shredded carrots
- 4 garlic cloves, thinly sliced
- 1 cup reduced-sodium chicken broth
- 3 oz. reduced-fat cream cheese
- 1 Tbsp. lemon juice
- 1½ cups frozen peas (about 6 oz.),
  thawed
- ⅓ cup shredded Parmesan cheese
- ¼ cup minced fresh basil
- 2 tsp. grated lemon peel
- ¼ tsp. salt
- ¼ tsp. pepper
- ¼ tsp. crushed red pepper flakes

1. Cook rotini according to package
directions. Meanwhile, in a large nonstick
skillet, heat oil over medium heat. Add
chicken; cook and stir until no longer pink.
Remove from pan.
2. Add mushrooms and carrots to same
skillet; cook and stir until tender. Add
garlic; cook 1 minute longer. Stir in broth,
cream cheese and lemon juice; stir until
cheese is melted.
3. Drain rotini; add to vegetable mixture.
Stir in chicken, peas, Parmesan cheese,
basil, lemon peel, salt, pepper and pepper
flakes; heat through.
1⅓ cups: 308 cal., 8g fat (4g sat. fat), 56mg
chol., 398mg sod., 31g carb. (5g sugars, 6g
fiber), 27g pro.
Diabetic exchanges:: 3 lean meat, 2 starch,
½ fat.

**CREAMY LENTILS WITH
KALE ARTICHOKE SAUTE**

CREAMY LENTILS WITH KALE ARTICHOKE SAUTE

*I've been trying to eat more meatless
meals, so I experimented with this hearty
saute and served it over brown rice.
It was so good even the non-kale lovers
gobbled it up.*
—Teri Rasey, Cadillac, MI

Takes: 30 min. • **Makes:** 4 servings

- ½ cup dried red lentils, rinsed and
  sorted
- ¼ tsp. dried oregano
- ⅛ tsp. pepper
- 1¼ cups vegetable broth
- ¼ tsp. sea salt, divided
- 1 Tbsp. olive oil or grapeseed oil
- 16 cups chopped fresh kale
  (about 12 oz.)
- 1 can (14 oz.) water-packed artichoke
  hearts, drained and chopped
- 3 garlic cloves, minced
- ½ tsp. Italian seasoning
- 2 Tbsp. grated Romano cheese
- 2 cups hot cooked brown
  or basmati rice

1. Place first four ingredients and ⅛ tsp.
salt in a small saucepan; bring to a boil.
Reduce heat; simmer, covered, until lentils
are tender and liquid is almost absorbed,
12-15 minutes. Remove from heat.
2. In a 6-qt. stockpot, heat oil over
medium heat. Add kale and remaining
salt; cook, covered, until kale is wilted,
4-5 minutes, stirring occasionally. Add
artichoke hearts, garlic and Italian
seasoning; cook and stir 3 minutes.
Remove from heat; stir in cheese.
3. Serve lentils and kale mixture over rice.
1 serving: 321 cal., 6g fat (2g sat. fat), 1mg
chol., 661mg sod., 53g carb. (1g sugars, 5g
fiber), 15g pro.

✳

TEST KITCHEN TIP
Lentils don't require soaking, but they
should be rinsed and sifted through to
look for stones before cooking.

CHILI-LIME MUSHROOM TACOS

I used to make this dish with beef, but substituting portobello mushrooms turned it into our vegetarian favorite.
—Greg Fontenot, The Woodlands, TX

Takes: 25 min. • **Makes:** 4 servings

- 4 large portobello mushrooms (about ¾ lb.)
- 1 Tbsp. olive oil
- 1 medium sweet red pepper, cut into strips
- 1 medium onion, halved and thinly sliced
- 2 garlic cloves, minced
- 1½ tsp. chili powder
- ½ tsp. salt
- ½ tsp. ground cumin
- ¼ tsp. crushed red pepper flakes
- 1 tsp. grated lime zest
- 2 Tbsp. lime juice
- 8 corn tortillas (6 in.), warmed
- 1 cup shredded pepper jack cheese

1. Remove stems from mushrooms; if desired, remove gills using a spoon. Cut mushrooms into ½-in. slices.

2. In a large skillet, heat oil over medium-high heat; saute mushrooms, red pepper and onion until mushrooms are tender, 5-7 minutes. Stir in garlic, seasonings, lime zest and juice; cook and stir 1 minute. Serve in tortillas; top with cheese.

2 tacos: 300 cal., 14g fat (6g sat. fat), 30mg chol., 524mg sod., 33g carb. (5g sugars, 6g fiber), 13g pro.

Diabetic exchanges: 2 vegetable, 1½ starch, 1 medium-fat meat, ½ fat.

* HEALTH TIP * These same tacos made with lean ground beef adds almost 4g saturated fat per serving. That's a good reason for a meatless Taco Tuesday!

QUICK SHRIMP CREOLE

(PICTURED ON P. 130)

My mother made shrimp Creole when I was growing up, so I've carried on the family tradition. For an extra bit of heat, pass the Louisiana hot sauce.
—Gina Norton, Wonder Lake, IL

Takes: 30 min. • **Makes:** 6 servings

- 3 cups uncooked instant brown rice
- 3 Tbsp. canola oil
- 2 medium onions, halved and sliced
- 1 medium sweet red pepper, coarsely chopped
- 1 medium green pepper, coarsely chopped
- ½ cup chopped celery
- 2 Tbsp. all-purpose flour
- 1 tsp. dried oregano
- ¾ tsp. pepper
- ½ tsp. salt
- 1 can (14½ oz.) diced tomatoes, undrained
- 1 can (8 oz.) tomato sauce
- 1 lb. uncooked shrimp (31-40 per lb.), peeled and deveined
  Louisiana-style hot sauce, optional

1. Cook rice according to package directions. Meanwhile, in a large skillet, heat oil over medium-high heat. Add onions, peppers and celery; cook and stir 6-8 minutes or until tender.

2. Stir in flour, oregano, pepper and salt until blended. Stir in tomatoes and tomato sauce. Bring to a boil, stirring constantly; cook and stir until thickened. Reduce heat; simmer, covered, 5-8 minutes or until flavors are blended, stirring occasionally.

3. Add shrimp; cook, covered, 4-5 minutes longer or until shrimp turn pink, stirring occasionally. Serve with rice and, if desired, hot sauce.

1 cup shrimp mixture with ⅔ cup rice: 356 cal., 10g fat (1g sat. fat), 92mg chol., 588mg sod., 48g carb. (6g sugars, 5g fiber), 19g pro.

Diabetic exchanges: 2½ starch, 2 lean meat, 1½ fat, 1 vegetable.

CHILI-LIME MUSHROOM TACOS

GLAZED ROSEMARY PORK

With a honey-rosemary glaze, this delicately seasoned pork is both fancy enough for a dinner party, but easy enough to make anytime.
—Barbara Sistrunk, Fultondale, AL

....

Takes: 30 min. • **Makes:** 6 servings

- ¼ cup reduced-sodium chicken broth
- 3 Tbsp. honey
- 1 Tbsp. minced fresh rosemary or 1 tsp. dried rosemary, crushed
- 1 Tbsp. Dijon mustard
- 1 tsp. balsamic vinegar
- ⅛ tsp. salt
- ⅛ tsp. pepper
- 2 pork tenderloins (1 lb. each)
- 2 Tbsp. olive oil, divided
- 4 garlic cloves, minced

1. Whisk together first seven ingredients. Cut tenderloins crosswise into 1-in. slices; pound each with a meat mallet to ½-in. thickness.
2. In a large nonstick skillet, heat 1 Tbsp. oil over medium-high heat. In batches, cook pork until a thermometer reads 145°, 3-4 minutes per side. Remove from the pan.
3. In same skillet, heat remaining oil over medium heat; saute garlic until tender, about 1 minute. Stir in broth mixture; bring to a boil, stirring to loosen browned bits from pan. Add pork, turning to coat; heat through.
4 oz. cooked pork: 255 cal., 10g fat (2g sat. fat), 85mg chol., 194mg sod., 10g carb. (9g sugars, 0 fiber), 31g pro.
Diabetic exchanges: ½ starch, 4 lean meat, 1 fat.

WHITE WINE GARLIC CHICKEN

This garlic chicken is great over cooked brown rice or your favorite pasta. Add a sprinkle of Parmesan cheese if you like.
—Heather Esposito, Rome, NY

....

Takes: 30 min. • **Makes:** 4 servings

- 4 boneless skinless chicken breast halves (6 oz. each)
- ½ tsp. salt
- ¼ tsp. pepper
- 1 Tbsp. olive oil
- 2 cups sliced baby portobello mushrooms (about 6 oz.)
- 1 medium onion, chopped
- 2 garlic cloves, minced
- ½ cup dry white wine or reduced-sodium chicken broth

1. Pound chicken breasts with a meat mallet to ½-in. thickness; sprinkle with salt and pepper. In a large skillet, heat oil over medium heat; cook chicken until no longer pink, 5-6 minutes per side. Remove from pan; keep warm.
2. Add mushrooms and onion to pan; cook and stir over medium-high heat until tender and lightly browned, 2-3 minutes. Add garlic; cook and stir 30 seconds. Add wine; bring to a boil, stirring to loosen browned bits from pan. Cook until liquid is slightly reduced, 1-2 minutes; serve over the chicken.
1 chicken breast half with ¼ cup mushroom mixture: 243 cal., 7g fat (2g sat. fat), 94mg chol., 381mg sod., 5g carb. (2g sugars, 1g fiber), 36g pro.
Diabetic exchanges: 5 lean meat, 1 fat.

WHITE WINE GARLIC CHICKEN

HERBED PORTOBELLO PASTA

GREEN PEPPER STEAK

For a delicious, fast meal, try this flavorful beef dinner loaded with tomatoes and peppers. What a perfect recipe to use garden vegetables of the season!
—Emmalee Thomas, Laddonia, MO

Takes: 30 min. • **Makes:** 4 servings

- 1 Tbsp. cornstarch
- ¼ cup reduced-sodium soy sauce
- ¼ cup water
- 2 Tbsp. canola oil, divided
- 1 lb. beef top sirloin steak, cut into ¼-in.-thick strips
- 2 small onions, cut into thin wedges
- 2 celery ribs, sliced diagonally
- 1 medium green pepper, cut into 1-in. pieces
- 2 medium tomatoes, cut into wedges
  Hot cooked rice

1. Mix cornstarch, soy sauce and water until smooth. In a large skillet, heat 1 Tbsp. oil over medium-high heat; stir-fry beef until browned, 2-3 minutes. Remove from the pan.
2. Stir-fry onions, celery and pepper in remaining oil 3 minutes. Stir cornstarch mixture; add to pan. Bring to a boil; cook and stir until thickened and bubbly, 1-2 minutes. Stir in tomatoes and beef; heat through. Serve with rice.

1 serving: 259 cal., 12g fat (2g sat. fat), 46mg chol., 647mg sod., 10g carb. (4g sugars, 2g fiber), 27g pro.
Diabetic exchanges: 3 lean meat, 2 vegetable, 1½ fat.

HERBED PORTOBELLO PASTA

Meaty mushrooms make this light pasta taste hearty and filling. It's my fast and fresh go-to weeknight dinner.
—Laurie Trombley, Stonyford, CA

Prep: 20 min. • **Cook:** 15 min
Makes: 4 servings

- ½ lb. uncooked multigrain angel hair pasta
- 4 large portobello mushrooms (¾ lb.), stems removed
- 1 Tbsp. olive oil
- 2 garlic cloves, minced
- 4 plum tomatoes, chopped
- ¼ cup pitted Greek olives
- ¼ cup minced fresh basil
- 1 tsp. minced fresh rosemary or ¼ tsp. dried rosemary, crushed
- 1 tsp. minced fresh thyme or ¼ tsp. dried thyme
- ¼ tsp. salt
- ⅛ tsp. pepper
- ⅔ cup crumbled feta cheese
- ¼ cup shredded Parmesan cheese

1. Cook pasta according to package directions for al dente. Meanwhile, cut mushrooms in half and thinly slice. In a large skillet, heat oil over medium heat. Add mushrooms; saute until tender, 8-10 minutes. Add garlic; cook 1 minute longer. Stir in tomatoes and olives. Reduce heat to low; cook, uncovered, until slightly thickened, about 5 minutes. Stir in herbs, salt and pepper.
2. Drain pasta, reserving ¼ cup pasta water. Toss pasta with mushroom mixture, adjusting consistency with reserved pasta water. Sprinkle with cheeses.

1½ cups: 375 cal., 12g fat (4g sat. fat), 14mg chol., 585mg sod., 48g carb. (5g sugars, 7g fiber), 18g pro.
Diabetic exchanges: 3 starch, 2 medium-fat meat, 2 fat, 1 vegetable.

✳

TEST KITCHEN TIP

Instead of reaching for the salt shaker, try zesting a little lemon over the pasta and squeezing a bit of juice over each serving. It brightens up the flavor and helps keep it healthy.

BLUSHING PENNE PASTA

BLUSHING PENNE PASTA

I reworked this recipe from an original that called for vodka and heavy whipping cream. My friends and family had a hard time believing a sauce this rich, flavorful and creamy could be light.
—Margaret Wilson, San Bernardino, CA

Takes: 30 min. • **Makes:** 8 servings

- 1 pkg. (16 oz.) penne pasta
- 2 Tbsp. butter
- 1 medium onion, halved and thinly sliced
- 2 Tbsp. minced fresh thyme or 2 tsp. dried thyme
- 2 Tbsp. minced fresh basil or 2 tsp. dried basil
- 1 tsp. salt
- 1½ cups half-and-half cream, divided
- ½ cup white wine or reduced-sodium chicken broth
- 1 Tbsp. tomato paste
- 2 Tbsp. all-purpose flour
- ½ cup shredded Parmigiano-Reggiano cheese, divided

1. In a 6-qt. stockpot, cook pasta according to package directions. Drain; return to pot.
2. Meanwhile, in a large nonstick skillet, heat butter over medium heat; saute onion until lightly browned, 8-10 minutes. Add herbs and salt; cook and stir 1 minute. Add 1 cup cream, wine and tomato paste; cook and stir until blended.
3. Mix flour and remaining cream until smooth; gradually stir into onion mixture. Bring to a boil; cook and stir until thickened, about 2 minutes. Stir in ¼ cup cheese. Stir into pasta. Serve with remaining cheese.

1 cup: 335 cal., 10g fat (6g sat. fat), 34mg chol., 431mg sod., 47g carb. (4g sugars, 2g fiber), 12g pro.

MAPLE-DIJON CHICKEN

MAPLE-DIJON CHICKEN

Eating dinner as a family every night is really important to us, and this recipe is one that we all love. It's our favorite skillet chicken dish.
—Courtney Stultz, Weir, KS

Takes: 30 min. • **Makes:** 4 servings

- 1 lb. boneless skinless chicken breasts, cut into 1-in.-thick strips
- ½ tsp. dried rosemary, crushed
- ½ tsp. dried thyme
- ½ tsp. pepper
- ¼ tsp. salt
- 1 Tbsp. coconut oil or olive oil
- ½ cup chopped onion
- 1 garlic clove, minced
- ⅓ cup Dijon mustard
- 3 Tbsp. maple syrup

Toss chicken with seasonings. In a large skillet, heat oil over medium heat; saute chicken 10 minutes. Add onion and garlic; cook and stir 5 minutes. Add mustard and syrup; cook and stir until chicken is no longer pink, 5-7 minutes.

1 serving: 221 cal., 6g fat (4g sat. fat), 63mg chol., 684mg sod., 13g carb. (10g sugars, 1g fiber), 23g pro.
Diabetic exchanges: 3 lean meat, 1 starch, ½ fat.

CHICKEN ARTICHOKE SKILLET

This fast chicken recipe shows off some of my favorite Greek flavors. I like to change up the olives every and now and then— Greek, green, black or a mixture.
—Carol Latimore, Arvada, CO

....

Takes: 25 min. • **Makes:** 4 servings

- 4 boneless skinless chicken breast halves (4 oz. each)
- ¼ tsp. salt
- ¼ tsp. pepper
- 2 tsp. olive oil
- 1 can (14 oz.) water-packed quartered artichoke hearts, rinsed and drained
- ⅔ cup reduced-sodium chicken broth
- ¼ cup halved pimiento-stuffed olives
- ¼ cup halved pitted Greek olives
- 2 Tbsp. minced fresh oregano or 2 tsp. dried oregano
- 1 Tbsp. lemon juice

1. Sprinkle chicken with salt and pepper. In a large skillet, heat oil over medium-high heat; brown chicken on both sides.

2. Add remaining ingredients; bring to a boil. Reduce heat; simmer, covered, until a thermometer inserted in chicken reads 165°, 4-5 minutes.

1 serving: 225 cal., 9g fat (1g sat. fat), 63mg chol., 864mg sod., 9g carb. (0 sugars, 0 fiber), 26g pro.

Diabetic exchanges: 3 lean meat, 1 vegetable.

MUSHROOM PEPPER STEAK

MUSHROOM PEPPER STEAK

Here's a stir-fry with lots of fresh veggies and all the classic flavors you'd expect. It's perfect over rice.
—Billie Moss, Walnut Creek, CA

....

Prep: 15 min. + marinating • **Cook:** 15 min.
Makes: 4 servings

- 6 Tbsp. reduced-sodium soy sauce, divided
- ⅛ tsp. pepper
- 1 lb. beef top sirloin steak, cut into thin strips
- 1 Tbsp. cornstarch
- ½ cup reduced-sodium beef broth
- 1 garlic clove, minced
- ½ tsp. minced fresh gingerroot
- 3 tsp. canola oil, divided
- 1 cup julienned sweet red pepper
- 1 cup julienned green pepper
- 2 cups sliced fresh mushrooms
- 2 medium tomatoes, cut into wedges
- 6 green onions, sliced
  Hot cooked rice, optional

1. In a shallow bowl, combine 3 Tbsp. soy sauce and pepper; add beef and turn to coat. Cover; refrigerate 30-60 minutes. In a small bowl, combine the cornstarch, broth and remaining soy sauce until smooth; set aside.

2. Drain beef, discarding marinade. In a large nonstick skillet or wok, stir-fry the garlic and ginger in 2 tsp. oil for 1 minute. Add the beef; stir-fry 4-6 minutes or until no longer pink. Remove beef; keep warm.

3. Stir-fry the peppers in remaining oil for 1 minute. Add mushrooms; stir-fry for 2 minutes longer or until peppers are crisp-tender. Stir broth mixture and add to vegetable mixture. Bring to a boil; cook and stir for 2 minutes or until thickened. Return beef to pan; add tomatoes and onions. Cook for 2 minutes or until heated through. Serve over rice if desired.

1¼ cups beef mixture: 241 cal., 10g fat (3g sat. fat), 64mg chol., 841mg sod., 13g carb. (5g sugars, 3g fiber), 25g pro.

Diabetic exchanges: 3 lean meat, 2 vegetable, 1 fat.

SHRIMP PUTTANESCA

I throw together these bold ingredients for a feisty seafood pasta.
—Lynda Balslev, Sausalito, CA

Takes: 30 min. • **Makes:** 4 servings

- 2 Tbsp. olive oil, divided
- 1 lb. uncooked shrimp (31-40 per lb.), peeled and deveined
- ¾ to 1 tsp. crushed red pepper flakes, divided
- ¼ tsp. salt
- 1 small onion, chopped
- 2 to 3 anchovy fillets, finely chopped
- 3 garlic cloves, minced
- 2 cups grape tomatoes or small cherry tomatoes
- ½ cup dry white wine or vegetable broth
- ⅓ cup pitted Greek olives, coarsely chopped
- 2 tsp. drained capers
  Sugar to taste
  Chopped fresh Italian parsley
  Hot cooked spaghetti, optional

1. In a large skillet, heat 1 Tbsp. oil; saute shrimp with ½ tsp. pepper flakes until shrimp turn pink, 2-3 minutes. Stir in salt; remove from pan.

2. In same pan, heat remaining oil over medium heat; saute onion until tender, about 2 minutes. Add anchovies, garlic and remaining pepper flakes; cook and stir until fragrant, about 1 minute. Stir in tomatoes, wine, olives and capers; bring to a boil. Reduce heat; simmer, uncovered, until tomatoes are softened and mixture is thickened, 8-10 minutes.

3. Stir in shrimp. Add sugar to taste; sprinkle with parsley. If desired, serve with spaghetti.

1 cup shrimp mixture: 228 cal., 12g fat (2g sat. fat), 140mg chol., 579mg sod., 8g carb. (3g sugars, 1g fiber), 20g pro.

GRECIAN CHICKEN

The caper, tomato and olive flavors whisk you away to the Greek isles in an easy skillet dish that's perfect for hectic weeknights.
—Jan Marler, Murchison, TX

Takes: 30 min. • **Makes:** 4 servings

- 3 tsp. olive oil, divided
- 1 lb. chicken tenderloins
- 2 medium tomatoes, sliced
- 1 cup sliced fresh mushrooms
- ½ cup chopped onion
- 1 Tbsp. capers, drained
- 1 Tbsp. lemon-pepper seasoning
- 1 Tbsp. salt-free Greek seasoning
- 1 medium garlic clove, minced
- ½ cup water
- 2 Tbsp. chopped ripe olives
  Hot cooked orzo pasta, optional

1. In a large skillet, heat 2 tsp. oil over medium heat. Add chicken; saute until no longer pink, 7-9 minutes. Remove and keep warm.

2. In same skillet, heat remaining oil; add next six ingredients. Cook and stir until onion is translucent, 2-3 minutes. Stir in garlic; cook 1 minute more. Add water; bring to a boil. Reduce heat; simmer, uncovered, until vegetables are tender, 3-4 minutes. Return chicken to skillet; add olives. Simmer, uncovered, until chicken is heated through, 2-3 minutes. If desired, serve with orzo.

1 serving: 172 cal., 5g fat (1g sat. fat), 56mg chol., 393mg sod., 6g carb. (3g sugars, 2g fiber), 28g pro.
Diabetic exchanges: 3 lean meat, 1 vegetable, 1 fat.

SHRIMP PUTTANESCA

OVEN
ENTREES

"*Spicy butternut squash makes a great base for vegetarian tacos. I'm always looking for quick and nutritious weeknight dinners like this for my family.*"
—Elisabeth Larsen, Pleasant Grove, UT

OVEN ENTREES

PASTA PIZZA

My family often requests this meatless main dish. It's a tempting cross between pizza and spaghetti.
—Andrea Quick, Columbus, OH

Prep: 25 min. • **Bake:** 10 min.
Makes: 4 servings

- 8 oz. uncooked angel hair pasta
- 4 tsp. olive oil, divided
- 2 cups sliced fresh mushrooms
- ½ cup chopped green pepper
- ¼ cup chopped onion
- 1 can (15 oz.) pizza sauce
- ¼ cup sliced ripe olives
- ½ cup shredded part-skim mozzarella cheese
- ¼ tsp. Italian seasoning

1. Preheat oven to 400°. Cook pasta according to package directions; drain.
2. In a large cast-iron or other ovenproof skillet, heat 1 tsp. oil over medium heat. Add mushrooms, green pepper and onion; saute until tender. Remove with a slotted spoon and keep warm. Increase heat to medium-high. In same skillet, heat the remaining oil. Spread pasta evenly in skillet to form a crust. Cook until lightly browned, 5-7 minutes.
3. Turn crust onto a large plate. Reduce heat to medium; slide crust back into skillet. Top with pizza sauce, sauteed vegetables and olives; sprinkle with cheese and Italian seasoning. Bake until cheese is melted, 10-12 minutes.
1 serving: 374 cal., 10g fat (3g sat. fat), 9mg chol., 532mg sod., 56g carb. (7g sugars, 5g fiber), 14g pro.

CHICKEN PESTO ROLL-UPS

One night I looked in the refrigerator and thought to myself, "What can I make with chicken, mushrooms, cheese and pesto?" This pretty dish was the result. Add Italian bread and fruit salad and you have a meal!
—Melissa Nordmann, Mobile, AL

Prep: 15 min. • **Bake:** 30 min.
Makes: 4 servings

- 4 boneless skinless chicken breast halves (6 oz. each)
- ½ cup prepared pesto, divided
- 1 lb. medium fresh mushrooms, sliced
- 4 slices reduced-fat provolone cheese, halved

1. Preheat oven to 350°. Pound chicken breasts with a meat mallet to ¼-in. thickness. Spread ¼ cup pesto over chicken breasts.
2. Coarsely chop half of the sliced mushrooms; scatter remaining sliced mushrooms in a 15x10x1-in. baking pan coated with cooking spray. Top each chicken breast with a fourth of the chopped mushrooms and a halved cheese slice. Roll up chicken from a short side; secure with toothpicks. Place seam side down on top of the sliced mushrooms.
3. Bake, covered, until chicken is no longer pink, 25-30 minutes. Preheat broiler; top chicken with remaining pesto and remaining cheese. Broil until cheese is melted and browned, 3-5 minutes longer. Discard toothpicks.
1 stuffed chicken breast half: 374 cal., 17g fat (5g sat. fat), 104mg chol., 582mg sod., 7g carb. (1g sugars, 1g fiber), 44g pro.
Diabetic exchanges: 5 lean meat, 2 fat.

GREEN CURRY SALMON WITH GREEN BEANS

Like a lot of people here in the beautiful Pacific Northwest, my boyfriend, Michael, loves to fish. Whenever we have an abundance of fresh salmon on hand, this is one way we cook it.
—Amy Paul Maynard, Albany, OR

Takes: 30 min. • **Makes:** 4 servings

    4 salmon fillets (4 oz. each)
    1 cup light coconut milk
    2 Tbsp. green curry paste
    1 cup uncooked instant brown rice
    1 cup reduced-sodium chicken broth
    ⅛ tsp. pepper
    ¾ lb. fresh green beans, trimmed
    1 tsp. sesame oil
    1 tsp. sesame seeds, toasted
       Lime wedges

1. Preheat oven to 400°. Place salmon fillets in an 8-in. square baking dish. Whisk together coconut milk and curry paste; pour over salmon. Bake, uncovered, until fish just begins to flake easily with a fork, 15-20 minutes.
2. Meanwhile, in a small saucepan, combine rice, broth and pepper; bring to a boil. Reduce heat; simmer, covered, 5 minutes. Remove from heat; let stand for 5 minutes.
3. In a large saucepan, place steamer basket over 1 in. of water. Place green beans in basket; bring water to a boil. Reduce heat to maintain a simmer; steam, covered, until the beans are crisp-tender, 7-10 minutes. Toss with sesame oil and sesame seeds.
4. Serve salmon with rice, beans and lime wedges. Spoon coconut sauce over the salmon.

Note: This recipe was tested with Thai Kitchen Green Curry Paste.

1 serving: 366 cal., 17g fat (5g sat. fat), 57mg chol., 340mg sod., 29g carb. (5g sugars, 4g fiber), 24g pro.

Diabetic exchanges: 3 lean meat, 2 starch, 1 fat.

✳ HEALTH TIP ✳ This nutrition-packed complete meal is gluten-free, heart-smart and diabetic-friendly.

MUSHROOM TURKEY TETRAZZINI

This creamy casserole is a fantastic way to use up that leftover Thanksgiving turkey. And it's a real family-pleaser!
—Linda Howe, Lisle, IL

Prep: 35 min. • **Bake:** 25 min.
Makes: 8 servings

    12 oz. uncooked multigrain spaghetti,
        broken into 2-in. pieces
     2 tsp. chicken bouillon granules
     2 Tbsp. butter
     ½ lb. sliced fresh mushrooms
     2 Tbsp. all-purpose flour
     ¼ cup sherry or additional pasta water
     ¾ tsp. salt-free lemon-pepper
        seasoning
     ½ tsp. salt
     ⅛ tsp. ground nutmeg
     1 cup fat-free evaporated milk
     ⅔ cup grated Parmesan cheese, divided
     4 cups cubed cooked turkey breast
     ¼ tsp. paprika, optional

1. Preheat oven to 375°. Cook spaghetti according to package directions for al dente. Drain, reserving 2½ cups pasta water; transfer spaghetti to a 13x9-in. baking dish coated with cooking spray. Dissolve bouillon in reserved pasta water
2. In a large nonstick skillet, heat butter over medium-high heat; saute mushrooms until tender. Stir in flour until blended. Gradually stir in sherry, reserved pasta water and seasonings. Bring to a boil; cook and stir until thickened, about 2 minutes.
3. Reduce heat to low; stir in milk and ⅓ cup cheese until blended. Add turkey; heat through, stirring constantly. Pour over spaghetti; toss to combine. Sprinkle with remaining cheese and, if desired, paprika.
4. Bake casserole, covered, until bubbly, 25-30 minutes.

1 cup: 357 cal., 7g fat (3g sat. fat), 71mg chol., 717mg sod., 38g carb. (5g sugars, 3g fiber), 34g pro.

Diabetic exchanges: 3 starch, 3 lean meat, ½ fat.

MUSHROOM TURKEY TETRAZZINI

BULGUR TURKEY MANICOTTI

BULGUR TURKEY MANICOTTI

The addition of wholesome bulgur gives extra nutrition to this Italian entree. It's so zesty and flavorful, your family will never realize it's good for them.
—Mary Gunderson, Conrad, IA

....

Prep: 20 min. + standing • **Bake:** 1¼ hours
Makes: 7 servings

- ¼ cup bulgur
- ⅔ cup boiling water
- ¾ lb. lean ground turkey
- 1 tsp. dried basil
- 1 tsp. dried oregano
- ¼ tsp. pepper
- 1½ cups (12 oz.) 2% cottage cheese
- 1 jar (24 oz.) meatless pasta sauce
- 1 can (8 oz.) no-salt-added tomato sauce
- ½ cup water
- 1 pkg. (8 oz.) manicotti shells
- 1 cup shredded part-skim mozzarella cheese

1. Combine bulgur and boiling water; let stand, covered, until liquid is absorbed, about 30 minutes. Drain; squeeze dry.
2. Preheat oven to 350°. In a large nonstick skillet, cook and crumble turkey over medium-high heat until no longer pink, 5-7 minutes. Stir in seasonings, cottage cheese and bulgur.
3. Mix pasta sauce, tomato sauce and ½ cup water. Spread 1 cup sauce mixture into a 13x9-in. baking dish coated with cooking spray. Fill uncooked manicotti shells with the turkey mixture; place in prepared dish. Top with the remaining sauce mixture.
4. Bake, covered, until bubbly and shells are tender, 70-75 minutes. Uncover and sprinkle with mozzarella cheese. Bake until cheese is melted, about 5 minutes.

2 manicotti: 346 cal., 9g fat (4g sat. fat), 46mg chol., 717mg sod., 42g carb. (12g sugars, 4g fiber), 25g pro.
Diabetic exchanges: 3 starch, 3 lean meat, ½ fat.

SASSY SALSA MEAT LOAVES

SASSY SALSA MEAT LOAVES

We still can't settle on our favorite salsa, but, honestly, why bother? There are so many fantastic options! We love trying them all in this twist on classic meat loaf. You can make these loaves ahead, and they'll last for a few days—perfect for meat loaf sandwiches topped with a little Monterey Jack cheese.
—Tasha Tully, Owings Mills, MD

....

Prep: 25 min. • **Bake:** 65 min. + standing
Makes: 2 loaves (6 servings each)

- ¾ cup uncooked instant brown rice
- 1 can (8 oz.) tomato sauce
- 1½ cups salsa, divided
- 1 large onion, chopped
- 1 large egg, lightly beaten
- 1 celery rib, finely chopped
- ¼ cup minced fresh parsley
- 2 Tbsp. minced fresh cilantro
- 2 garlic cloves, minced
- 1 Tbsp. chili powder
- 1½ tsp. salt
- ½ tsp. pepper
- 2 lbs. lean ground beef (90% lean)
- 1 lb. ground turkey
- ½ cup shredded reduced-fat Monterey Jack cheese or Mexican cheese blend

1. Preheat oven to 350°. Cook rice according to package directions; cool slightly. In a large bowl, combine tomato sauce, ½ cup salsa, onion, egg, celery, parsley, cilantro, garlic and seasonings; stir in rice. Add beef and turkey; mix lightly but thoroughly.
2. Shape mixture into two 8x4-in. loaves in a greased 15x10x1-in. baking pan. Bake until a thermometer inserted in center reads 165°, 1-1¼ hours.
3. Spread with the remaining salsa and sprinkle with cheese; bake until cheese is melted, about 5 minutes. Let stand for 10 minutes before slicing.

Freeze option: Bake meat loaves without topping. Cool; securely wrap in plastic, then foil. To use, partially thaw in the refrigerator overnight. Unwrap meat loaves; place in a greased 15x10x1-in. baking pan. Reheat in a preheated 350° oven 40-45 minutes or until a thermometer inserted in center reads 165°; top as directed.

1 slice: 237 cal., 11g fat (4g sat. fat), 91mg chol., 634mg sod., 9g carb. (2g sugars, 1g fiber), 25g pro.
Diabetic exchanges: 3 lean meat, ½ starch, ½ fat.

TORTILLA PIE

My husband and I especially like this delicious dinner pie because it's lighter tasting than traditional lasagnas made with pasta. Even our two young daughters get excited when I bring it to the table.
—Lisa King, Caledonia, MI

....

Takes: 30 min. • **Makes:** 4 servings

- ½ lb. lean ground beef (90% lean)
- ½ cup chopped onion
- 2 garlic cloves, minced
- 1 tsp. chili powder
- ½ tsp. ground cumin
- 1 can (14½ oz.) Mexican diced tomatoes, drained
- ¾ cup reduced-fat ricotta cheese
- ¼ cup shredded part-skim mozzarella cheese
- 3 Tbsp. minced fresh cilantro, divided
- 4 whole wheat tortillas (8 in.)
- ½ cup shredded cheddar cheese

1. Preheat oven to 400°. In a large skillet, cook and crumble beef with onion and garlic over medium heat until no longer pink, 4-6 minutes. Stir in spices and tomatoes. Bring to a boil; remove from heat. In a small bowl, mix ricotta cheese, mozzarella cheese and 2 Tbsp. cilantro.
2. Place one tortilla in a 9-in. round baking pan coated with cooking spray. Layer with half of the meat sauce, one tortilla, ricotta mixture, another tortilla and remaining meat sauce. Top with the remaining tortilla; sprinkle with cheddar cheese and remaining cilantro.
3. Bake, covered, until heated through, 15-20 minutes.

1 serving: 356 cal., 14g fat (6g sat. fat), 65mg chol., 574mg sod., 32g carb. (7g sugars, 5g fiber), 25g pro.
Diabetic exchanges: 3 medium-fat meat, 2 starch.

TORTILLA PIE

TURKEY ROULADES

(PICTURED ON P. 171)

The filling in this recipe goes so well with turkey. I love the hint of lemon, and the savory combo of apples, mushrooms and spinach. The bread-crumb coating adds a nice crunch, too.
—Kari Wheaton, South Beloit, IL

....

Prep: 40 min. • **Bake:** 40 min.
Makes: 8 servings

- 1 cup diced peeled tart apple
- 1 cup chopped fresh mushrooms
- ½ cup finely chopped onion
- 2 tsp. olive oil
- 5 oz. frozen chopped spinach, thawed and squeezed dry
- 2 Tbsp. lemon juice
- 2 tsp. grated lemon zest
- ¾ tsp. salt, divided
  Pinch ground nutmeg
- 4 turkey breast tenderloins (8 oz. each)
- ¼ tsp. pepper
- 1 large egg, lightly beaten
- ½ cup seasoned bread crumbs

1. In a large skillet coated with cooking spray, saute the apple, mushrooms and onion in oil until tender. Remove from the heat; stir in the spinach, lemon juice, lemon zest, ¼ tsp. salt and nutmeg.
2. Make a lengthwise slit down center of each tenderloin to within ½ in. of bottom. Open tenderloins so they lie flat; cover with plastic wrap. Flatten meat to ¼-in. thickness. Remove plastic; sprinkle turkey with pepper and remaining salt.
3. Spread spinach mixture over the tenderloins to within 1 in. of edges. Roll up jelly-roll style, starting with a short side; tie with kitchen string. Place egg and bread crumbs in separate shallow bowls. Dip the roulades in egg, then roll in crumbs.
4. Place in an 11x7-in. baking pan coated with cooking spray. Bake, uncovered, at 375° until a thermometer reads 170°, 40-45 minutes. Let stand for 5 minutes before slicing.

½ roulade: 184 cal., 4g fat (1g sat. fat), 82mg chol., 405mg sod., 9g carb. (3g sugars, 1g fiber), 29g pro.
Diabetic exchanges: 3 lean meat, ½ starch.

MUSHROOM BROCCOLI PIZZA

TANGY PARMESAN TILAPIA

If you want fish with a gluten-free coating, this works beautifully! Some reduced-fat mayos may contain gluten, though, so check the label on yours to be sure.
—Deborah Purdue, Westland, MI

Takes: 15 min. • **Makes:** 4 servings

- ¼ cup grated Parmesan cheese
- 2 Tbsp. reduced-fat mayonnaise
- 1 Tbsp. butter, softened
- 1 Tbsp. lime juice
- ⅛ tsp. garlic powder
- ⅛ tsp. dried basil
- ⅛ tsp. pepper
- Dash onion powder
- 4 tilapia fillets (5 oz. each)
- ¼ tsp. salt

1. Preheat broiler. Combine the first eight ingredients.
2. Line a 15x10x1-in. baking pan with foil; coat foil with cooking spray. Place tilapia in pan; sprinkle with salt.
3. Broil 3-4 in. from heat 2-3 minutes per side. Spread cheese mixture over fillets. Broil until topping is golden brown and fish just begins to flake easily with a fork, 1-2 minutes.

1 fillet: 191 cal., 8g fat (4g sat. fat), 84mg chol., 359mg sod., 2g carb. (0 sugars, 0 fiber), 28g pro.
Diabetic exchanges: 4 lean meat, 1½ fat.

MUSHROOM BROCCOLI PIZZA

I wouldn't say I'm a vegetarian, but I do like meatless entrees. Since I enjoy gardening, I often cook with homegrown veggies, finding creative ways to use them up, like in this fresh, satisfying pizza.
—Kathleen Kelley, Roseburg, OR

Prep: 30 min. + rising • **Bake:** 15 min.
Makes: 6 slices

- 1 pkg. (¼ oz.) active dry yeast
- ¾ cup warm water (110° to 115°)
- 1 tsp. olive oil
- ½ tsp. sugar
- ½ cup whole wheat flour
- ½ tsp. salt
- 1½ cups all-purpose flour

TOPPINGS
- 1 Tbsp. olive oil
- 1 cup sliced fresh mushrooms
- ¼ cup chopped onion
- 4 garlic cloves, minced
- 3 cups broccoli florets
- 2 Tbsp. water
- ½ cup pizza sauce
- 4 plum tomatoes, sliced
- ¼ cup chopped fresh basil
- 1½ cups shredded part-skim mozzarella cheese
- ⅓ cup shredded Parmesan cheese

1. In a bowl, dissolve yeast in warm water. Add oil and sugar; mix well. Combine whole wheat flour and salt; stir into yeast mixture until smooth. Stir in enough all-purpose flour to form a soft dough.
2. Turn onto a floured surface; knead until smooth and elastic, 6-8 minutes. Place in a bowl coated with cooking spray, turning once to coat top. Cover; let rise in a warm place until doubled, about 1½ hours. Preheat oven to 425°.
3. Punch down dough; press onto a 12-in. pizza pan coated with cooking spray. Prick dough several times with a fork. Bake until edges of crust are light golden brown, 10-12 minutes.
4. In a nonstick skillet, heat oil over medium-high heat; saute mushrooms, onion and garlic until tender. Place broccoli and water in a microwave-safe bowl; microwave, covered, on high until broccoli is crisp-tender, about 2 minutes. Drain well.
5. Spread pizza sauce over crust. Top with mushroom mixture, tomatoes, broccoli, basil and cheeses. Bake until crust is golden brown and the cheese is melted, 12-14 minutes.

1 slice: 317 cal., 11g fat (5g sat. fat), 21mg chol., 558mg sod., 40g carb. (4g sugars, 4g fiber), 16g pro.
Diabetic exchanges: 2 starch, 2 medium-fat meat, 1 vegetable, ½ fat.

CREAMY SKINNY PASTA CASSEROLE

1⅔ cups: 445 cal., 13g fat (6g sat. fat), 78mg chol., 559mg sod., 49g carb. (6g sugars, 7g fiber), 33g pro.
* HEALTH TIP * Whole wheat pasta is a great way to get whole grains into your daily diet. If you're unaccustomed to its chewy texture, try using half whole wheat and half regular pasta.

MEXICAN-STYLE STUFFED PEPPERS

We've always liked stuffed peppers, but everyone is pleasantly surprised at this mildly spicy version. For convenience, you can assemble these pretty peppers ahead of time and bake them later.
—LaDonna Reed, Ponca City, OK

Prep: 20 min. • **Bake:** 50 min.
Makes: 6 servings

1 lb. lean ground beef (90% lean)
⅓ cup chopped onion
⅓ cup chopped celery
2 tsp. chili powder
¼ tsp. salt
1 Tbsp. canned chopped green chiles
1¼ cups salsa, divided
3 cups cooked rice
6 medium sweet red or green peppers
¼ cup water
1 cup shredded reduced-fat Mexican cheese blend

1. Preheat oven to 350°. In a large skillet, cook and crumble beef with onion and celery over medium-high heat until no longer pink, 5-7 minutes. Stir in the chili powder, salt, green chiles, 1 cup salsa and cooked rice.
2. Cut off and discard tops from peppers; remove seeds. Fill peppers with beef mixture. Place in a 13x9-in. baking dish coated with cooking spray. Add water to baking dish.
3. Bake, covered, until peppers are tender and the filling is heated through, 45-50 minutes. Top peppers with remaining salsa and cheese. Bake, uncovered, until cheese is melted, 2-3 minutes.

1 stuffed pepper: 322 calories, 11g fat (5g saturated fat), 57mg cholesterol, 506mg sodium, 33g carbohydrate (5g sugars, 3g fiber), 23g protein.
Diabetic exchanges: 3 lean meat, 2 starch.

CREAMY SKINNY PASTA CASSEROLE

Baked pasta is a favorite potluck dish, so I altered some of the ingredients in my traditional recipe to make it more calorie-friendly! Try it with ground beef, too.
—Andrea Bolden, Unionville, TN

Takes: 30 min. • **Makes:** 6 servings

12 oz. uncooked whole wheat penne pasta
1 lb. lean ground chicken
1 small onion, finely chopped
1 tsp. garlic powder, divided
1 tsp. Italian seasoning
½ tsp. salt
¼ tsp. pepper
1 can (14½ oz.) diced tomatoes, undrained
3 oz. reduced-fat cream cheese
½ cup reduced-fat sour cream
1 cup shredded part-skim mozzarella cheese, divided
Minced fresh parsley and crushed red pepper flakes, optional

1. Preheat oven to 400°. Cook pasta according to package directions for al dente. Drain, reserving ⅓ cup pasta water; return all to pot.
2. Meanwhile, in a large skillet, cook and crumble chicken with onion, ½ tsp. garlic powder and remaining seasonings over medium-high heat until no longer pink, 5-7 minutes. Stir in tomatoes; bring to a boil. Add to pasta; toss to combine. Transfer to a 13x9-in. baking dish coated with cooking spray.
3. Mix cream cheese, sour cream, ½ cup mozzarella cheese and remaining garlic powder. Drop mixture by tablespoonfuls over pasta. Sprinkle with remaining mozzarella cheese.
4. Bake, uncovered, until the cheese is melted, 8-10 minutes. If desired, sprinkle with parsley and pepper flakes.

MEXICAN-STYLE STUFFED PEPPERS

HONEY-ROASTED CHICKEN & ROOT VEGETABLES

HONEY-ROASTED CHICKEN & ROOT VEGETABLES

When my whole family comes over for dinner, I make a big platter of roast chicken with sweet potatoes, carrots and fennel. My dad leads the fan club.
—Kelly Ferguson, Conshohocken, PA

Prep: 25 min. • **Cook:** 40 min.
Makes: 6 servings

- 1 tsp. salt
- 1 tsp. pepper
- 1 tsp. minced fresh rosemary
- 1 tsp. minced fresh thyme
- 2 Tbsp. olive oil, divided
- 1 Tbsp. butter
- 6 boneless skinless chicken breast halves (6 oz. each)
- ½ cup white wine
- 3 Tbsp. honey, divided
- 3 peeled medium sweet potatoes, chopped
- 4 medium peeled carrots, chopped
- 2 medium fennel bulbs, chopped
- 2 cups chicken stock
- 3 bay leaves

1. Preheat oven to 375°. Combine salt, pepper, rosemary and thyme. In a large skillet, heat 1 Tbsp. olive oil and butter over medium-high heat. Sprinkle half the seasoning mixture over chicken breasts. Add to skillet; cook until golden brown, 2-3 minutes per side. Remove and set aside. Add the wine and 2 Tbsp. honey to pan; cook for 2-3 minutes, stirring to loosen browned bits.
2. Combine sweet potatoes, carrots and fennel in a microwave-safe bowl. Add remaining olive oil, seasonings and honey to vegetables; stir to combine. Microwave, covered, until potatoes are just tender, 10 minutes.
3. Transfer the vegetables to a shallow roasting pan. Add chicken stock, wine mixture and bay leaves; top vegetables with chicken. Roast until a thermometer inserted in chicken reads 165°, 25-30 minutes. Discard bay leaves. Serve with vegetables and sauce.

1 serving: 432 cal., 11g fat (3g sat. fat), 99mg chol., 543mg sod., 42g carb. (23g sugars, 6g fiber), 39g pro.
Diabetic exchanges: 5 lean meat, 3 starch, 1½ fat.

SWEET & SPICY PORK CHOPS

My husband used to come home from work before I did, and one night he threw together these amazing chops. We've followed his recipe ever since.
—Kathy Kirkland, Denham Springs, LA

Takes: 20 min. • **Makes:** 2 servings

- 2 Tbsp. brown sugar
- 1 Tbsp. finely chopped onion
- 1 to 1½ tsp. chili powder
- ½ tsp. garlic powder
- ½ tsp. prepared mustard
- 2 boneless pork loin chops (4 oz. each)
  Dash salt and pepper

1. Preheat broiler. In a small bowl, mix the first five ingredients.
2. Place chops on a broiler pan; sprinkle with salt and pepper. Broil 4 in. from heat 5 minutes. Turn; top with brown sugar mixture. Broil 4-5 minutes longer or until a thermometer reads 145°. Let stand for 5 minutes before serving.

1 pork chop: 212 cal., 7g fat (2g sat. fat), 55mg chol., 137mg sod., 15g carb. (14g sugars, 1g fiber), 22g pro.
Diabetic exchanges: 4 lean meat, 1 starch.

PHILLY CHEESESTEAK ROLLS

My light take on cheesesteak gets straight to the tender meat, creamy cheese and sweet and tangy veggies.
—Paige Day, North Augusta, SC

Prep: 30 min. • **Bake:** 15 min.
Makes: 4 servings

- ½ lb. sliced fresh mushrooms
- 1 medium onion, halved and sliced
- 1 small green pepper, cut into thin strips
- 1 beef top round steak (1 lb.)
- 4 wedges The Laughing Cow light Swiss cheese
- ¼ tsp. pepper
- 3 cups hot mashed potatoes

1. Preheat oven to 450°. Place a large skillet coated with cooking spray over medium-high heat. Add mushrooms, onion and green pepper; cook and stir until tender, 8-10 minutes. Remove from pan; cool slightly.

2. Cut steak into four pieces; pound with a meat mallet to ¼-in. thickness. Spread with cheese. Sprinkle with pepper; top with mushroom mixture. Roll up from a short side; secure with toothpicks. Place in a foil-lined 15x10x1-in. baking pan.

3. Bake rolls until the meat reaches desired doneness (for medium-rare, a thermometer should read 135°; medium, 140°; medium-well, 145°), 12-17 minutes. Let stand for 5 minutes before serving. Serve with mashed potatoes.

1 roll with ¾ cup mashed potatoes: 364 cal., 10g fat (3g sat. fat), 68mg chol., 822mg sod., 34g carb. (5g sugars, 4g fiber), 33g pro.
Diabetic exchanges: 4 lean meat, 2 starch, 1 vegetable.

ITALIAN HOT DISH
(PICTURED ON P. 170)

My husband had a poor perception of healthy food until he tried this meaty casserole. The combination of pasta, oregano, mushrooms and green peppers makes it a favorite in our house.
—Theresa Smith, Sheboygan, WI

Prep: 30 min. • **Bake:** 40 min.
Makes: 4 servings

- 1½ cups uncooked multigrain bow tie pasta (about 4 oz.)
- 1 lb. lean ground beef (90% lean)
- 1 cup sliced fresh mushrooms, divided
- ½ cup chopped onion
- ½ cup chopped green pepper
- 1 tsp. dried oregano
- ½ tsp. garlic powder
- ¼ tsp. onion powder
- ⅛ tsp. pepper
- 1 can (15 oz.) tomato sauce
- ½ cup shredded part-skim mozzarella cheese, divided
- 2 Tbsp. grated Parmesan cheese, divided

1. Preheat oven to 350°. Cook pasta according to package directions for al dente; drain.

2. Meanwhile, in a large skillet coated with cooking spray, cook and crumble beef with ½ cup mushrooms, onion and green pepper over medium-high heat until no longer pink, 5-7 minutes. Stir in seasonings and tomato sauce; bring to a boil. Reduce heat; simmer, covered, 15 minutes.

3. Place pasta in an 8-in. square baking dish coated with cooking spray. Top with meat sauce and remaining mushrooms. Sprinkle with ¼ cup mozzarella cheese and 1 Tbsp. Parmesan cheese.

4. Bake, covered, 35 minutes. Uncover; sprinkle with remaining cheeses. Bake until heated through and cheese is melted, 5-10 minutes.

1 serving: 394 cal., 15g fat (6g sat. fat), 82mg chol., 704mg sod., 32g carb. (5g sugars, 5g fiber), 34g pro.
Diabetic exchanges: 2 starch, 3 lean meat, 2 vegetable, ½ fat.

PHILLY CHEESESTEAK ROLLS

TERRIFIC TURKEY MEAT LOAF

TERRIFIC TURKEY MEAT LOAF

You'll love this moist, tender entree. Not only is it loaded with flavor, but it's low in carbohydrates and saturated fat.
—Wanda Bannister, New Bern, NC

Prep: 15 min. • **Bake:** 50 min.
Makes: 4 servings

- 1 large egg white, lightly beaten
- ½ cup oat bran
- ½ cup chopped green pepper
- ¼ cup finely chopped onion
- 3 Tbsp. ketchup
- 2 Tbsp. chopped ripe olives
- 1 Tbsp. Worcestershire sauce
- 1 garlic clove, minced
- ½ tsp. Dijon mustard
- ¼ tsp. celery salt
- ¼ tsp. dried marjoram
- ¼ tsp. rubbed sage
- ¼ tsp. pepper
- 1 lb. ground turkey

1. Preheat oven to 375°. In a large bowl, combine all ingredients except turkey. Add turkey; mix lightly but thoroughly. Pat into a loaf in an 11x7-in. baking dish coated with cooking spray.

2. Bake, uncovered, until a thermometer reads 165°, 50-60 minutes.

1 serving: 226 cal., 10g fat (2g sat. fat), 75mg chol., 381mg sod., 14g carb. (5g sugars, 3g fiber), 25g pro.
Diabetic exchanges: 3 lean meat, ½ starch.

PASTRY-TOPPED TURKEY CASSEROLE

My friends tell me I make the best potpie. Hearty and full-flavored, this comforting classic never lets on that it's also low in fat and a good source of fiber.
—Agnes Ward, Stratford, ON

Prep: 45 min. • **Bake:** 20 min. + standing
Makes: 6 servings

- 2 cups diced red potatoes
- 1 large onion, finely chopped
- 2 celery ribs, chopped
- 2 tsp. chicken bouillon granules
- ½ tsp. dried rosemary, crushed
- ¼ tsp. garlic powder
- ¼ tsp. dried thyme
- ⅛ tsp. pepper
- 1 can (14½ oz.) reduced-sodium chicken broth
- ½ cup water
- 3 Tbsp. all-purpose flour
- ⅔ cup fat-free evaporated milk
- 3 cups frozen mixed vegetables, thawed and drained
- 2 cups cubed cooked turkey breast

CRUST
- ¼ cup all-purpose flour
- ¼ cup whole wheat flour
- ½ tsp. baking powder
- ⅛ tsp. salt
- 4 Tbsp. fat-free milk, divided
- 1 Tbsp. canola oil
  Paprika

1. Preheat oven to 400°. Place the first 10 ingredients in a large saucepan; bring to a boil. Reduce heat; simmer, covered, until potatoes are tender, 10-15 minutes.

2. Whisk flour and evaporated milk until smooth; stir into pan. Bring to a boil, stirring constantly; cook and stir until thickened, about 2 minutes. Add frozen vegetables and turkey; heat through, stirring occasionally. Transfer to an ungreased 8-in. square baking dish.

3. For crust, whisk together flours, baking powder and salt; stir in 3 Tbsp. milk and oil. On a lightly floured surface, roll dough to ⅛-in. thickness; cut into short strips. Arrange over filling. Brush strips with remaining milk; sprinkle with paprika.

4. Bake, uncovered, until filling is bubbly, 20-25 minutes. Let stand 10 minutes before serving.

1 serving: 280 cal., 4g fat (1g sat. fat), 39mg chol., 696mg sod., 38g carb. (9g sugars, 6g fiber), 23g pro.
Diabetic exchanges: 2 starch, 2 lean meat, 1 vegetable, ½ fat.

PASTRY-TOPPED
TURKEY CASSEROLE

PEPPERED BEEF TENDERLOIN ROAST

A pepper rub gives this delicious beef roast a bit of a zippy flavor. It takes just minutes to prepare, and the meat slices well. Lining the baking pan with foil makes it a breeze to clean up, too.
—Denise Bitner, Reedsville, PA

Prep: 10 min. • **Bake:** 40 min. + standing
Makes: 12 servings

- 3 Tbsp. coarsely ground pepper
- 2 Tbsp. olive oil
- 1 Tbsp. grated lemon zest
- 2 garlic cloves, minced
- 1 tsp. salt
- 1 beef tenderloin roast (3 to 4 lbs.)

1. Preheat oven to 400°. Mix the first five ingredients.
2. Place roast on a rack in a roasting pan; rub with pepper mixture. Roast until desired doneness (for medium-rare, a thermometer should read 135°; medium, 140°), 40-60 minutes. Remove roast from oven; tent with foil. Let stand 15 minutes before slicing.

3 oz. cooked beef: 188 cal., 9g fat (3g sat. fat), 49mg chol., 197mg sod., 1g carb. (0 sugars, 1g fiber), 24g pro.
Diabetic exchanges: 3 lean meat, ½ fat.

HORSERADISH-CRUSTED TURKEY TENDERLOINS

HORSERADISH-CRUSTED TURKEY TENDERLOINS

This zesty and delicious low-carb entree won a recipe contest and was featured on the menu at one of our local restaurants.
—Ellen Cross, Hubbardsville, NY

Prep: 20 min. • **Bake:** 15 min.
Makes: 4 servings

- 2 Tbsp. reduced-fat mayonnaise
- 2 Tbsp. prepared horseradish
- ½ cup soft bread crumbs
- 1 green onion, chopped
- 2 Tbsp. minced fresh parsley
- 1 lb. turkey breast tenderloins

SAUCE
- ¼ cup reduced-fat mayonnaise
- ¼ cup fat-free plain yogurt
- 2 Tbsp. fat-free milk
- 1 Tbsp. prepared horseradish
- 1 Tbsp. Dijon mustard
- ¼ tsp. paprika

1. Preheat oven to 425°. Mix mayonnaise and horseradish. In a shallow bowl, toss the bread crumbs with green onion and parsley. Spread tenderloins with the mayonnaise mixture; dip in the crumb mixture to coat. Place in a greased 15x10x1-in. pan.
2. Bake until a thermometer reads 165°, 12-15 minutes. Let stand for 5 minutes before slicing.
3. Mix sauce ingredients. Serve with the turkey.
Note: To make soft bread crumbs, tear bread into pieces and place in a food processor or blender. Cover and pulse until crumbs form. One slice of bread yields ½-¾ cup crumbs.

1 serving: 230 cal., 9g fat (1g sat. fat), 53mg chol., 386mg sod., 8g carb. (3g sugars, 1g fiber), 30g pro.
Diabetic exchanges: ½ starch, 3 lean meat, 2 fat.

ZUCCHINI LASAGNA

I plant zucchini every year, and we always seem to have more than we can use! This recipe is a particularly delicious way to use our abundant crop.

—Charlotte McDaniel, Williamsville, IL

....

Prep: 20 min. • **Bake:** 40 min. + standing
Makes: 6 servings

- 1 lb. lean ground beef (90% lean)
- ¼ cup chopped onion
- ½ tsp. dried oregano
- ½ tsp. dried basil
- ¼ tsp. salt
- ¼ tsp. pepper
- 1 can (15 oz.) tomato sauce
- 1 large egg, lightly beaten
- 1 cup 2% cottage cheese
- 4 medium zucchini (about 1¾ lbs.)
- 3 Tbsp. all-purpose flour
- 1 cup shredded part-skim mozzarella cheese
  Additional shredded mozzarella cheese, optional

1. Preheat 375°. In large skillet, cook and crumble beef with onion over medium-high heat until no longer pink, 5-7 minutes. Stir in seasonings and tomato sauce. Bring to boil; simmer, uncovered, 5 minutes. In a bowl, mix egg and cottage cheese.

2. Trim ends of zucchini; cut lengthwise into ¼-in.-thick slices. Layer half of the slices in a 13x9-in. baking dish coated with cooking spray; dust with half of the flour. Top with cottage cheese mixture and half of the meat sauce. Add remaining zucchini; dust with remaining flour. Spread with remaining meat sauce; sprinkle with 1 cup mozzarella cheese.

3. Bake, uncovered, until heated through, about 40 minutes. If desired, sprinkle with additional cheese. Let stand 10 minutes before serving.

1 serving: 273 cal., 13g fat (5g sat. fat), 92mg chol., 725mg sod., 14g carb. (6g sugars, 3g fiber), 27g pro.
Diabetic exchanges: 3 lean meat, 1 starch, 1 fat.

LAMB WITH MINT SALSA

This flavorful entree is well-seasoned with an herb rub of basil, garlic, rosemary and thyme. Tender slices of meat are served with a refreshing salsa that will have even non-lamb lovers licking their lips.

—*Taste of Home* Test Kitchen

....

Prep: 15 min. + chilling • **Bake:** 20 min.
Makes: 8 servings (2 cups salsa)

- 5 tsp. olive oil
- 2 garlic cloves, minced
- 1 tsp. each dried basil, thyme and rosemary, crushed
- ½ tsp. salt
- ¼ tsp. pepper
- 2 racks of lamb (8 ribs each)

MINT SALSA
- 1 cup minced fresh mint
- 1 small cucumber, peeled, seeded and chopped
- ½ cup seeded chopped tomato
- ⅓ cup finely chopped onion
- ⅓ cup chopped sweet yellow pepper
- 1 jalapeno pepper, seeded and chopped
- 3 Tbsp. lemon juice
- 2 Tbsp. sugar
- 2 garlic cloves, minced
- ¾ tsp. ground ginger
- ¼ tsp. salt

1. In a small bowl, combine the oil, garlic and seasonings. Rub over lamb. Place in a roasting pan; cover and refrigerate for 1 hour. In a bowl, combine the salsa ingredients; cover and refrigerate until serving.

2. Bake lamb, uncovered, at 425° for 20-30 minutes or until meat reaches desired doneness (for medium-rare, a thermometer should read 135°; medium, 140°; medium-well, 145°). Cover loosely with foil and let stand for 5-10 minutes before slicing. Serve with mint salsa.

Note: Wear disposable gloves when cutting hot peppers; the oils can burn skin. Avoid touching your face.

2 lamb chops with ¼ cup salsa: 184 cal., 10g fat (3g sat. fat), 49mg chol., 270mg sod., 7g carb. (4g sugars, 1g fiber), 15g pro.
Diabetic exchanges: 2 lean meat, ½ starch, ½ fat.

ZUCCHINI LASAGNA

ROAST PORK WITH APPLES & ONIONS

ROAST PORK WITH APPLES & ONIONS

The sweetness of the apples and onions really complements roast pork. With its crisp skin and melt-in-your-mouth flavor, this is my family's favorite weekend dinner.
—Lily Julow, Lawrenceville, GA

Prep: 30 min. • **Bake:** 45 min. + standing
Makes: 8 servings

- 1 boneless pork loin roast (2 lbs.)
- ¼ tsp. salt
- ¼ tsp. pepper
- 1 Tbsp. olive oil
- 3 large Golden Delicious apples, cut into 1-in. wedges
- 2 large onions, cut into ¾-in. wedges
- 5 garlic cloves, peeled
- 1 Tbsp. minced fresh rosemary or 1 tsp. dried rosemary, crushed

1. Preheat oven to 350°. Sprinkle roast with salt and pepper. In a large nonstick skillet, heat oil over medium heat; brown roast on all sides. Transfer to a roasting pan coated with cooking spray. Place apples, onions and garlic around roast; sprinkle with rosemary.

2. Roast until a thermometer inserted in pork reads 145°, 45-55 minutes, turning apples, onion and garlic once. Remove from oven; tent with foil. Let stand for 10 minutes before slicing roast. Serve with apple mixture.

1 serving: 210 cal., 7g fat (2g sat. fat), 57mg chol., 109mg sod., 14g carb. (9g sugars, 2g fiber), 23g pro.
Diabetic exchanges: 3 lean meat, 1 starch, ½ fat.

WHOLE WHEAT VEGGIE PIZZA

A wonderful crust layered with herbed tomato sauce and toppings encourages my family of six to dig right in to this low-fat main course.
—Denise Warner, Red Lodge, MT

Prep: 40 min. + rising • **Bake:** 20 min.
Makes: 2 pizzas (6 slices each)

- ½ cup whole wheat flour
- 2 pkg. (¼ oz. each) quick-rise yeast
- 1 tsp. garlic powder
- ½ tsp. salt
- 2½ cups all-purpose flour
- 1 cup water
- 2 Tbsp. olive oil

SAUCE
- 1 can (14½ oz.) diced tomatoes, undrained
- 1 Tbsp. minced fresh parsley
- 1½ tsp. sugar
- 1½ tsp. Italian seasoning
- 1½ tsp. dried basil
- ½ tsp. garlic powder
- ¼ tsp. pepper

TOPPINGS
- 1 tsp. olive oil
- 1 cup chopped zucchini
- 1 cup sliced fresh mushrooms
- ½ cup chopped green or red pepper
- ¼ cup chopped onion
- 1¼ cups shredded part-skim mozzarella cheese

1. In a large bowl, mix first four ingredients and 1 cup all-purpose flour. In a small saucepan, heat water and oil to 120°-130°. Add to dry ingredients; beat on medium speed 3 minutes. Stir in enough remaining flour to form a soft dough.

2. Turn onto a floured surface; knead until smooth and elastic, about 5 minutes. Place in a greased bowl, turning once to grease the top. Cover and let rise in a warm place until doubled, about 30 minutes.

3. In a small saucepan, bring the sauce ingredients to a boil. Reduce heat; simmer, uncovered, until slightly thickened, 15-18 minutes, stirring occasionally. Remove from heat.

4. Preheat oven to 400°. Punch down dough. On a lightly floured surface, divide dough in half and roll each into a 12-in. circle. Place on two greased 12-in. pizza pans; prick with a fork. Bake until lightly browned, 8-10 minutes.

5. Meanwhile, in a skillet, heat oil over medium-high heat; saute vegetables until zucchini is crisp-tender. Spread crusts with sauce; top with vegetables and cheese. Bake until cheese is melted, 12-15 minutes.

1 slice: 190 cal., 6g fat (2g sat. fat), 8mg chol., 234mg sod., 28g carb. (3g sugars, 3g fiber), 7g pro.
Diabetic exchanges: 1½ starch, ½ vegetable, ½ fat.

WHOLE WHEAT VEGGIE PIZZA

BAKED BUFFALO CHICKEN

When I make this tangy chicken, I have to double the recipe because it disappears so quickly. Better to have leftovers, especially since they make great salads and sandwiches.
—Beth Zimmerman, Willingboro, NJ

Prep: 20 min. + marinating • **Bake:** 25 min.
Makes: 4 servings

- ¾ cup Buffalo wing sauce, divided
- 4 boneless skinless chicken breast halves (6 oz. each)
- ¾ cup all-purpose flour
- ¾ tsp. dried tarragon
- ½ tsp. pepper
- 1¼ cups panko (Japanese) bread crumbs

1. Pour 5 Tbsp. wing sauce into a shallow dish. Add chicken breasts and turn to coat. Let stand 15 minutes or refrigerate, covered, up to 24 hours.
2. Preheat oven to 400°. Drain chicken, discarding marinade. In a shallow bowl, mix flour, tarragon and pepper. Place bread crumbs and remaining wing sauce in separate shallow bowls. Dip chicken in flour mixture to coat all sides; shake off excess. Dip in wing sauce, then in bread crumbs, patting to help coating adhere.
3. Place chicken on a rack in a 15x10x1-in. baking pan. Bake 25-30 minutes or until a thermometer reads 165°.

1 chicken breast half : 277 cal., 5g fat (1g sat. fat), 94mg chol., 811mg sod., 18g carb. (1g sugars, 1g fiber), 37g pro.
Diabetic exchanges: 5 lean meat, 1 starch.

SALMON WITH HORSERADISH PISTACHIO CRUST

SALMON WITH HORSERADISH PISTACHIO CRUST

Impress everyone at your table with this elegant but easy salmon that's delicious and nutritious. You can substitute green onions for shallots if you like.
—Linda Press Wolfe, Cross River, NY

Takes: 30 min. • **Makes:** 6 servings

- 6 salmon fillets (4 oz. each)
- ⅓ cup sour cream
- ⅔ cup dry bread crumbs
- ⅔ cup chopped pistachios
- ½ cup minced shallots
- 2 Tbsp. olive oil
- 1 to 2 Tbsp. prepared horseradish
- 1 Tbsp. snipped fresh dill or 1 tsp. dill weed
- ½ tsp. grated lemon or orange zest
- ¼ tsp. crushed red pepper flakes
- 1 garlic clove, minced

Preheat oven to 350°. Place salmon, skin side down, in an ungreased 15x10x1-in.

baking pan. Spread sour cream over each fillet. Combine remaining ingredients. Pat crumb-nut mixture onto tops of salmon fillets, pressing to help coating adhere. Bake until fish just begins to flake easily with a fork, 12-15 minutes.

1 salmon fillet: 376 cal., 25g fat (5g sat. fat), 60mg chol., 219mg sod., 15g carb. (3g sugars, 2g fiber), 24g pro.
Diabetic exchanges: 3 lean meat, 2 fat.

DID YOU KNOW?

Wild salmon is 20% leaner than farm-raised fish, and it's higher in heart-healthy omega-3 fatty acids. Some people prefer its flavor over farm-raised fish, too. Fresh wild salmon is available from May through October, as the different species travel upstream to spawn.

ROSEMARY TURKEY BREAST

(PICTURED ON P. 170)

I season turkey with a blend of rosemary, garlic and paprika. Because I rub half of the mixture directly on the meat under the skin, I can remove the skin before serving and not lose any of the flavor. The result is an entree that's lower in fat, yet delicious—the perfect centerpiece for holiday meals.

—Dorothy Pritchett, Wills Point, TX

Prep: 10 min. • **Bake:** 1½ hours + standing
Makes: 15 servings

- 2 Tbsp. olive oil
- 8 to 10 garlic cloves, peeled
- 3 Tbsp. chopped fresh rosemary or 3 tsp. dried rosemary, crushed
- 1 tsp. salt
- 1 tsp. paprika
- ½ tsp. coarsely ground pepper
- 1 bone-in turkey breast (5 lbs.)

1. In a food processor, combine the oil, garlic, rosemary, salt, paprika and pepper; cover and process until garlic is coarsely chopped.

2. With your fingers, carefully loosen the skin from both sides of turkey breast. Spread half of the garlic mixture over the meat under the skin. Smooth skin over meat and secure to underside of breast with toothpicks. Spread remaining garlic mixture over turkey skin.

3. Place turkey on a rack in a shallow roasting pan. Bake, uncovered, at 325° for 1½-2 hours or until a thermometer reads 170°. Let stand for 15 minutes before slicing. Discard toothpicks.

4 oz. cooked turkey: 148 cal., 3g fat (0 sat. fat), 78mg chol., 207mg sod., 1g carb. (0 sugars, 0 fiber), 29g pro.
Diabetic exchanges: 4 lean meat.

★ ★ ★ ★ ★ **READER REVIEW**

"Great flavor, moist, simple and delicious! A winner!"

CYNANDTOM TASTEOFHOME.COM

BLACK BEAN & RICE ENCHILADAS

I love Mexican food, and I'm always looking for ways to make it more healthy. I renovated a dish that I have enjoyed in restaurants to suit my taste and lifestyle.
—Christie Ladd, Mechanicsburg, PA

Prep: 40 min. • **Bake:** 30 min.
Makes: 8 servings

- 1 Tbsp. olive oil
- 1 green pepper, chopped
- 1 medium onion, chopped
- 3 garlic cloves, minced
- 1 can (15 oz.) black beans, rinsed and drained
- 1 can (14½ oz.) diced tomatoes and green chiles
- ¼ cup picante sauce
- 1 Tbsp. chili powder
- 1 tsp. ground cumin
- ¼ tsp. crushed red pepper flakes
- 2 cups cooked brown rice
- 8 flour tortillas (6 in.), warmed
- 1 cup salsa
- 1 cup shredded reduced-fat cheddar cheese
- 3 Tbsp. chopped fresh cilantro leaves

1. Preheat oven to 350°. In a large nonstick skillet, heat oil over medium heat. Add green pepper, onion and garlic; saute until tender. Add next six ingredients; bring to a boil. Reduce heat; simmer, uncovered, until heated through. Add the rice; cook 5 minutes longer.

2. Spoon a rounded ½ cup of rice mixture down center of each tortilla. Fold sides over filling and roll up. Place seam side down in a 13x9-in. baking dish coated with cooking spray. Spoon remaining rice mixture along sides of dish. Top tortillas with salsa. Bake, covered, for 25 minutes. Uncover; sprinkle with cheese. Bake until cheese is melted, 2-3 minutes longer. Sprinkle with cilantro before serving.

1 enchilada: 279 cal., 8g fat (2g sat. fat), 10mg chol., 807mg sod., 39g carb. (4g sugars, 5g fiber), 11g pro.
Diabetic exchanges: 2½ starch, 1 lean meat, 1 vegetable.

BLACK BEAN &
RICE ENCHILADAS

FISH TACOS WITH BERRY SALSA

FISH TACOS WITH BERRY SALSA

I dreamed up this dish while lying in bed one night. I wasn't sure how the recipe would turn out, but when I tried it, I was so proud to call it mine. If you can't find jicama, just substitute a tart apple.

—Emily Rigsbee, Bloomington, IN

Takes: 30 min. • **Makes:** 4 servings

- 1 cup chopped peeled jicama
- 1 cup chopped fresh strawberries
- 1 jalapeno pepper, seeded and finely chopped
- 3 Tbsp. minced fresh cilantro
- 2 Tbsp. lime juice
- ½ tsp. salt, divided
- 4 tilapia fillets (6 oz. each)
- ¼ tsp. pepper
- 8 corn tortillas (6 in.)
- ½ cup crumbled cotija cheese

1. Preheat broiler. For salsa, in a small bowl, combine the first five ingredients; stir in ¼ tsp. salt.
2. Place fillets on a foil-lined 15x10x1-in. baking pan; sprinkle with pepper and remaining salt. Broil 4-6 in. from heat until fish just begins to flake easily with a fork, 5-7 minutes. Serve fish in tortillas with salsa and cheese.

Note: Wear disposable gloves when cutting hot peppers; the oils can burn skin. Avoid touching your face.

2 tacos: 329 cal., 8g fat (3g sat. fat), 98mg chol., 599mg sod., 29g carb. (3g sugars, 6g fiber), 38g pro.

Diabetic exchanges: 5 lean meat, 2 starch.

* HEALTH TIP * Tilapia is low in calories, rich in high-quality protein and a good source of many B vitamins.

ORANGE-GLAZED PORK LOIN

ORANGE-GLAZED PORK LOIN

Here's one of the best pork recipes I've ever tried. My family looks forward to this roast for dinner, and guests always want the recipe. The flavorful rub and a glaze sparked with orange juice are outstanding on pork chops, too.

—Lynnette Miete, Alna, ME

Prep: 10 min. • **Bake:** 1 hour 20 min. + standing • **Makes:** 16 servings

- 1 tsp. salt
- 1 garlic clove, minced
- 2 to 3 fresh thyme sprigs or ¼ tsp. dried thyme
- ¼ tsp. ground ginger
- ¼ tsp. pepper
- 1 boneless pork loin roast (5 lbs.)

GLAZE

- 1 cup orange juice
- ¼ cup packed brown sugar
- 1 Tbsp. Dijon mustard
- ⅓ cup cold water
- 1 Tbsp. cornstarch

1. Preheat oven to 350°. Combine the first five ingredients; rub over roast. Place fat side up on a rack in a shallow roasting pan. Bake, uncovered, for 1 hour.
2. Meanwhile, in a saucepan over medium heat, combine orange juice, brown sugar and mustard. In a small bowl, mix water and cornstarch until smooth. Add to the orange juice mixture. Bring to a boil; cook and stir 2 minutes. Reserve 1 cup glaze for serving; brush half of remaining glaze over the roast.
3. Bake until a thermometer reads 145°, 20-40 minutes longer, brushing the pork occasionally with remaining glaze. Let stand 10 minutes before slicing. Reheat reserved glaze; serve with roast.

4 oz. cooked pork with 1 Tbsp. glaze: 199 cal., 7g fat (2g sat. fat), 71mg chol., 212mg sod., 6g carb. (5g sugars, 0 fiber), 28g pro.

Diabetic exchanges: 4 lean meat, ½ starch.

CIDER-GLAZED PORK TENDERLOIN

This super easy recipe is full of the fall flavors all of us love. The natural sweetness of the maple syrup really shines through.
—Susan Stetzel, Gainesville, NY

Takes: 30 min. • **Makes:** 4 servings

- 1 pork tenderloin (1 lb.)
- ¼ tsp. salt
- ½ tsp. pepper, divided
- 1 Tbsp. olive oil
- ¾ cup apple cider or juice
- ¼ cup maple syrup
- 2 Tbsp. cider vinegar

1. Preheat oven to 425°. Cut tenderloin in half to fit skillet; sprinkle with salt and ¼ tsp. pepper. In a large skillet, heat oil over medium-high heat; brown pork on all sides. Transfer to a 15x10x1-in. pan. Roast until a thermometer reads 145°, 12-15 minutes.
2. Meanwhile, in same skillet, bring cider, syrup, vinegar and remaining pepper to a boil, stirring to loosen browned bits from pan. Cook, uncovered, until mixture is reduced to a glaze consistency, about 5 minutes.
3. Remove pork from oven; let stand 5 minutes before slicing. Serve with glaze.

3 oz. cooked pork with 1 Tbsp. glaze: 239 cal., 7g fat (2g sat. fat), 64mg chol., 200mg sod., 19g carb. (17g sugars, 0 fiber), 23g pro.
Diabetic exchanges: 3 lean meat, 1 starch, 1 fat.

VEGETABLE & BEEF STUFFED RED PEPPERS

VEGETABLE & BEEF STUFFED RED PEPPERS

I love to make this stuffed pepper recipe. It's one of the few ways I can get my husband to eat veggies. Make it meatless by replacing the beef with eggplant and adding more vegetables like mushrooms or squash. You can also replace the rice with barley, couscous or even orzo.
—Jennifer Zimmerman, Avondale, AZ

Prep: 35 min. • **Bake:** 40 min.
Makes: 6 servings

- 6 medium sweet red peppers
- 1 lb. lean ground beef (90% lean)
- 1 Tbsp. olive oil
- 1 medium zucchini, chopped
- 1 medium yellow summer squash, chopped
- 1 medium onion, finely chopped
- ⅓ cup finely chopped green pepper
- 2 cups coarsely chopped fresh spinach
- 4 garlic cloves, minced
- 1 cup ready-to-serve long grain and wild rice
- 1 can (8 oz.) tomato sauce
- ½ cup shredded part-skim mozzarella cheese
- ¼ tsp. salt
- 3 slices reduced-fat provolone cheese, halved

1. Preheat oven to 350°. Cut and discard tops from red peppers; remove seeds. In a 6-qt. stockpot, cook peppers in boiling water until crisp-tender, 3-5 minutes; drain and rinse in cold water.
2. In a large skillet, cook the beef over medium heat until no longer pink, breaking into crumbles, 6-8 minutes. Remove with a slotted spoon; pour off the drippings.
3. In same pan, heat oil over medium heat; saute zucchini, yellow squash, onion and green pepper until tender, 4-5 minutes. Add spinach and garlic; cook and stir until wilted, about 1 minute. Stir in cooked beef, rice, tomato sauce, mozzarella cheese and salt.
4. Place red peppers in a greased 8-in. square baking dish. Fill with meat mixture. Bake, covered, until peppers are tender, 35-40 minutes. Top with provolone cheese; bake, uncovered, until cheese is melted, about 5 minutes.

1 stuffed pepper: 287 cal., 13g fat (5g sat. fat), 57mg chol., 555mg sod., 21g carb. (8g sugars, 5g fiber), 23g pro.
Diabetic exchanges: 3 lean meat, 2 vegetable, 1 fat, ½ starch.

COD & ASPARAGUS BAKE

The lemon pulls this flavorful and healthy dish together. You can also use grated Parmesan cheese instead of Romano.
—Thomas Faglon, Somerset, NJ

Takes: 30 min. • **Makes:** 4 servings

    4   cod fillets (4 oz. each)
    1   lb. fresh thin asparagus, trimmed
    1   pint cherry tomatoes, halved
    2   Tbsp. lemon juice
    1½ tsp. grated lemon zest
    ¼   cup grated Romano cheese

1. Preheat oven to 375°. Place cod and asparagus in a 15x10x1-in. baking pan brushed with oil. Add tomatoes, cut side down. Brush fish with lemon juice; sprinkle with lemon zest. Sprinkle the fish and vegetables with Romano cheese. Bake until fish just begins to flake easily with a fork, about 12 minutes.

2. Remove baking pan from oven; preheat broiler. Broil cod mixture 3-4 in. from the heat until vegetables are lightly browned, 2-3 minutes.

1 serving: 141 cal., 3g fat (2g sat. fat), 45mg chol., 184mg sod., 6g carb. (3g sugars, 2g fiber), 23g pro.

Diabetic exchanges: 3 lean meat, 1 vegetable.

TEST KITCHEN TIP

If asparagus isn't in season, fresh green beans make a great substitution and will cook in about the same amount of time.

COD & ASPARAGUS BAKE

SEASONED CHICKEN STRIPS

These strips are designed for kids, but tasty enough for company. The tender strips are moist and juicy and would also be great on a salad.
—Becky Oliver, Fairplay, CO

Takes: 25 min. • **Makes:** 4 servings

    ⅓   cup egg substitute or 1 large egg
    1   Tbsp. prepared mustard
    1   garlic clove, minced
    ¾   cup dry bread crumbs
    2   tsp. dried basil
    1   tsp. paprika
    ½   tsp. salt
    ¼   tsp. pepper
    1   lb. chicken tenderloins

1. Preheat oven to 400°. In a shallow bowl, whisk together egg substitute, mustard and garlic. In another shallow bowl, toss bread crumbs with seasonings. Dip chicken in egg mixture, then coat with crumb mixture.

2. Place on a baking sheet coated with cooking spray. Bake until exterior is golden brown and chicken is no longer pink, 10-15 minutes.

3 oz. cooked chicken: 194 cal., 2g fat (0 sat. fat), 56mg chol., 518mg sod., 14g carb. (1g sugars, 1g fiber), 31g pro.

Diabetic exchanges: 3 lean meat, 1 starch.

LENTIL LOAF

This lentil loaf is so flavorful, you won't miss the meat. And it's packed with fiber and nutrients.
—Tracy Fleming, Phoenix, AZ

....

Prep: 35 min. • **Bake:** 45 min. + standing
Makes: 6 servings

- ¾ cup brown lentils, rinsed
- 1 can (14½ oz.) vegetable broth
- 1 Tbsp. olive oil
- 1¾ cups shredded carrots
- 1 cup finely chopped onion
- 1 cup chopped fresh mushrooms
- 2 Tbsp. minced fresh basil or 2 tsp. dried basil
- 1 Tbsp. minced fresh parsley
- 1 cup shredded part-skim mozzarella cheese
- ½ cup cooked brown rice
- 1 large egg
- 1 large egg white
- ½ tsp. salt
- ½ tsp. garlic powder
- ¼ tsp. pepper
- 2 Tbsp. tomato paste
- 2 Tbsp. water

1. Place lentils and broth in a small saucepan; bring to a boil. Reduce the heat; simmer, covered, until tender, about 30 minutes.
2. Preheat oven to 350°. Line a 9x5-in. loaf pan with parchment, letting the ends extend up the sides. Coat paper with cooking spray.
3. In a large skillet, heat oil over medium heat. Add carrots, onion and mushrooms; saute until tender, about 10 minutes. Stir in herbs. Transfer to a large bowl; cool slightly.
4. Add cheese, rice, egg, egg white, seasonings and lentils to vegetables; mix well. Mix tomato paste and water; spread over loaf.
5. Bake until a thermometer inserted into the center reads 160°, 45-50 minutes. Let stand 10 minutes before slicing.

1 slice: 213 cal., 5g fat (3g sat. fat), 43mg chol., 580mg sod., 29g carb. (5g sugars, 5g fiber), 14g pro.
Diabetic exchanges: 2 lean meat, 1½ starch, 1 vegetable, ½ fat.

THAI SALMON BROWN RICE BOWLS

THAI SALMON BROWN RICE BOWLS

This speedy salmon recipe couldn't be any easier. The ginger-sesame dressing saves times and boosts the flavor of this healthy dish.
—Naylet LaRochelle, Miami, FL

....

Takes: 15 min. • **Makes:** 4 servings

- 4 salmon fillets (4 oz. each)
- ½ cup sesame ginger salad dressing, divided
- 3 cups hot cooked brown rice
- ½ cup chopped fresh cilantro
- ¼ tsp. salt
- 1 cup julienned carrot
  Thinly sliced red cabbage, optional

1. Preheat oven to 400°. Place salmon in a foil-lined 15x10x1-in. pan; brush with ¼ cup dressing. Bake until fish just begins to flake easily with a fork, 8-10 minutes. Meanwhile, toss rice with cilantro and salt.
2. To serve, divide rice mixture among four bowls. Top with salmon, carrots and, if desired, red cabbage. Drizzle with the remaining dressing.

1 serving: 486 cal., 21g fat (4g sat. fat), 57mg chol., 532mg sod., 49g carb. (8g sugars, 3g fiber), 24g pro.

TEST KITCHEN TIP

People seem to either love or hate cilantro. If it's not your favorite, go ahead and omit it. Just add some chopped fresh parsley instead.

LENTIL LOAF

CHICKEN TOSTADA CUPS

Several years ago I tried a version of these cups at a restaurant in Santa Fe, and I wanted to give it my own spin. These are great for gatherings where you can let everyone add their own favorite toppings.
—Marla Clark, Moriarty, NM

Prep: 25 min. • **Bake:** 15 min.
Makes: 6 servings

- 12 corn tortillas (6 in.), warmed
  Cooking spray
- 2 cups shredded rotisserie chicken
- 1 cup salsa
- 1 can (16 oz.) refried beans
- 1 cup shredded reduced-fat Mexican cheese blend
  Optional toppings: shredded lettuce, reduced-fat sour cream, sliced ripe olives, sliced green onions, chopped cilantro, sliced radishes, diced avocado and additional salsa

1. Preheat oven to 425°. Press warm tortillas into 12 muffin cups coated with cooking spray, pleating sides as needed. Spritz tortillas with additional cooking spray.

2. Bake until lightly browned, 5-7 minutes. Toss chicken with salsa. Layer each cup with beans, chicken mixture and cheese.

3. Bake until heated through, 9-11 minutes. Serve with toppings as desired.

2 tostada cups: 338 cal., 11g fat (4g sat. fat), 52mg chol., 629mg sod., 35g carb. (2g sugars, 6g fiber), 25g pro.

Diabetic exchanges: 3 lean meat, 2 starch, 1 fat.

PEPPER-CRUSTED PORK TENDERLOIN

Guests will be impressed by this elegant entree and its golden crumb coating with peppery pizazz. The meat slices up so moist and tender, you can serve it without sauce and still enjoy a succulent main dish.
—Ellen Riley, Murfreesboro, TN

Prep: 25 min. • **Bake:** 30 min.
Makes: 6 servings

- 3 Tbsp. Dijon mustard
- 1 Tbsp. buttermilk
- 2 tsp. minced fresh thyme
- 1 to 2 tsp. coarsely ground pepper
- ¼ tsp. salt
- 2 pork tenderloins (¾ lb. each)
- ⅔ cup soft bread crumbs

1. Preheat oven to 425°. Mix first five ingredients. To make a double roast, arrange tenderloins side by side, thick end to thin end; tie together with kitchen string at 1½-in. intervals. Place on a rack in a 15x10x1-in. pan. Spread with mustard mixture; cover with the bread crumbs, pressing to adhere.

2. Bake until a thermometer inserted in pork reads 145°, 30-40 minutes. (Tent loosely with foil if needed to prevent overbrowning.) Let stand 5 minutes. Cut into slices; remove string before serving.

Note: To make soft bread crumbs, tear bread into pieces and place in a food processor or blender. Cover and pulse until crumbs form. One slice of bread yields ½-¾ cup crumbs.

1 serving: 155 cal., 4g fat (1g sat. fat), 64mg chol., 353mg sod., 3g carb. (0 sugars, 0 fiber), 23g pro.

Diabetic exchanges: 3 lean meat.

PEPPER-CRUSTED PORK TENDERLOIN

ROASTED BUTTERNUT SQUASH TACOS

(PICTURED ON P. 171)

Spicy butternut squash makes a great base for vegetarian tacos. I'm always looking for quick and nutritious weeknight dinners like this for my family.
—Elisabeth Larsen, Pleasant Grove, UT

Prep: 10 min. • **Bake:** 30 min.
Makes: 6 servings

- 2 Tbsp. canola oil
- 1 Tbsp. chili powder
- ½ tsp. ground cumin
- ½ tsp. ground coriander
- ½ tsp. salt
- ¼ tsp. cayenne pepper
- 1 medium butternut squash (3 to 4 lbs.), peeled and cut into ½-in. pieces
- 12 corn tortillas (6 in.), warmed
- 1 cup crumbled queso fresco or feta cheese
- 1 medium ripe avocado, peeled and sliced thin
- ¼ cup diced red onion
  Pico de gallo, optional

1. Preheat oven to 425°. Combine first six ingredients. Add squash cubes; toss to coat. Transfer to a foil-lined 15x10x1-in. baking pan. Bake, stirring occasionally, until tender, 30-35 minutes.
2. Divide squash evenly among tortillas. Top with queso fresco, avocado and red onion. If desired, serve with pico de gallo.

2 tacos: 353 cal., 13g fat (3g sat. fat), 13mg chol., 322mg sod., 54g carb. (7g sugars, 13g fiber), 11g pro.

MAKEOVER MEATLESS LASAGNA

If you've never tried tofu before, this is the best way to give it a try. It blends in with all the other ingredients, adding protein without the fat and calories of ground beef.
—Mary Lou Moeller, Wooster, OH

Prep: 30 min. • **Bake:** 45 min. + standing
Makes: 12 servings

- 10 uncooked whole wheat lasagna noodles
- 1½ cups sliced fresh mushrooms

MAKEOVER MEATLESS LASAGNA

- ¼ cup chopped onion
- 2 garlic cloves, minced
- 1 can (14½ oz.) Italian diced tomatoes, undrained
- 1 can (12 oz.) tomato paste
- 1 pkg. (14 oz.) firm tofu, drained and cubed
- 2 large eggs, lightly beaten
- 3 cups 2% cottage cheese
- ½ cup grated Parmesan cheese
- ½ cup packed fresh parsley leaves
- ½ tsp. pepper
- 2 cups shredded part-skim mozzarella cheese, divided

1. Preheat oven to 375°. Cook noodles according to package directions for al dente. Meanwhile, in a large saucepan, cook mushrooms and onion over medium heat until tender. Add garlic; cook for 1 minute. Add tomatoes and tomato paste; cook and stir until heated through.
2. Pulse tofu in a food processor until smooth. Add next five ingredients; pulse until combined. Drain noodles.
3. Place five lasagna noodles in a 13x9-in. baking dish coated with cooking spray, overlapping as needed. Layer with half the tofu mixture, half the sauce and half the mozzarella. Top with remaining noodles, tofu mixture and sauce.
4. Bake, covered, 35 minutes. Sprinkle with remaining mozzarella. Bake the lasagna, uncovered, until cheese is melted, 10-15 minutes. Let stand for 10 minutes before serving.

1 piece: 258 cal., 9g fat (4g sat. fat), 48mg chol., 498mg sod., 26g carb. (9g sugars, 3g fiber), 19g pro.
Diabetic exchanges: 2 medium-fat meat, 1½ starch.

TEST KITCHEN TIP

If you don't tell your guests, they'll never know there is tofu in this dish. Pureed with cottage cheese, it has a very similar taste and texture to ricotta.

LAMB MARSALA

LAMB MARSALA

Lamb was a special treat for my family when I was growing up. I've had this recipe for more than 30 years.
—Bonnie Silverstein, Denver, CO

....

Prep: 10 min. • **Bake:** 1 hour
Makes: 6 servings

- ¾ cup Marsala wine or ½ cup chicken broth, ¼ cup white grape juice and 1 Tbsp. white wine vinegar
- 1 garlic clove, minced
- 1 Tbsp. dried oregano
- 1 Tbsp. olive oil
- 1 boneless leg of lamb (2½ lbs.), rolled and tied
- ½ tsp. salt
- ¼ tsp. pepper
- 1 lb. fresh mushrooms, quartered

1. In a small bowl, combine the wine, garlic and oregano; set aside. Rub oil over lamb, then sprinkle with salt and pepper. Place roast on a rack in a shallow roasting pan; spoon some of wine mixture over roast. Set aside remaining wine mixture.
2. Bake, uncovered, at 325° for 1-1½ hours or until meat reaches desired doneness (for medium-rare, a thermometer should read 135°; medium, 140°; medium-well, 145°), basting occasionally with some of reserved wine mixture. Remove from the oven; cover loosely with foil for 10-15 minutes.
3. Meanwhile, pour pan drippings into a measuring cup; skim fat. In a large skillet coated with cooking spray, saute the mushrooms until tender. Add the pan drippings and any remaining wine mixture; heat through. Slice lamb and serve with mushroom sauce.

1 serving: 330 cal., 13g fat (5g sat. fat), 114mg chol., 296mg sod., 7g carb. (4g sugars, 1g fiber), 38g pro.
Diabetic exchanges: 5 lean meat, 1 vegetable.

SHEET PAN PINEAPPLE CHICKEN FAJITAS

SHEET PAN PINEAPPLE CHICKEN FAJITAS

I combined chicken and pineapple for a different take on fajitas. This is more on the sweet side but my family loved it!
—Nancy Heishman, Las Vegas, NV

....

Prep: 20 min. • **Cook:** 20 min.
Makes: 6 servings

- 2 Tbsp. coconut oil, melted
- 3 tsp. chili powder
- 2 tsp. ground cumin
- 1 tsp. garlic powder
- ¾ tsp. kosher salt
- 1½ lbs. chicken tenderloins, halved lengthwise
- 1 large red or sweet onion, halved and sliced (about 2 cups)
- 1 large sweet red pepper, cut into ½-in. strips
- 1 large green pepper, cut into ½-in. strips
- 1 Tbsp. minced seeded jalapeno pepper
- 2 cans (8 oz. each) unsweetened pineapple tidbits, drained
- 2 Tbsp. honey
- 2 Tbsp. lime juice
- 12 corn tortillas (6 in.), warmed

Optional toppings: pico de gallo, sour cream, shredded Mexican cheese blend and sliced avocado
Lime wedges, optional

1. Preheat oven to 425°. In a large bowl, mix first five ingredients; stir in chicken. Add onion, peppers, pineapple, honey and lime juice; toss to combine. Spread evenly in two greased 15x10x1-in. baking pans.
2. Roast 10 minutes, rotating baking pans halfway through cooking. Remove the pans from oven; preheat broiler.
3. Broil chicken mixture, one pan at a time, 3-4 in. from heat until vegetables are lightly browned and chicken is no longer pink, 3-5 minutes. Serve in tortillas, with toppings and lime wedges as desired.

2 fajitas: 359 cal., 8g fat (4g sat. fat), 56mg chol., 372mg sod., 45g carb. (19g sugars, 6g fiber), 31g pro.
Diabetic exchanges: 3 starch, 3 lean meat, 1 fat.

TEST KITCHEN TIP

If you love pineapple, add even more as a topping, or serve the fajitas with a fruity sauce like peach or pineapple salsa. And if you don't have coconut oil, substitute canola or vegetable oil.

GRILLED DINNERS

"*I love the zesty taste of this grilled tenderloin. The cumin, avocado and jalapeno give it southwestern flair. It's an easy, elegant way to prepare pork.*"
—Josephine Piro, Easton, PA

California Burger Wraps (p. 211) **Grilled Chicken & Mango Skewers** (p. 206) **Chicken Ole Foil Supper** (p. 206)
Chinese Pork Tenderloin (p. 213) **Grilled Pork with Avocado Salsa** (p. 202) **The Ultimate Fish Tacos** (p. 213)

GRILLED PORK WITH AVOCADO SALSA
(PICTURED ON P. 201)

I love the zesty taste of this grilled tenderloin. The cumin, avocado and jalapeno give it southwestern flair. It's an easy, elegant way to prepare pork.
—Josephine Piro, Easton, PA

Prep: 25 min. + marinating • **Grill:** 10 min.
Makes: 6 servings

- ½ cup chopped sweet onion
- ½ cup lime juice
- ¼ cup finely chopped seeded jalapeno peppers
- 2 Tbsp. olive oil
- 4 tsp. ground cumin
- 1½ lbs. pork tenderloin, cut into ¾-in. slices
- 3 Tbsp. jalapeno pepper jelly

SALSA
- 2 medium ripe avocados, peeled and chopped
- 1 small cucumber, seeded and chopped
- 2 plum tomatoes, seeded and chopped
- 2 green onions, chopped
- 2 Tbsp. minced fresh cilantro
- 1 Tbsp. honey
- ¼ tsp. salt
- ¼ tsp. pepper

1. For marinade, mix first five ingredients. In a large bowl, toss the pork with ½ cup of the marinade; refrigerate, covered, for up to 2 hours.

2. For glaze, place jelly and ⅓ cup of the remaining marinade in a small saucepan; bring to a boil. Cook and stir until slightly thickened, 1-2 minutes; remove from heat. Place salsa ingredients in a large bowl; toss lightly with remaining marinade.

3. Drain pork, discarding marinade. Place the pork on a lightly oiled grill rack over medium heat. Grill pork, covered, until a thermometer reads 145°, 4-5 minutes per side, brushing with glaze during the last 3 minutes. Serve with salsa.

Note: Wear disposable gloves when cutting hot peppers; the oils can burn skin. Avoid touching your face.

3 oz. cooked pork with ⅓ cup salsa: 300 cal., 15g fat (3g sat. fat), 64mg chol., 155mg sod., 19g carb. (10g sugars, 4g fiber), 24g pro.
Diabetic exchanges: 1 starch, 3 lean meat, 2 fat.

TANDOORI CHICKEN PITA PIZZAS

TANDOORI CHICKEN PITA PIZZAS

My family and I are big picnickers, and I'm always looking for new dishes to try in the great outdoors. The amazing flavors at our favorite Indian restaurant inspired these mini pizzas.
—Angela Spengler, Niceville, FL

Takes: 25 min. • **Makes:** 4 servings

- 1 cup plain Greek yogurt, divided
- 2 Tbsp. chopped fresh cilantro
- ½ tsp. ground coriander
- ½ tsp. ground cumin
- ½ tsp. ground ginger
- ½ tsp. ground turmeric
- ½ tsp. paprika
- ½ tsp. cayenne pepper
- ¾ lb. boneless skinless chicken breasts, cut into ½-in.-thick strips
- 4 whole wheat pita breads (6 in.)
- ⅔ cup crumbled feta cheese
- ⅓ cup chopped seeded tomato
- ⅓ cup chopped fresh Italian parsley

1. For the sauce, mix ½ cup yogurt and cilantro. In a large bowl, mix spices and remaining yogurt; stir in chicken to coat.

2. Place the chicken on an oiled grill rack over medium heat; grill, covered, until no longer pink, 2-3 minutes per side. Grill the pita breads until warmed, about 1 minute per side.

3. Spread pitas with the sauce. Top with chicken, cheese, tomato and parsley.

1 pizza: 380 cal., 12g fat (6g sat. fat), 72mg chol., 598mg sod., 41g carb. (5g sugars, 5g fiber), 29g pro.
Diabetic exchanges: 3 lean meat, 2½ starch.

DIJON GRILLED PORK CHOPS

My mom gave me the recipe for these savory chops with a sweet and tangy marinade. The apple juice and Dijon mustard complement the pork nicely. With a vegetable and some rice or pasta, you have a meal.

—Babette Watterson, Atglen, PA

Prep: 10 min. + marinating • **Grill:** 10 min.
Makes: 4 servings

- 6 Tbsp. brown sugar
- 6 Tbsp. Dijon mustard
- 3 Tbsp. unsweetened apple juice
- 3 Tbsp. Worcestershire sauce
- 4 bone-in pork loin chops (8 oz. each)

1. For marinade, in a small bowl, mix the first four ingredients. Place pork chops and ⅔ cup marinade in a large resealable plastic bag; seal bag and turn to coat. Reserve remaining marinade; cover and refrigerate with pork 8 hours or overnight.

2. Place chops on a lightly oiled grill rack over medium heat; discard the marinade remaining in the bag. Grill chops, covered, until a thermometer reads 145°, 4-6 minutes per side, basting with reserved marinade during the last 3 minutes. Let stand 5 minutes before serving.

1 pork chop: 295 cal., 10g fat (4g sat. fat), 98mg chol., 408mg sod., 13g carb. (12g sugars, 0 fiber), 34g pro.
Diabetic exchanges: 1 starch, 4 lean meat.

DID YOU KNOW?

Worcestershire sauce was originally considered a mistake. In 1835, an English lord commissioned two chemists to duplicate a sauce he had tried in India. The pungent batch was disappointing and wound up in their cellar. When the pair stumbled upon the aged concoction two years later, they were pleasantly surprised by its unique taste.

GRILLED SALMON WITH NECTARINES

My family (including two small children) liked this recipe so well, I made it for a potluck the very next day after we'd tried it. Everyone there raved about it, too, including people who aren't particularly fond of fish.

—Kerin Benjamin, Citrus Heights, CA

Takes: 15 min. • **Makes:** 4 servings

- 4 salmon fillets (4 oz. each)
- ½ tsp. salt, divided
- ⅛ tsp. pepper
- 1 Tbsp. honey
- 1 Tbsp. lemon juice
- 1 Tbsp. olive oil
- 3 medium nectarines, thinly sliced
- 1 Tbsp. minced fresh basil

1. Sprinkle salmon with ¼ tsp. salt and pepper. Place on an oiled grill, skin side down. Grill, covered, over medium heat until fish just begins to flake easily with a fork, 8-10 minutes.

2. Meanwhile, in a bowl, mix honey, lemon juice, oil and the remaining salt. Stir in the nectarines and basil. Serve with salmon.

1 fillet with ⅓ cup nectarines: 307 cal., 16g fat (3g sat. fat), 67mg chol., 507mg sod., 17g carb. (13g sugars, 2g fiber), 23g pro.
Diabetic exchanges: 3 lean meat, 1½ fat, 1 fruit.

DIJON GRILLED PORK CHOPS

TUNA TERIYAKI KABOBS

TUNA TERIYAKI KABOBS

I love to barbecue but don't always want a heavy dinner. Kabobs are perfect in the spring, and you'll have room for dessert!
—Holly Battiste, Barrington, NJ

Prep: 25 min. + marinating • **Grill:** 15 min.
Makes: 8 kabobs

1½ lbs. tuna steaks, cut into
1½-in. chunks
2 medium sweet red peppers, cut into
1-in. pieces
1 large sweet onion, cut into
1-in. pieces

MARINADE/DRESSING
¼ cup minced fresh cilantro
¼ cup sesame oil
3 Tbsp. lime juice
2 Tbsp. soy sauce
2 Tbsp. extra virgin olive oil
1 Tbsp. minced fresh gingerroot
2 garlic cloves, minced

SALAD
1 pkg. (5 oz.) fresh baby spinach
1 medium sweet yellow pepper, cut
into 1-in. pieces
8 cherry tomatoes, halved

1. Thread tuna onto four metal or soaked wooden skewers. Thread pepper and onion pieces onto four more skewers. Place skewers in a 13x9-in. baking dish.
2. Whisk together marinade ingredients. Reserve half of mixture for salad dressing. Pour remaining marinade over skewers; refrigerate, covered, 30 minutes.
3. Grill kabobs, covered, on a greased grill rack over medium heat, turning kabobs occasionally, until tuna is slightly pink in center for medium-rare (2-3 minutes per side) and vegetables are crisp-tender (10-12 minutes). Remove tuna kabobs from direct heat and keep warm while vegetables finish grilling.
4. For salad, toss spinach, yellow pepper and cherry tomatoes with the reserved dressing. For each portion, serve a tuna kabob and vegetable kabob over salad.

2 kabobs: 389 cal., 16g fat (2g sat. fat), 66mg chol., 444mg sod., 15g carb. (9g sugars, 4g fiber), 45g pro.
Diabetic exchanges: 5 lean meat, 2 vegetable, 2 fat.

GINGER HALIBUT WITH BRUSSELS SPROUTS

GINGER HALIBUT WITH BRUSSELS SPROUTS

I moved to the United States from Russia and love cooking Russian food for family and friends. Halibut with soy sauce, ginger and pepper is a favorite.
—Margarita Parker, New Bern, NC

Takes: 25 min. • **Makes:** 4 servings

4 tsp. lemon juice
4 halibut fillets (4 to 6 oz. each)
1 tsp. minced fresh gingerroot
¼ to ¾ tsp. salt, divided
¼ tsp. pepper
½ cup water
10 oz. (about 2½ cups) fresh Brussels sprouts, halved
Crushed red pepper flakes
1 Tbsp. canola oil
5 garlic cloves, sliced lengthwise
2 Tbsp. sesame oil
2 Tbsp. soy sauce
Lemon slices, optional

1. Brush lemon juice over halibut fillets. Sprinkle with minced ginger, ¼ tsp. salt and pepper.
2. Place the fish on an oiled grill rack, skin side down. Grill, covered, over medium heat (or broil 6 in. from heat) until fish just begins to flake easily with a fork, 6-8 minutes.
3. In a large skillet, bring water to a boil over medium-high heat. Add Brussels sprouts, pepper flakes and, if desired, the remaining salt. Cook, covered, until tender, 5-7 minutes. Meanwhile, in a small skillet, heat oil over medium heat. Add garlic; cook until golden brown. Drain on paper towels.
4. Drizzle sesame oil and soy sauce over halibut. Serve with Brussels sprouts; sprinkle with sauteed garlic. If desired, serve with lemon slices.

1 fillet with Brussels sprouts: 234 cal., 12g fat (2g sat. fat), 56mg chol., 701mg sod., 7g carb. (2g sugars, 3g fiber), 24g pro.
Diabetic exchanges: 3 lean meat, 2 fat, 1 vegetable.

GRILLED CHICKEN & MANGO SKEWERS

GRILLED CHICKEN & MANGO SKEWERS

This recipe was inspired by charbroiled chicken skewers we ate while strolling along Calle Ocho in Miami on Sunday afternoons. I like to garnish my skewers with sesame seeds.
—Wolfgang Hanau, West Palm Beach, FL

Takes: 30 min. • **Makes:** 4 servings

- **3** medium ears sweet corn
- **1** Tbsp. butter
- **⅓** cup plus 3 Tbsp. sliced green onions, divided
- **1** lb. boneless skinless chicken breasts, cut into 1-in. cubes
- **½** tsp. salt
- **¼** tsp. pepper
- **1** medium mango, peeled and cut into 1-in. cubes
- **1** Tbsp. extra virgin olive oil
  Lime wedges, optional

1. Cut corn from cobs. In a large skillet, heat butter over medium-high heat; saute cut corn until crisp-tender, about 5 minutes. Stir in ⅓ cup green onions. Keep warm.

2. Toss chicken with salt and pepper. Alternately thread chicken and mango onto four metal or soaked wooden skewers. Brush with oil.

3. Grill, covered, over medium heat or broil 4 in. from heat until chicken is no longer pink, 10-12 minutes, turning occasionally. Serve with corn mixture; sprinkle with remaining green onions. If desired, serve with lime wedges.

1 skewer with ½ cup corn mixture:
297 cal., 10g fat (3g sat. fat), 70mg chol., 387mg sod., 28g carb. (16g sugars, 3g fiber), 26g pro.
Diabetic exchanges: 3 lean meat, 2 starch, 1½ fat.

CHICKEN OLE FOIL SUPPER
(PICTURED ON P. 201)

These Mexican-style chicken packets can be assembled ahead and frozen if you like. Just thaw them overnight in the fridge, then grill as directed. I like to serve them with warm tortillas and fresh fruit or a big green salad on the side.
—Mary Peck, Salina, KS

Takes: 30 min. • **Makes:** 4 servings

- **1** can (15 oz.) black beans, rinsed and drained
- **2** cups fresh or frozen corn (about 10 oz.), thawed
- **1** cup salsa
- **4** boneless skinless chicken breast halves (4 oz. each)
- **¼** tsp. garlic powder
- **¼** tsp. pepper
- **⅛** tsp. salt
- **1** cup shredded cheddar cheese
- **2** green onions, chopped

1. Mix the beans, corn and salsa; divide among four 18x12-in. pieces of heavy-duty foil. Top with chicken. Mix the seasonings; sprinkle over chicken. Fold foil over the chicken, sealing tightly.

2. Grill packets, covered, over medium heat until a thermometer inserted in chicken reads 165°, 15-20 minutes. Open foil carefully to allow steam to escape. Sprinkle with cheese and green onions.

1 serving: 405 cal., 13g fat (6g sat. fat), 91mg chol., 766mg sod., 34g carb. (8g sugars, 6g fiber), 37g pro.
Diabetic exchanges: 4 lean meat, 2 starch, 1 fat.

BRUSCHETTA STEAK

My husband and I love bruschetta with fresh tomatoes and herbs from our garden, even without the usual bread.
—Kristy Still, Broken Arrow, OK

Takes: 25 min. • **Makes:** 4 servings

- 3 medium tomatoes, chopped
- 3 Tbsp. minced fresh basil
- 3 Tbsp. chopped fresh parsley
- 2 Tbsp. olive oil
- 1 tsp. minced fresh oregano or ½ tsp. dried oregano
- 1 garlic clove, minced
- ¾ tsp. salt, divided
- 1 beef flat iron or top sirloin steak (1 lb.), cut into four portions
- ¼ tsp. pepper
  Grated Parmesan cheese, optional

1. Combine first six ingredients; stir in ¼ tsp. salt.
2. Sprinkle the beef with pepper and remaining salt. Grill meat, covered, over medium heat or broil 4 in. from heat until meat reaches desired doneness (for medium-rare, a thermometer should read 135°; medium, 140°), 4-6 minutes per side. Top with tomato mixture. If desired, sprinkle with cheese.

1 steak with ½ cup tomato mixture: 280 cal., 19g fat (6g sat. fat), 73mg chol., 519mg sod., 4g carb. (2g sugars, 1g fiber), 23g pro.
Diabetic exchanges: 3 lean meat, 1½ fat, 1 vegetable.

FLAVORFUL GRILLED PORK TENDERLOIN

My wife likes it when I do the cooking, and folks can always find me grilling, no matter the weather. This tenderloin has a ton of flavor thanks to its special spice blend, and it doesn't get much easier to make.
—Steve Ehrhart, Villa Park, IL

Takes: 30 min. • **Makes:** 8 servings

- ¾ tsp. salt
- ¾ tsp. seasoned salt
- ¾ tsp. poultry seasoning
- ¾ tsp. onion powder
- ¾ tsp. garlic powder
- ¾ tsp. chili powder
- ⅛ tsp. cayenne pepper
- 2 pork tenderloins (1 lb. each)

Mix seasonings; sprinkle over tenderloins. Grill, covered, over medium heat until a thermometer reads 145°, 20-25 minutes, turning occasionally. Let stand 5 minutes before slicing.

3 oz. cooked pork: 135 cal., 4g fat (1g sat. fat), 64mg chol., 416mg sod., 1g carb. (0 sugars, 0 fiber), 23g pro.
Diabetic exchanges: 3 lean meat.

★ ★ ★ ★ ★ **READER REVIEW**
"I love this recipe. My kids felt that it was a little too spicy, so I make one tenderloin without the cayenne pepper for them."
KBPAULSON TASTEOFHOME.COM

BRUSCHETTA STEAK

CILANTRO & LEMON MARINATED CHICKEN KABOBS

STEAK FAJITAS

A zesty salsa and tender strips of steak make these traditional fajitas extra special.
—Rebecca Baird, Salt Lake City, UT

Takes: 30 min. • **Makes:** 6 servings

2 large tomatoes, seeded and chopped
½ cup diced red onion
¼ cup lime juice
1 jalapeno pepper, seeded and minced
3 Tbsp. minced fresh cilantro
2 tsp. ground cumin, divided
¾ tsp. salt, divided
1 beef flank steak (about 1½ lbs.)
1 Tbsp. canola oil
1 large onion, halved and sliced
6 whole wheat tortillas (8 in.), warmed
Sliced avocado and lime wedges, optional

1. For salsa, place the first five ingredients in a small bowl; stir in 1 tsp. of the cumin and ¼ tsp. salt. Let stand until serving.
2. Sprinkle steak with remaining cumin and salt. Grill, covered, over medium heat or broil 4 in. from heat until meat reaches desired doneness (for medium-rare, a thermometer should read 135°; medium, 140°), 6-8 minutes. Let stand 5 minutes.
3. Meanwhile, in a skillet, heat oil over medium-high heat; saute the onion until crisp-tender. Slice steak thinly across the grain; serve in tortillas with onion and salsa. If desired, serve with avocado and lime wedges.

Note: Wear disposable gloves when cutting hot peppers; the oils can burn skin. Avoid touching your face.

1 fajita: 329 cal., 12g fat (4g sat. fat), 54mg chol., 498mg sod., 29g carb. (3g sugars, 5g fiber), 27g pro.

Diabetic exchanges: 3 lean meat, 2 starch, ½ fat.

CILANTRO & LEMON MARINATED CHICKEN KABOBS

Cook the onions first so there's plenty of room on the grill for the chicken skewers. Give the whole platter a spritz of lemon for a sunshiny delight.
—Moumita Ghosh, Kolkata, West Bengal

Prep: 40 min. + marinating • **Grill:** 20 min.
Makes: 6 servings

1½ lbs. boneless skinless chicken breasts, cut into 1-in. pieces
3 Tbsp. lemon juice
1½ tsp. salt
½ cup water
¼ cup plain yogurt
1 cup fresh cilantro leaves
⅓ cup fresh mint leaves
2 serrano peppers, sliced
1 piece fresh gingerroot (1 in.), coarsely chopped
4 garlic cloves, sliced
3 medium sweet onions, cut crosswise into ½-in. slices
4 Tbsp. canola oil, divided
Lemon wedges

1. In a large bowl, toss the chicken with lemon juice and salt; let stand 15 minutes. Meanwhile, place water, yogurt, herbs, peppers, ginger and garlic in a blender; cover and process until smooth. Stir into the chicken mixture; refrigerate, covered, 2 hours.
2. Oil grill rack lightly. Brush onions with 2 Tbsp. oil. Grill, covered, over medium heat or broil 4 in. from heat until tender, turning occasionally, 10-12 minutes.
3. Remove chicken from the marinade; discard marinade. Thread chicken onto six metal or soaked wooden skewers. Grill, covered, over medium heat or broil 4 in. from heat until chicken is no longer pink, 10-12 minutes, turning occasionally and brushing with remaining oil during the last 4 minutes. Serve with grilled onions and lemon wedges.

Note: Wear disposable gloves when cutting hot peppers; the oils can burn skin. Avoid touching your face.

1 kabob with ½ grilled onion: 224 cal., 12g fat (2g sat. fat), 63mg chol., 651mg sod., 4g carb. (3g sugars, 1g fiber), 24g pro.

Diabetic exchanges: 3 lean meat, 2 fat, 1 vegetable.

STEAK FAJITAS

SPICED SALMON

This fish is so quick and easy to prepare. What a great way to enjoy salmon.
—Donna Reynolds, Innisfail, AB

Takes: 20 min. • **Makes:** 8 servings

- 2 Tbsp. packed brown sugar
- 1 Tbsp. soy sauce
- 1 Tbsp. butter, melted
- 1 Tbsp. olive oil
- ½ tsp. garlic powder
- ½ tsp. ground mustard
- ½ tsp. paprika
- ½ tsp. pepper
- ¼ tsp. dill weed
  - Dash salt
  - Dash dried tarragon
  - Dash cayenne pepper
- 1 salmon fillet (2 lbs.)

Mix first 12 ingredients; brush over the salmon. Place salmon, skin side down, on an oiled grill rack or a lightly oiled baking sheet. Grill, covered, over medium heat or broil 4 in. from heat until fish just begins to flake easily with a fork, 10-15 minutes.

3 oz. cooked salmon: 256 cal., 17g fat (4g sat. fat), 65mg chol., 330mg sod., 5g carb. (5g sugars, 0 fiber), 20g pro.
Diabetic exchanges: 3 lean meat, 1½ fat.

How To Serve Whole Salmon
After grilling, gently remove the salmon to a serving platter with one or two large spatulas. The fish will separate from the skin easily so you can serve up portions of the cooked fillet.

SPICY SHRIMP & WATERMELON KABOBS

My three sons can polish off a watermelon in one sitting. Before they dig in, I set aside a few slices to make these zesty kabobs.
—Jennifer Fisher, Austin, TX

Takes: 30 min. • **Makes:** 4 servings

- 1 Tbsp. reduced-sodium soy sauce
- 1 Tbsp. Sriracha Asian hot chili sauce
- 1 Tbsp. honey
- 1 garlic clove, minced
- 4 cups cubed seedless watermelon (1 in.), divided
- 1 lb. uncooked shrimp (16-20 per lb.), peeled and deveined
- 1 medium red onion, cut into 1-in. pieces
- ½ tsp. sea salt
- ¼ tsp. coarsely ground pepper
  - Minced fresh cilantro, optional

1. For glaze, place soy sauce, chili sauce, honey, garlic and 2 cups watermelon in a blender; cover and process until pureed. Transfer to a small saucepan; bring to a boil. Cook, uncovered, over medium-high heat until the mixture is reduced by half, about 10 minutes. Set aside ¼ cup glaze for serving.

2. On four metal or soaked wooden skewers, alternately thread shrimp, onion and remaining watermelon. Sprinkle with salt and pepper.

3. Place kabobs on an oiled grill rack over medium heat. Grill, covered, 3-4 minutes on each side or until shrimp turns pink, brushing with remaining glaze during the last 2 minutes. If desired, sprinkle with cilantro. Serve with reserved glaze.

1 kabob with 1 Tbsp. glaze: 172 cal., 2g fat (0 sat. fat), 138mg chol., 644mg sod., 23g carb. (19g sugars, 2g fiber), 20g pro.
Diabetic exchanges: 3 lean meat, 1 fruit, ½ starch.
* HEALTH TIP * A serving of fruit with dinner? Check—along with 20 percent of recommended daily vitamin C.

SPICY SHRIMP & WATERMELON KABOBS

CALIFORNIA BURGER WRAPS

ZESTY APRICOT TURKEY

You see a lot of steak, chicken and chops at cookouts, but how about something different? With its apricot-chile pepper glaze, this juicy grilled turkey is one of our picnic faves.
—Wendy Moylan, Crystal Lake, IL

Takes: 30 min. • **Makes:** 4 servings

- ⅓ cup apricot spreadable fruit
- 1 Tbsp. white wine vinegar
- 1 Tbsp. honey
- 1 garlic clove, minced
- ½ tsp. grated lemon zest
- ⅛ tsp. hot pepper sauce
- 2 turkey breast tenderloins (8 oz. each)
- ½ tsp. salt
- ¼ tsp. pepper

1. In a microwave, melt spreadable fruit; stir in vinegar, honey, garlic, lemon zest and pepper sauce. Reserve ¼ cup sauce for serving.
2. Sprinkle turkey with salt and pepper; place on an oiled grill rack over medium heat. Grill, covered, until a thermometer reads 165°, 7-10 minutes per side; brush with remaining sauce during the last minute of cooking. Let stand 5 minutes before slicing. Serve with reserved sauce.

3 oz. cooked turkey with 1 Tbsp. sauce: 200 cal., 2g fat (0 sat. fat), 65mg chol., 424mg sod., 18g carb. (15g sugars, 0 fiber), 27g pro.
Diabetic exchanges: 3 lean meat, 1 starch.

CALIFORNIA BURGER WRAPS

I love the way these delicious flavors blend! Plus it's a snap to throw the wraps together for a quick, healthy lunch using leftover burgers. You can serve the tasty burgers on buns, of course, or give your guests the option of lettuce anytime you happen to be grilling fresh burgers.
—Rachelle McCalla, Atlantic, IA

Takes: 30 min. • **Makes:** 4 servings

- 1 lb. lean ground beef (90% lean)
- ½ tsp. salt
- ¼ tsp. pepper
- 8 Bibb lettuce leaves
- ⅓ cup crumbled feta cheese
- 2 Tbsp. Miracle Whip Light
- ½ medium ripe avocado, peeled and cut into 8 slices
- ¼ cup chopped red onion
  Chopped cherry tomatoes, optional

1. In a large bowl, combine the beef, salt and pepper, mixing lightly but thoroughly. Shape into eight ½-in.-thick patties.
2. Grill burgers, covered, over medium heat or broil 3-4 in. from heat on each side or until a thermometer reads 160°, for 3-4 minutes. Place burgers in lettuce leaves. Combine feta and Miracle Whip; spread over burgers. Top with avocado, red onion and if desired, tomatoes.

2 wraps: 252 cal., 15g fat (5g sat. fat), 78mg chol., 518mg sod., 5g carb. (2g sugars, 2g fiber), 24g pro.
Diabetic exchanges: 3 lean meat, 2 fat.

TEST KITCHEN TIP

If you don't keep Miracle Whip on hand, mayonnaise with a pinch of sugar would be a good substitute.

CHINESE PORK TENDERLOIN

CHINESE PORK TENDERLOIN

Marinated in soy sauce, lime juice, red pepper and ginger, the meat takes on plenty of flavor, which makes it special enough for company.

—Margaret Haugh Heilman, Houston, TX

Prep: 5 min. + marinating • **Grill:** 15 min.
Makes: 4 servings

- 3 Tbsp. lime juice
- 3 Tbsp. reduced-sodium soy sauce
- 3 Tbsp. stir-fry sauce
- 4½ tsp. grated fresh gingerroot
- 1 tsp. crushed red pepper flakes
- 3 garlic cloves, minced
- 1 pork tenderloin (1 lb.)

In a bowl, combine the first six ingredients. Place the pork in a shallow container with a lid; add half of the marinade. Turn pork to coat; cover and refrigerate for 2 hours, turning occasionally. Cover and refrigerate the remaining marinade for basting. Drain marinade from pork and discard. Grill the pork, covered, over hot heat until a thermometer reads 160° and juices run clear, 15-20 minutes, basting occasionally with reserved marinade.

3 oz. cooked pork: 155 cal., 4g fat (1g sat. fat), 64mg chol., 662mg sod., 4g carb. (2g sugars, 0 fiber), 24g pro.
Diabetic exchanges: 3 lean meat.

HERBED BALSAMIC CHICKEN

HERBED BALSAMIC CHICKEN

Our kitchen is tiny and cramped, so we try to grill simple (but tasty) meals outside as often as possible during the hot summer months. Dried herbs work OK here, but in summer we use herbs fresh from the garden for the best taste.

—Kelly Evans, Denton, TX

Takes: 30 min. • **Makes:** 6 servings

- ½ cup balsamic vinegar
- 3 Tbsp. extra virgin olive oil
- 1 Tbsp. minced fresh basil
- 1 Tbsp. minced fresh chives
- 2 tsp. grated lemon peel
- 1 garlic clove, minced
- ¾ tsp. salt
- ¼ tsp. pepper
- 6 boneless skinless chicken thighs (1½ lbs.)

1. Whisk together all ingredients except chicken. In a bowl, toss chicken with ⅓ cup vinegar mixture; let stand 10 minutes.
2. Grill chicken, covered, over medium heat or broil 4 in. from the heat until a thermometer reads 170°, 6-8 minutes per side. Drizzle chicken with the remaining vinegar mixture before serving.

1 chicken thigh with 2 tsp. sauce: 245 cal., 15g fat (3g sat. fat), 76mg chol., 358mg sod., 6g carb. (5g sugars, 0 fiber), 21g pro.
Diabetic exchanges: 3 lean meat, 1½ fat.

THE ULTIMATE FISH TACOS
(PICTURED ON P. 201)

This recipe is my favorite meal to prepare. Adding my own personal touch to the marinade makes these tacos pop with flavor. Warm corn tortillas on the grill, then add green cilantro, purple cabbage and fresh lime juice to your fish tacos.

—Yvonne Molina, Moreno Valley, CA

Prep: 20 min. + marinating • **Grill:** 10 min.
• **Makes:** 6 servings

- ¼ cup olive oil
- 1 tsp. ground cardamom
- 1 tsp. paprika
- 1 tsp. salt
- 1 tsp. pepper
- 6 mahi mahi fillets (6 oz. each)
- 12 corn tortillas (6 in.)
- 2 cups chopped red cabbage
- 1 cup chopped fresh cilantro
   Salsa verde, optional
- 2 medium limes, cut into wedges
   Hot pepper sauce (Tapatio preferred)

1. In a 13x9-in. baking dish, whisk the first five ingredients. Add fillets; turn to coat. Refrigerate, covered, 30 minutes.
2. Drain fish and discard marinade. On an oiled grill rack, grill mahi mahi, covered, over medium-high heat (or broil 4 in. from heat) until the fish flakes easily with a fork, 4-5 minutes per side. Remove fish. Place tortillas on grill rack; heat 30-45 seconds. Keep warm.
3. To assemble, divide fish among the tortillas; layer with red cabbage, cilantro and, if desired, salsa verde. Squeeze a little lime juice and hot pepper sauce over fish mixture; fold sides of tortilla over mixture. Serve with lime wedges and additional pepper sauce.

2 tacos: 284 cal., 5g fat (1g sat. fat), 124mg chol., 278mg sod., 26g carb. (2g sugars, 4g fiber), 35g pro.
Diabetic exchanges: 5 lean meat, 1½ starch, ½ fat.

SLOW-COOKED SUPPERS

"Here's a fun, simple chicken taco recipe for a casual dinner with friends or family. For variety, use any leftover filling as a topping for a taco salad."
—Tracy Gunter, Boise, ID

Slow-Cooker Pork & Apple Curry (p. 224) **Slow-Cooked Sirloin** (p. 217) **North African Chicken & Rice** (p. 221)
Slow-Cooked Orange Chipotle Chicken (p. 225) **Lime Chicken Tacos** (p. 220) **Spicy Lentil & Chickpea Stew** (p. 226)

CHICKEN WITH SUGAR PUMPKINS & APRICOTS

CHICKEN WITH SUGAR PUMPKINS & APRICOTS

When we have family gatherings, we give the slow cooker kitchen duty. This yummy chicken with pumpkin and apricots has the warm flavors of Morocco.
—Nancy Heishman, Las Vegas, NV

Prep: 20 min. • **Cook:** 4 hours
Makes: 8 servings

- 3 Sugar Baby pumpkins, peeled and cubed (5 to 6 cups each)
- 1 Tbsp. canola oil
- 8 boneless skinless chicken thighs (4 oz. each)
- 1 medium red onion, chopped
- 2 garlic cloves, minced
- ¾ cup dried Turkish apricots, diced
- ½ cup apricot nectar
- ⅓ cup apricot preserves
- 2 Tbsp. lemon juice
- 1 tsp. ground ginger
- 1 tsp. ground cinnamon
- 1 tsp. salt
- ½ tsp. pepper
- 3 Tbsp. minced fresh parsley
  Hot cooked rice, optional
- ½ cup pomegranate seeds, optional

1. Place pumpkin in a 5-qt. slow cooker coated with cooking spray.

2. In a large nonstick skillet, heat oil over medium-high heat; brown chicken thighs on all sides. Transfer chicken to slow cooker. In same skillet, saute onions and garlic 1-2 minutes; transfer to slow cooker.
3. Add next eight ingredients to slow cooker. Cook, covered, on low until meat is tender, 4-5 hours. Top with parsley. If desired, serve with hot cooked rice and sprinkle with pomegranate seeds.
Note: If Sugar Baby pumpkins are unavailable, you may substitute one large (5-6 pound) butternut squash, peeled and cut into 1-in. cubes. You should have 15-18 cups of cubed squash.

1 chicken thigh with 1 cup pumpkin: 318 cal., 10g fat (3g sat. fat), 76mg chol., 376mg sod., 36g carb. (20g sugars, 3g fiber), 24g pro.
Diabetic exchanges: 2 starch, 3 lean meat, ½ fat.

LEMON CHICKEN WITH BASIL
No matter when I eat it, this tangy slow-cooked chicken reminds me of summer meals with friends and family.
—Deborah Posey, Virginia Beach, VA

Prep: 5 min. • **Cook:** 3 hours
Makes: 4 servings

- 4 boneless skinless chicken breast halves (6 oz. each)
- 2 medium lemons
- 1 bunch fresh basil leaves (¾ oz.)
- 2 cups chicken stock
  Additional grated lemon zest and chopped basil, optional

1. Place chicken breasts in a 3-qt. slow cooker. Finely grate enough zest from lemons to measure 4 teaspoons. Cut lemons in half; squeeze juice. Add zest and juice to slow cooker.
2. Tear the basil leaves directly into slow cooker. Add chicken stock. Cook, covered, on low until the meat is tender, 3-4 hours. When cool enough to handle, shred meat with two forks. If desired, stir in additional lemon zest and chopped basil.

1 chicken breast half: 200 cal., 4g fat (1g sat. fat), 94mg chol., 337mg sod., 3g carb. (1g sugars, 0 fiber), 37g pro.
Diabetic exchanges: 5 lean meat.

TEST KITCHEN TIP

For a sweet and savory treat, layer chicken, butter lettuce leaves and apple slices on toasted raisin bread.

ITALIAN TURKEY MEATBALLS

What's not to love about moist and tender homemade Italian meatballs? Because they're made with lean turkey, these are low in saturated fat, too!
—Mary Berg, Lake Elmo, MN

Prep: 45 min. • **Cook:** 4 hours
Makes: 12 servings

- 3 slices white bread, torn into small pieces
- ½ cup fat-free milk
- 2 lbs. lean ground turkey
- ¼ cup grated Parmesan cheese
- ¼ cup minced fresh parsley
- 2 large eggs, lightly beaten
- 3 garlic cloves, minced
- 2 tsp. Italian seasoning
- ½ tsp. salt
- ½ tsp. pepper

SAUCE
- 2 medium onions, chopped
- 1 medium green pepper, chopped
- 2 cans (28 oz. each) crushed tomatoes in puree
- 2 cans (6 oz. each) tomato paste
- 4 garlic cloves, minced
- 1 Tbsp. sugar
- 2 tsp. Italian seasoning
- ½ tsp. salt
- ½ tsp. pepper
- 2 bay leaves
  Hot cooked pasta
  Additional minced fresh parsley and grated Parmesan cheese, optional

1. Preheat broiler. Combine bread and milk in a large bowl; let stand until liquid is absorbed. Add next eight ingredients; mix lightly but thoroughly. Shape into 1½-in. balls; place on a greased rack of a broiler pan. Broil 5-6 in. from heat until lightly browned, 4-5 minutes.
2. For the sauce, in a 6-qt. slow cooker, mix the next nine ingredients. Add bay leaves and meatballs; gently stir into sauce.
3. Cook, covered, on low until meatballs are cooked through, 4-5 hours. Discard bay leaves. Serve with pasta; if desired, sprinkle with additional parsley and Parmesan cheese.
Freeze option: Omitting additional parsley and Parmesan cheese, freeze cooled meatball mixture in freezer containers. To use, partially thaw in refrigerator overnight. Microwave, covered, on high in a microwave-safe dish until heated through, stirring gently and adding a little water if necessary. If desired, sprinkle with additional parsley and Parmesan.

3 meatballs with ⅔ cup sauce: 239 cal., 8g fat (2g sat. fat), 85mg chol., 588mg sod., 23g carb. (11g sugars, 4g fiber), 22g pro.
Diabetic exchanges: 3 lean meat, 1½ starch.

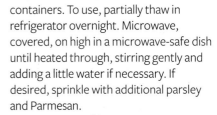

SLOW-COOKED SIRLOIN
(PICTURED ON P. 214)

My family of five likes to eat beef, so this recipe is a favorite. I usually serve it with homemade bread or rolls to soak up the tasty gravy.
—Vicki Tormaschy, Dickinson, ND

Prep: 20 min. • **Cook:** 3½ hours
Makes: 6 servings

- 1 beef top sirloin steak (1½ lbs.)
- 1 medium onion, cut into 1-in. chunks
- 1 medium green pepper, cut into 1-in. chunks
- 1 can (14½ oz.) reduced-sodium beef broth
- ¼ cup Worcestershire sauce
- ¼ tsp. dill weed
- ¼ tsp. dried thyme
- ¼ tsp. pepper
  Dash crushed red pepper flakes
- 2 Tbsp. cornstarch
- 2 Tbsp. cold water

1. In a large nonstick skillet, brown beef on both sides. Place onion and green pepper in a 3-qt. slow cooker. Top with beef. Combine broth, Worcestershire sauce, dill, thyme, pepper and pepper flakes; pour over beef. Cover and cook on high until meat reaches desired doneness and vegetables are crisp-tender, 3-4 hours.
2. Remove beef and keep warm. Combine cornstarch and water until smooth; gradually stir into cooking juices. Cover and cook on high until slightly thickened, about 30 minutes. Return beef to the slow cooker; heat through.

3 oz. beef with ¼ cup vegetables and ½ cup gravy: 199 cal., 6g fat (2g sat. fat), 68mg chol., 305mg sod., 8g carb. (2g sugars, 1g fiber), 26g pro.
Diabetic exchanges: 3 lean meat, 1 vegetable.

ITALIAN TURKEY MEATBALLS

3. Cook, covered, on low until vegetables are tender, 5-6 hours. Sprinkle with cilantro. Serve with rice, lime wedges and, if desired, yogurt.

1⅔ cups curry: 304 cal., 8g fat (2g sat. fat), 2mg chol., 696mg sod., 49g carb. (12g sugars, 12g fiber), 9g pro.

* HEALTH TIP * Chickpeas are a smart way to add a dose of protein to a meatless main. They are also a good source of fiber, folate and vitamin B6.

SLOW-COOKER PORK CHOPS

Everyone will enjoy these fork-tender pork chops with a creamy, light gravy. Serve with a green vegetable, mashed potatoes and coleslaw or a salad.
—Sue Bingham, Madisonville, TN

Prep: 15 min. • **Cook:** 2 hours
Makes: 4 servings

- ½ cup all-purpose flour, divided
- ½ tsp. ground mustard
- ½ tsp. garlic pepper blend
- ¼ tsp. seasoned salt
- 4 boneless pork loin chops (4 oz. each)
- 2 Tbsp. canola oil
- 1 can (14½ oz.) chicken broth

1. In a shallow bowl, combine ¼ cup flour, mustard, garlic pepper and seasoned salt. Add pork chops, one at a time, and dredge to coat. In a large skillet, brown chops in oil on both sides.
2. Transfer to a 5-qt. slow cooker. Pour broth over chops. Cook, covered, on low for 2-3 hours or until meat is tender.
3. Remove pork to a serving plate and keep warm. Whisk the remaining flour into cooking juices until smooth; cook, covered, on high until gravy is thickened.

1 pork chop: 279 cal., 14g fat (3g sat. fat), 57mg chol., 606mg sod., 12g carb. (1g sugars, 0 fiber), 24g pro.

Diabetic exchanges: 3 lean meat, 1½ fat, 1 starch.

SLOW-COOKED VEGETABLE CURRY

I love the fuss-free nature of the slow cooker, but I don't want to sacrifice flavor for convenience. This cozy, spiced-up dish provides both.
—Susan Smith, Mead, WA

Prep: 35 min. • **Cook:** 5 hours
Makes: 6 servings

- 1 Tbsp. canola oil
- 1 medium onion, finely chopped
- 4 garlic cloves, minced
- 3 tsp. ground coriander
- 1½ tsp. ground cinnamon
- 1 tsp. ground ginger
- 1 tsp. ground turmeric
- ½ tsp. cayenne pepper
- 2 Tbsp. tomato paste
- 2 cans (15 oz. each) garbanzo beans or chickpeas, rinsed and drained
- 3 cups cubed peeled sweet potatoes (about 1 lb.)

- 3 cups fresh cauliflower florets (about 8 oz.)
- 4 medium carrots, cut into ¾-in. pieces (about 2 cups)
- 2 medium tomatoes, seeded and chopped
- 2 cups chicken broth
- 1 cup light coconut milk
- ½ tsp. pepper
- ¼ tsp. salt
  Minced fresh cilantro
  Hot cooked brown rice
  Lime wedges
  Plain yogurt, optional

1. In a large skillet, heat oil over medium heat; saute onion until soft and lightly browned, 5-7 minutes. Add garlic and spices; cook and stir 1 minute. Stir in tomato paste; cook 1 minute. Transfer to a 5- or 6-qt. slow cooker.
2. Mash 1 can of beans until smooth; add to slow cooker. Stir in remaining beans, vegetables, broth, coconut milk, pepper and salt.

SLOW-COOKED VEGETABLE CURRY

SLOW COOKER PORK CHOPS

SPICY COWBOY CHILI

Toasting the peppers for this chili releases their earthy flavors — but do wear gloves when handling dried peppers and seeds.

—Rachel Sprinkel, Hilo, HI

Prep: 45 min. • **Cook:** 7 hours
Makes: 14 servings (3½ qt.)

- 1 whole garlic bulb
- 2 to 3 Tbsp. olive oil, divided
- 2 dried ancho chiles
- 2 dried chipotle chiles
- 1 bottle (12 oz.) dark beer
- 3 lbs. beef stew meat, cut into ¾-in. pieces
- 2 large onions, chopped
- 3 cans (16 oz. each) kidney beans, rinsed and drained
- 3 cans (14½ oz. each) diced tomatoes, undrained
- 2 cans (8 oz. each) tomato sauce
- 2 Tbsp. Worcestershire sauce
- 1 Tbsp. chili powder
- 1 tsp. pepper
- ½ tsp. salt
  Shredded cheddar cheese, optional

1. Preheat oven to 425°. Remove papery outer skin from garlic bulb, but do not peel or separate the cloves. Cut off top of garlic bulb, exposing individual cloves. Brush cut cloves with 1 tsp. oil. Wrap in foil. Bake until garlic cloves are soft, 30-35 minutes. Unwrap and cool slightly. Squeeze garlic from skins; mash with a fork.

2. Meanwhile, in a large dry skillet over medium-high heat, toast chiles on both sides until puffy, 3-6 minutes. (Do not blacken.) Cool. Remove stems and seeds; coarsely chop chiles. Place in a small bowl; cover with beer. Let stand until softened, about 30 minutes.

3. In the same skillet, heat 1 Tbsp. oil over medium-high heat. Brown beef in batches, adding additional oil if needed; transfer to a 6-qt. slow cooker. In the skillet, heat 2 tsp. oil over medium heat. Add onions; cook and stir until tender. Add to beef.

4. Stir in the remaining ingredients, mashed garlic and dried chiles mixture. Cover and cook on low until meat is tender, 7-9 hours. If desired, serve with shredded cheese.

SPICY COWBOY CHILI

Note: Wear disposable gloves when cutting hot peppers; the oils can burn skin. Avoid touching your face.

1 cup: 301 cal., 9g fat (3g sat. fat), 60mg chol., 588mg sod., 27g carb. (7g sugars, 8g fiber), 27g pro.

Diabetic exchanges: 4 lean meat, 1½ starch, 1 vegetable.

LIME CHICKEN TACOS

(PICTURED ON P. 215)

Here's a fun, simple chicken taco recipe for a casual dinner with friends or family. For variety, use any leftover filling as a topping for a taco salad.

—Tracy Gunter, Boise, ID

Prep: 10 min. • **Cook:** 5½ hours
Makes: 6 servings

- 1½ lbs. boneless skinless chicken breast halves
- 3 Tbsp. lime juice
- 1 Tbsp. chili powder
- 1 cup frozen corn, thawed
- 1 cup chunky salsa
- 12 fat-free flour tortillas (6 in.), warmed
  Sour cream, pickled onions, shredded lettuce and shredded cheddar or cotija cheese, optional

1. Place chicken in a 3-qt. slow cooker. Combine lime juice and chili powder; pour over chicken. Cook, covered, on low until chicken is tender, 5-6 hours.

2. Remove chicken. When cool enough to handle, shred meat with two forks; return to slow cooker. Stir in corn and salsa. Cook, covered, on low until heated through, about 30 minutes. Place filling on tortillas; if desired, serve with sour cream, pickled onions, lettuce and cheese.

2 tacos: 291 cal., 3g fat (1g sat. fat), 63mg chol., 674mg sod., 37g carb. (2g sugars, 2g fiber), 28g pro.

Diabetic exchanges: 3 lean meat, 2½ starch.

NORTH AFRICAN CHICKEN & RICE

I'm always looking to try recipes from different cultures and this one is a huge favorite. We love the spice combinations. This cooks equally well in a slow cooker or pressure cooker.
—Courtney Stultz, Weir, KS

Prep: 10 min. • **Cook:** 4 hours
Makes: 8 servings

- 1 medium onion, diced
- 1 Tbsp. olive oil
- 8 boneless skinless chicken thighs (about 2 lbs.)
- 1 Tbsp. minced fresh cilantro
- 1 tsp. ground turmeric
- 1 tsp. paprika
- 1 tsp. sea salt
- ½ tsp. pepper
- ½ tsp. ground cinnamon
- ½ tsp. chili powder
- 1 cup golden raisins
- ½ to 1 cup chopped pitted green olives
- 1 medium lemon, sliced
- 2 garlic cloves, minced
- ½ cup chicken broth or water
- 4 cups hot cooked brown rice

In a 3- or 4-qt. slow cooker, combine the diced onion and oil. Place chicken thighs on top of onion; sprinkle with next seven ingredients. Top with raisins, olives, lemon and garlic. Add broth. Cook, covered, on low until the chicken is tender, 4-5 hours. Serve with hot cooked rice.

1 serving: 386 cal., 13g fat (3g sat. fat), 76mg chol., 556mg sod., 44g carb. (12g sugars, 3g fiber), 25g pro.

TEST KITCHEN TIP

If green olives aren't your favorite, don't leave them out entirely—go with ½ cup. They add a nice underlying flavor as well as a little saltiness to the dish.

NORTH AFRICAN CHICKEN & RICE

MOIST ITALIAN TURKEY BREAST

This recipe makes some of the juiciest turkey I have ever eaten. High in lean protein, it's a smart entree for any special occasion.
—Jessica Kunz, Springfield, IL

Prep: 25 min. • **Cook:** 5 hours + standing
Makes: 12 servings

- 1 lb. carrots, cut into 2-in. pieces
- 2 medium onions, cut into wedges
- 3 celery ribs, cut into 2-in. pieces
- 1 can (14½ oz.) chicken broth
- 1 bone-in turkey breast (6 to 7 lbs.), thawed and skin removed
- 2 Tbsp. olive oil
- 1½ tsp. seasoned salt
- 1 tsp. Italian seasoning
- ½ tsp. pepper

1. Place vegetables and broth in a 6- or 7-qt. slow cooker; top with turkey breast. Brush turkey with oil; sprinkle with seasonings.
2. Cook, covered, on low until a thermometer inserted in turkey reads at least 170°, 5-6 hours. Remove turkey from slow cooker; let stand, covered, 15 minutes before carving. Serve with vegetables. If desired, strain cooking juices and thicken for gravy.

1 serving: 360 cal., 15g fat (4g sat. fat), 123mg chol., 477mg sod., 6g carb. (3g sugars, 2g fiber), 48g pro.

SOUTHERN LOADED SWEET POTATOES

For a taste of a southern classic, we make sweet potatoes stuffed with pulled pork and coleslaw and manage to sidestep the calorie overload.

—Amy Burton, Fuquay Varina, NC

Prep: 15 min. • **Cook:** 6 hours
Makes: 8 servings

- 1 boneless pork loin roast (2 to 3 lbs.)
- ½ cup Dijon mustard, divided
- 1 Tbsp. brown sugar
- 1 Tbsp. garlic powder
- 1 tsp. cayenne pepper
- ½ tsp. salt
- 1 cup reduced-sodium beef broth
- 8 medium sweet potatoes (about 5 lbs.)
- 3 cups coleslaw mix
- ½ cup fat-free plain Greek yogurt
- ½ cup reduced-fat mayonnaise
- 2 Tbsp. cider vinegar
- ½ tsp. celery seed
- ¼ tsp. garlic salt

1. Place roast in a 3-qt. slow cooker. In a small bowl, mix ⅓ cup mustard, brown sugar, garlic powder, cayenne and ¼ tsp. salt; brush over pork. Add beef broth; cook, covered, on low 6-8 hours or until meat is tender.

2. Meanwhile, preheat oven to 400°. Scrub potatoes; pierce several times with a fork. Bake 45-50 minutes or until tender.

3. Place coleslaw mix in a large bowl. In a small bowl, whisk yogurt, mayonnaise, vinegar, celery seed, garlic salt and remaining mustard and salt; pour over coleslaw mix and toss to coat.

4. Remove roast; cool slightly. Shred the pork with two forks; return to slow cooker.

5. With a sharp knife, cut an "X" in each potato. Fluff pulp with a fork. Using a slotted spoon, place pork mixture and coleslaw over each potato.

1 potato with ⅔ cup pork mixture and ¼ cup coleslaw: 428 cal., 10g fat (3g sat. fat), 62mg chol., 784mg sod., 52g carb. (23g sugars, 6g fiber), 28g pro.

APPLE CHICKEN STEW

APPLE CHICKEN STEW

My husband and I enjoy visiting the apple orchards in nearby Nebraska City. We always make sure to buy extra cider to use in this sensational slow-cooked stew.

—Carol Mathias, Lincoln, NE

Prep: 35 min. • **Cook:** 3 hours
Makes: 8 servings

- 1½ tsp. salt
- ¾ tsp. dried thyme
- ½ tsp. pepper
- ¼ to ½ tsp. caraway seeds
- 1½ lbs. potatoes (about 4 medium), cut into ¾-in. pieces
- 4 medium carrots, cut into ¼-in. slices
- 1 medium red onion, halved and sliced
- 1 celery rib, thinly sliced
- 2 lbs. boneless skinless chicken breasts, cut into 1-in. pieces
- 2 Tbsp. olive oil
- 1 bay leaf
- 1 large tart apple, peeled and cut into 1-in. cubes
- 1 Tbsp. cider vinegar
- 1¼ cups apple cider or juice
  Minced fresh parsley

1. Mix first four ingredients. In a 5-qt. slow cooker, layer vegetables; sprinkle with half of the salt mixture.

2. Toss chicken with oil and remaining salt mixture. In a large skillet over medium-high heat, brown chicken in batches. Add to slow cooker. Top with bay leaf and apple. Add vinegar and cider.

3. Cook, covered, on high until chicken is no longer pink and vegetables are tender, 3-3½ hours. Discard bay leaf. Stir before serving. Sprinkle with parsley.

1 cup: 284 cal., 6g fat (1g sat. fat), 63mg chol., 533mg sod., 31g carb. (9g sugars, 4g fiber), 26g pro.

Diabetic exchanges: 3 lean meat, 2 starch, 1 fat.

SLOW-COOKER PORK & APPLE CURRY

Here's a gentle curry dish that's sure to please American palates. For fun, try varying the garnish—add a few chopped peanuts or a little chutney.
—Nancy Reck, Mill Valley, CA

Prep: 15 min. • **Cook:** 5½ hours
Makes: 8 servings

- 2 lbs. boneless pork loin roast, cut into 1-in. cubes
- 1 medium apple, peeled and chopped
- 1 small onion, chopped
- ½ cup orange juice
- 1 Tbsp. curry powder
- 1 tsp. chicken bouillon granules
- 1 garlic clove, minced
- ½ tsp. salt
- ½ tsp. ground ginger
- ¼ tsp. ground cinnamon
- 2 Tbsp. cornstarch
- 2 Tbsp. cold water
  Hot cooked rice, optional
- ¼ cup raisins
- ¼ cup sweetened shredded coconut, toasted

CARNE GUISADA

1. In a 3-qt. slow cooker, combine the first 10 ingredients. Cover and cook on low for 5-6 hours or until meat is tender.

2. Increase heat to high. In a small bowl, combine cornstarch and water until smooth; stir into slow cooker. Cover and cook for 30 minutes or until thickened, stirring once.

3. Serve with rice if desired. Sprinkle with raisins and coconut.

⅔ cup: 174 cal., 6g fat (2g sat. fat), 57mg chol., 287mg sod., 8g carb. (4g sugars, 1g fiber), 22g pro.
Diabetic exchanges: 3 lean meat, ½ starch.

CARNE GUISADA

While living away from Texas for a while, my boyfriend and I grew homesick for the spicy flavors of home. We've made this recipe a few times now, and it goes really well with homemade flour tortillas. We love it over rice, too.
—Kelly Evans, Denton, TX

Prep: 25 min. • **Cook:** 7 hours
Makes: 12 servings (about 2 qt.)

- 1 bottle (12 oz.) beer
- ¼ cup all-purpose flour
- 2 Tbsp. tomato paste
- 1 jalapeno pepper, seeded and chopped
- 4 tsp. Worcestershire sauce
- 1 bay leaf
- 2 to 3 tsp. crushed red pepper flakes
- 2 tsp. chili powder
- 1½ tsp. ground cumin
- ½ tsp. salt
- ½ tsp. paprika
- 2 garlic cloves, minced
- ½ tsp. red wine vinegar
  Dash liquid smoke, optional
- 1 boneless pork shoulder butt roast (3 lbs.), cut into 2-in. pieces
- 2 large unpeeled red potatoes, chopped
- 1 medium onion, chopped
  Whole wheat tortillas or hot cooked brown rice, lime wedges and chopped fresh cilantro, optional

1. In a 4- or 5-qt. slow cooker, mix the first 13 ingredients and, if desired, liquid smoke. Stir in pork, potatoes and onion. Cook, covered, on low until pork is tender, 7-9 hours.

2. Discard bay leaf; skim fat from cooking juices. Shred pork slightly with two forks. Serve with optional ingredients as desired.
Note: Wear disposable gloves when cutting hot peppers; the oils can burn skin. Avoid touching your face.

⅔ cup: 261 cal., 12g fat (4g sat. fat), 67mg chol., 200mg sod., 16g carb. (3g sugars, 2g fiber), 21g pro.
Diabetic exchanges: 3 medium-fat meat, 1 starch.

SLOW-COOKED ORANGE CHIPOTLE CHICKEN
(PICTURED ON P. 214)

Even though this chicken dish cooks for hours, the citrus keeps things fresh. We're big on spice at our house, so sometimes I use two chipotle peppers.
—Deborah Biggs, Omaha, NE

Prep: 10 min. • **Cook:** 4 hours
Makes: 6 servings

- ½ cup thawed orange juice concentrate
- ¼ cup barbecue sauce
- 1 chipotle pepper in adobo sauce
- ¼ tsp. salt
- ¼ tsp. garlic powder
- 6 boneless skinless chicken breast halves (6 oz. each)
- ¼ cup chopped red onion
- 4 tsp. cornstarch
- 3 Tbsp. cold water
  Grated orange zest

1. Place first five ingredients in a blender; cover and process until blended.
2. Place chicken and onion in a 3-qt. slow cooker; top with juice mixture. Cook, covered, on low until a thermometer inserted in chicken reads at least 165°, 4-5 hours.
3. Remove chicken from slow cooker; keep warm. Transfer cooking juices to a saucepan; bring to a boil. In a small bowl, mix cornstarch and water until smooth; gradually stir into juices. Return to a boil, stirring constantly; cook and stir until thickened, 1-2 minutes. Spoon over chicken; top with orange zest.

1 chicken breast with ¼ cup sauce: 246 cal., 4g fat (1g sat. fat), 94mg chol., 315mg sod., 15g carb. (11g sugars, 1g fiber), 35g pro.
Diabetic exchanges: 5 lean meat, 1 starch.

TEST KITCHEN TIP
Chipotle peppers are spicy, so you don't need much to add smoky heat. Freeze leftover peppers individually in ice cube trays, then store in a freezer container.

GARLIC LOVER'S BEEF STEW

Wine gives a mellow flavor to this beef and carrot stew. We like to serve it over mashed potatoes, but you could also use egg noodles.
—Alissa Brown, Fort Washington, PA

Prep: 30 min. • **Cook:** 8 hours
Makes: 10 servings

- 1 boneless beef chuck roast (3 lbs.), cut into 2-in. pieces
- 1¼ tsp. salt
- ¾ tsp. coarsely ground pepper
- ½ cup all-purpose flour
- 2 Tbsp. olive oil
- 12 garlic cloves, minced
- 1 cup dry red wine or reduced-sodium beef broth
- 2 cans (14½ oz. each) diced tomatoes, undrained
- 1 can (14½ oz.) reduced-sodium beef broth
- 6 medium carrots, thinly sliced
- 2 medium onions, chopped
- 2 Tbsp. tomato paste
- 2 tsp. minced fresh rosemary or ½ tsp. dried rosemary, crushed
- 2 tsp. minced fresh thyme or ½ tsp. dried thyme
- 2 bay leaves
  Dash ground cloves
  Hot mashed potatoes

1. Sprinkle beef with salt, pepper and flour; toss to coat.
2. In a large skillet, heat oil over medium-high heat. Brown beef in batches. Remove with a slotted spoon. Reduce heat to medium. Add garlic; cook and stir for 1 minute.
3. Add wine to skillet, stirring to loosen browned bits from pan. Transfer to a 5- or 6-qt. slow cooker. Stir in tomatoes, broth, carrots, onions, tomato paste, rosemary, thyme, bay leaves, cloves and beef.
4. Cook, covered, on low 8-10 hours or until beef is tender. Remove bay leaves. Serve with mashed potatoes.

1 cup: 330 cal., 16g fat (5g sat. fat), 89mg chol., 586mg sod., 17g carb. (6g sugars, 3g fiber), 29g pro.
Diabetic exchanges: 4 lean meat, 1 starch, 1 fat.

GARLIC LOVER'S BEEF STEW

**SPICE TRADE
BEANS & BULGUR**

SPICY LENTIL & CHICKPEA STEW

This recipe came to me from a friend and previous co-worker at a health food store. I changed a few things until I found a version that my family loves. My son doesn't like things too spicy, so I make the stew milder for him and add a sprinkle of extra spice in mine. My husband, who farms, works outdoors for long hours at a time and finds this soup substantial enough to keep him satisfied.
—Melanie MacFarlane, Bedeque, PE

Prep: 25 min. • **Cook:** 8 hours
Makes: 8 servings (2¾ qt.)

- 2 tsp. olive oil
- 1 medium onion, thinly sliced
- 1 tsp. dried oregano
- ½ tsp. crushed red pepper flakes
- 2 cans (15 oz. each) chickpeas or garbanzo beans, rinsed and drained
- 1 cup dried lentils, rinsed
- 1 can (2¼ oz.) sliced ripe olives, drained
- 3 tsp. smoked paprika
- 4 cups vegetable broth
- 4 cans (8 oz. each) no-salt-added tomato sauce
- 4 cups fresh baby spinach
- ¾ cup fat-free plain yogurt

1. In a small skillet, heat oil over medium-high heat. Add onion, oregano and pepper flakes; cook and stir 8-10 minutes or until onion is tender. Transfer to a 5- or 6-qt. slow cooker.

2. Add chickpeas, lentils, olives and paprika; stir in broth and tomato sauce. Cook, covered, on low 8-10 hours or until lentils are tender. Stir in spinach. Top servings with yogurt.

1⅓ cups: 266 cal., 4g fat (0 sat. fat), 0 chol., 712mg sod., 45g carb. (11g sugars, 10g fiber), 14g pro.
Diabetic exchanges: 2 starch, 2 vegetable, 1 lean meat.

SPICE TRADE BEANS & BULGUR

A rich blend of treasured spices flavors tender, nutritious bulgur and chickpeas in a yummy stew that offers just the right amount of heat. It's a savory one-dish meal. The hint of sweetness from golden raisins provides the perfect accent.
—Faith Cromwell, San Francisco, CA

Prep: 30 min. • **Cook:** 3½ hours
Makes: 10 servings

- 3 Tbsp. canola oil, divided
- 2 medium onions, chopped
- 1 medium sweet red pepper, chopped
- 5 garlic cloves, minced
- 1 Tbsp. ground cumin
- 1 Tbsp. paprika
- 2 tsp. ground ginger
- 1 tsp. pepper
- ½ tsp. ground cinnamon
- ½ tsp. cayenne pepper
- 1½ cups bulgur
- 1 can (28 oz.) crushed tomatoes
- 1 can (14½ oz.) diced tomatoes, undrained
- 1 carton (32 oz.) vegetable broth
- 2 Tbsp. brown sugar
- 2 Tbsp. soy sauce
- 1 can (15 oz.) garbanzo beans or chickpeas, rinsed and drained
- ½ cup golden raisins
  Minced fresh cilantro, optional

1. In a large skillet, heat 2 Tbsp. oil over medium-high heat. Add onions and pepper; cook and stir 3-4 minutes or until tender. Add garlic and seasonings; cook 1 minute longer. Transfer mixture to a 5-qt. slow cooker.

2. In same skillet, heat remaining oil over medium-high heat. Add bulgur; cook and stir 2-3 minutes or until lightly browned.

3. Add bulgur, tomatoes, broth, brown sugar and soy sauce to slow cooker. Cook, covered, on low 3-4 hours or until bulgur is tender. Stir in beans and raisins; cook 30 minutes longer. If desired, sprinkle with fresh cilantro.

1¼ cups: 245 cal., 6g fat (0 sat. fat), 0 chol., 752mg sod., 45g carb. (15g sugars, 8g fiber), 8g pro.

SPICY LENTIL &
CHICKPEA STEW

TREAT
YOURSELF

> *"With dried apples and cranberries, these crispy cereal bars are perfect for snacks or brown-bag lunches. Store the leftovers —if you have any!—in a covered container. "*
> —Giovanna Kranenberg, Cambridge, MN

GROSSMUTTER'S PEPPERNUTS

Before Christmas, my grandmother would bake peppernuts and store them until the big day. When we came home from school, the whole house would smell like anise and we knew the holiday season was about to begin.
—Marilyn Kutzli, Clinton, IA

Prep: 40 min. + chilling
Bake: 10 min./batch
Makes: about 30 dozen

- 3 large eggs, room temperature
- 2 cups sugar
- 2¾ cups all-purpose flour
- 1 tsp. anise extract or crushed aniseed

1. Beat eggs and sugar at medium speed for 15 minutes. Reduce speed; gradually add the flour and anise. Beat until well combined. On a lightly floured surface, shape the dough into ½-in.-thick ropes. Refrigerate, covered, for 1 hour.
2. Preheat oven to 350°. Cut ropes into ½-in. pieces; place on greased baking sheets. Bake until set, 6-8 minutes. Cool completely on baking sheets on wire racks. Cookies will harden upon standing. Store in airtight containers.

6 cookies: 51 cal., 0 fat (0 sat. fat), 9mg chol., 4mg sod., 11g carb. (7g sugars, 0 fiber), 1g pro.
Diabetic exchanges: 1 starch.

CHOCOLATE-GLAZED BROWNIES

CHOCOLATE-GLAZED BROWNIES

These moist and fudgy squares are bursting with such rich chocolate flavor, you'd never guess they're low in fat. The brownies are ideal for taking to bake sales and family gatherings or sharing with co-workers. For holidays, I like to dress them up with colorful candy sprinkles.
—Deb Anderson, Joplin, MO

Prep: 15 min. • **Bake:** 20 min. + cooling
Makes: 1 dozen

- ⅓ cup butter, softened
- 1 cup sugar
- 1 tsp. vanilla extract
- 3 large egg whites, room temperature
- ⅔ cup all-purpose flour
- ½ cup baking cocoa
- ½ tsp. baking powder
- ¼ tsp. salt

GLAZE
- ⅔ cup confectioners' sugar
- 2 Tbsp. baking cocoa
- ¼ tsp. vanilla extract
- 3 to 4 tsp. hot water

1. Preheat oven to 350°. Cream butter and sugar until light and fluffy. Beat in the vanilla and egg whites, one at a time. In a small bowl, whisk together the flour, cocoa, baking powder and salt; gradually add to creamed mixture. Spread into an 8-in. square baking pan coated with cooking spray.
2. Bake until a toothpick inserted in center comes out clean, 20-25 minutes. Cool completely on a wire rack.
3. Mix glaze ingredients; spread over brownies. Cut into bars.

1 brownie: 180 cal., 6g fat (3g sat. fat), 14mg chol., 124mg sod., 31g carb. (23g sugars, 1g fiber), 3g pro.
Diabetic exchanges: 2 starch, 1 fat.

MAKEOVER PEACH UPSIDE-DOWN CAKE

This peachy delight has charmed folks for years. Our lightened-up version is even better, with less fat and calories than other similar recipes.
—*Taste of Home* Test Kitchen

Prep: 20 min. • **Bake:** 30 min. + cooling
Makes: 8 servings

- 1 can (15 oz.) sliced peaches in juice
- ⅓ cup packed brown sugar
- 4 Tbsp. butter, melted, divided
- ¼ tsp. ground cinnamon
- ⅛ tsp. ground nutmeg
- 1½ cups all-purpose flour
- ⅔ cup sugar
- ¾ tsp. baking powder
- ¼ tsp. baking soda
- ¼ tsp. salt
- 1 large egg, room temperature
- 1 tsp. vanilla extract
- 1 cup buttermilk

1. Preheat oven to 350°. Drain peaches, reserving 2 Tbsp. juice. Cut peach slices lengthwise in half; pat dry.
2. In a small bowl, mix the brown sugar, 1 Tbsp. melted butter, spices and reserved juice; spread into a 9-in. round baking pan coated with cooking spray. Arrange peach slices over top.
3. In a large bowl, whisk together flour, sugar, baking powder, baking soda and salt. In another bowl, whisk together egg, vanilla, buttermilk and remaining butter. Add to the dry ingredients; stir just until moistened. Spoon over peaches.
4. Bake until a toothpick inserted in center comes out clean, 30-35 minutes. Cool 10 minutes before inverting onto a serving plate. Serve warm.

1 piece: 226 cal., 1g fat (0 sat. fat), 24mg chol., 231mg sod., 50g carb. (31g sugars, 1g fiber), 4g pro.

PUMPKIN SEED CRANBERRY BISCOTTI

(PICTURED ON P. 228)

A hint of pumpkin seed and almond gives this biscotti recipe a wonderful flavor that's just right for fall. Try these with a cup of coffee or hot cocoa!
—Nancy Renner, Eugene, OR

Prep: 30 min. • **Bake:** 35 min. + cooling
Makes: about 2½ dozen

- 2 large eggs, room temperature
- ¼ cup canola oil
- ¾ cup sugar
- 1½ tsp. vanilla extract
- ½ tsp. almond extract
- 2 cups all-purpose flour
- 1 tsp. baking powder
- ½ tsp. salt
- 1 cup salted pumpkin seeds or pepitas, toasted
- ½ cup dried cranberries

1. Preheat oven to 350°. In a large bowl, beat the first five ingredients until well blended. In another bowl, whisk together flour, baking powder and salt. Add to egg mixture; mix just until moistened (dough will be sticky). Stir in the pumpkin seeds and cranberries.
2. Divide dough in half. On a baking sheet coated with cooking spray, shape each portion into a 12x2-in. rectangle using lightly floured hands. Bake until golden brown, 25-30 minutes.
3. Carefully remove rectangles to wire racks; cool 10 minutes. Transfer to a cutting board. Using a serrated knife, cut diagonally into ¾-in. slices. Return biscotti to baking sheets, cut side down.
4. Bake until firm, about 5 minutes. Turn; bake until lightly browned, 5-10 minutes. Remove from pans to wire racks to cool. Store in an airtight container.

1 cookie: 103 cal., 4g fat (1g sat. fat), 12mg chol., 71mg sod., 14g carb. (7g sugars, 1g fiber), 2g pro.
Diabetic exchanges: 1 starch, 1 fat.

MAKEOVER PEACH UPSIDE-DOWN CAKE

CHOCOLATE-COCONUT ANGEL CUPCAKES

My guests are never satisfied with just one of these, but that's OK because they are so light. The meringuelike tops make them different, and the chocolate and coconut make them memorable.
—Bernice Janowski, Stevens Point, WI

....

Prep: 20 min. • **Bake:** 30 min. + cooling
Makes: 1½ dozen

- 6 large egg whites, room temperature
- ⅔ cup all-purpose flour
- ¼ cup baking cocoa
- ½ tsp. baking powder
- 1⅓ cups sugar, divided
- 1 tsp. almond extract
- ½ tsp. cream of tartar
- ¼ tsp. salt
- 1 cup sweetened shredded coconut
  Confectioners' sugar, optional

1. Place the egg whites in a large bowl. Preheat oven to 350°. Line 18 muffin cups with cupcake liners.
2. Sift together the flour, cocoa, baking powder and 1 cup of the sugar twice.
3. Add almond extract, cream of tartar and salt to egg whites; beat on medium speed until soft peaks form. Gradually add remaining sugar, 1 Tbsp. at a time, beating on high after each addition until sugar is dissolved. Continue beating until stiff glossy peaks form. Gradually fold in flour mixture, about ½ cup at a time. Gently fold in coconut.
4. Fill prepared cups two-thirds full. Bake until top appears dry, 30-35 minutes.
5. Cool in the pans 10 minutes before removing to wire racks; cool completely. If desired, dust with confectioners' sugar.
1 cupcake: 110 cal., 2g fat (2g sat. fat), 0 chol., 78mg sod., 22g carb. (17g sugars, 1g fiber), 2g pro.
Diabetic exchanges: 1½ starch.

MOCHA NUT ROLL

I've enjoyed this cake several times at a friend's house and it never ceases to be delightful. Tender and impressive, it's the perfect indulgence for anyone who loves coffee and chocolate.
—Susan Bettinger, Battle Creek, MI

....

Prep: 35 min. • **Bake:** 10 min. + cooling
Makes: 12 servings

MOCHA NUT ROLL

- 4 large eggs, separated, room temperature
- ⅓ cup plus ½ cup sugar
- ½ tsp. vanilla extract
- ½ cup all-purpose flour
- 1 tsp. baking powder
- ¼ tsp. salt
- ¼ cup finely chopped walnuts

MOCHA FILLING
- ½ cup sugar
- 3 Tbsp. all-purpose flour
- 2 tsp. instant coffee granules
- ¼ tsp. salt
- 1¼ cups whole milk
- 1 oz. unsweetened chocolate, chopped
- 1 large egg, lightly beaten
- 1 Tbsp. butter
- 1 tsp. vanilla extract
  Confectioners' sugar and chocolate curls, optional

1. Line a greased 15x10x1-in. baking pan with waxed paper; grease and set aside.
2. In a large bowl, beat the egg yolks on high speed until thick and lemon-colored, 5 minutes. Gradually beat in ⅓ cup sugar. Beat in vanilla. Combine the flour, baking powder and salt; gradually add to yolk mixture and mix well (batter will be very thick). Stir in walnuts.
3. In a small bowl with clean beaters, beat egg whites on medium speed until soft peaks form. Gradually beat in remaining

sugar 1 Tbsp. at a time, on high until stiff peaks form. Gradually fold into the batter. Spread evenly into prepared pan.
4. Bake at 375° until cake springs back when lightly touched, 10-15 minutes. Cool in pan for 5 minutes. Invert onto a kitchen towel dusted with confectioners' sugar. Gently peel off waxed paper. Roll up cake in the towel jelly-roll style, starting with a short side. Cool completely on a wire rack.
5. Meanwhile, in a small saucepan, combine the sugar, flour, coffee granules, and salt. Stir in milk and chocolate. Bring to a boil. Cook and stir for 2 minutes.
6. Remove from the heat. Stir a small amount of hot mixture into egg; return all to pan, stirring constantly. Bring to a gentle boil. Cook and stir until mixture reaches 160°, 2-3 minutes. Remove from heat; gently stir in butter and vanilla. Cool to room temperature.
7. Unroll cake; spread filling evenly over cake to within ½ in. of edges. Roll up again. Place seam side down on a serving platter. If desired, just before serving sprinkle the cake with confectioners' sugar and garnish with chocolate curls.
1 slice: 195 cal., 7g fat (3g sat. fat), 93mg chol., 179mg sod., 30g carb. (24g sugars, 1g fiber), 5g pro.
Diabetic exchanges: 2 starch, 1 fat.

TREAT YOURSELF

GHOST CUPCAKE CONES

Scare up a good treat using prepared cake mix, ice cream cones and whipped topping. These ghosts are as easy as child's play so don't wait for Halloween.
—*Taste of Home* Test Kitchen

Prep: 35 min. • **Bake:** 20 min. + cooling
Makes: 2½ dozen

- 1 pkg. yellow cake mix (regular size)
- 30 ice cream cake cones (about 3 in. tall)
- 1 carton (12 oz.) frozen whipped topping, thawed
  Black decorating icing

1. Preheat oven to 350°. Cover two 13x9-in. pans with foil, tightly securing edges around pan. For each pan, cut fifteen small holes in foil, about 2½ in. apart. Carefully stand a cone in each hole.
2. Prepare the cake batter according to package directions. Fill cones to within ½ in. of tops (scant 3 Tbsp.); do not overfill. Bake until a toothpick inserted in center comes out clean, 17-20 minutes. Cool completely on wire racks.

3. To serve, pipe or dollop whipped topping over tops to resemble ghosts. Decorate with black icing. Refrigerate leftover cones.

1 cupcake cone: 139 cal., 6g fat (3g sat. fat), 19mg chol., 119mg sod., 18g carb. (8g sugars, 0 fiber), 2g pro.
Diabetic exchanges: 1 starch, 1 fat.

GRILLED PEACHES & BERRIES
(PICTURED ON P. 229)

Highlight the natural sweetness of peak summertime fruit with brown sugar, butter and a squeeze of lemon juice. Foil packets make this a go-anywhere dessert.
—Sharon Bickett, Chester, SC

Takes: 30 min. • **Makes:** 2 servings

- 2 medium ripe peaches, halved and pitted
- ½ cup fresh blueberries
- 1 Tbsp. brown sugar
- 2 tsp. lemon juice
- 4 tsp. butter

1. Place two peach halves, cut side up, on each of two double thicknesses of heavy-duty foil (12 in. square). Sprinkle each with blueberries, brown sugar and lemon juice; dot with butter. Fold foil over peaches and seal tightly.
2. Grill, covered, over medium-low heat until tender, 18-20 minutes. Open the foil carefully to allow steam to escape.

1 serving: 156 cal., 8g fat (5g sat. fat), 20mg chol., 57mg sod., 23g carb. (19g sugars, 2g fiber), 1g pro.
Diabetic exchanges: 2 fat, 1 fruit, ½ starch.

★ ★ ★ ★ ★ **READER REVIEW**

"Words can not describe how delicious this dish was. Next time I will be serving it next to a slice of pound or angel food cake to soak up all that syrup. Yum yum."

CCHAP_82 TASTEOFHOME.COM

WHITE CHIP CRANBERRY BLONDIES

We created these delicious blondies to satisfy any health-conscious cook. Applesauce moistens the batter, while dried cranberries, white chocolate and heart-healthy pecans flavor each bite.
—*Taste of Home* Test Kitchen

Prep: 15 min. • **Bake:** 15 min. + cooling
Makes: 20 bars

- 2 large eggs, room temperature
- ¼ cup canola oil
- ¼ cup unsweetened applesauce
- 1½ tsp. vanilla extract
- 1⅓ cups all-purpose flour
- ⅔ cup packed brown sugar
- 1 tsp. baking powder
- ½ tsp. salt
- 1 cup dried cranberries, divided
- ½ cup white baking chips
- ½ cup chopped pecans

1. In a large bowl, beat the eggs, oil, applesauce and vanilla. Combine the flour, brown sugar, baking powder and salt; stir into the egg mixture until blended. Stir in ½ cup cranberries (batter will be thick).
2. Spread batter into a 13x9-in. baking pan coated with cooking spray. Top with chips, pecans and remaining cranberries; gently press toppings down.
3. Bake at 350° until a toothpick inserted in center comes out clean, 15-20 minutes. Cool on a wire rack. Cut into bars.

1 bar: 154 cal., 7g fat (1g sat. fat), 22mg chol., 92mg sod., 22g carb. (12g sugars, 1g fiber), 2g pro.
Diabetic exchanges: 1½ starch, 1 fat.

WHITE CHIP CRANBERRY BLONDIES

PATRIOTIC FROZEN DELIGHT

My husband and I pick lots of fruit at berry farms in the area and freeze it to enjoy all year. This frozen dessert showcases both blueberries and strawberries and also has a refreshing lemon flavor.
—Bernice Russ, Bladenboro, NC

Prep: 10 min. + freezing
Makes: 12 servings

- 1 can (14 oz.) sweetened condensed milk
- ⅓ cup lemon juice
- 2 tsp. grated lemon zest
- 2 cups plain yogurt
- 2 cups miniature marshmallows
- ½ cup chopped pecans
- 1 cup sliced fresh strawberries
- 1 cup fresh blueberries

In a bowl, combine milk, lemon juice and zest. Stir in yogurt, marshmallows and pecans. Spread half into an ungreased 11x7-in. dish. Sprinkle with half of the strawberries and blueberries. Cover with the remaining yogurt mixture; top with remaining berries. Cover and freeze. Remove from the freezer 15-20 minutes before serving.

1 serving: 223 cal., 9g fat (4g sat. fat), 21mg chol., 84mg sod., 32g carb. (29g sugars, 1g fiber), 6g pro.
Diabetic exchanges: 2 starch, 2 fat.

LEMON MERINGUE ANGEL CAKE

EASY APPLE STRUDEL

My family always loves it when I make this wonderful dessert. Old-fashioned strudel was too fattening and time-consuming, but this revised classic tastes just as good. It's best served warm from the oven.
—Joanie Fuson, Indianapolis, IN

Prep: 30 min. • **Bake:** 35 min.
Makes: 6 servings

- ⅓ cup raisins
- 2 Tbsp. water
- ¼ tsp. almond extract
- 3 cups coarsely chopped peeled apples
- ⅓ cup plus 2 tsp. sugar, divided
- 3 Tbsp. all-purpose flour
- ¼ tsp. ground cinnamon
- 8 sheets phyllo dough (14x9-in. size)
- 2 Tbsp. butter, melted
- 2 Tbsp. canola oil
  Confectioners' sugar, optional

1. Preheat oven to 350°. Place raisins, water and extract in a large microwave-save bowl; microwave, uncovered, on high for 1½ minutes. Let stand for 5 minutes. Drain. Add apples, ⅓ cup sugar, flour and cinnamon; toss to combine.
2. In a small bowl, mix melted butter and oil; remove 2 tsp. mixture for brushing top. Place one sheet of phyllo dough on a work surface; brush lightly with some of the butter mixture. (Keep the remaining phyllo covered with a damp towel to prevent it from drying out.) Layer with seven additional phyllo sheets, brushing each layer with some butter mixture. Spread apple mixture over phyllo dough to within 2 in. of one long side.
3. Fold the short edges over filling. Roll up jelly-roll style, starting from the side with a 2-in. border. Transfer to a baking sheet coated with cooking spray. Brush strudel with reserved butter mixture; sprinkle with remaining sugar. With a sharp knife, cut diagonal slits in top of strudel.
4. Bake until golden brown, 35-40 minutes. Cool on a wire rack. If desired, dust strudel with confectioners' sugar before serving.

1 slice: 229 cal., 9g fat (3g sat. fat), 10mg chol., 92mg sod., 37g carb. (24g sugars, 2g fiber), 2g pro.

LEMON MERINGUE ANGEL CAKE

I've been told that this dessert tastes just like lemon meringue pie and that it's the best angel food cake anyone could ask for. You can't beat the two flavors together.
—Sharon Kurtz, Emmaus, PA

Prep: 40 min. + standing • **Bake:** 35 min.
Makes: 14 servings

- 12 large egg whites, room temperature
- 1½ cups sugar, divided
- 1 cup cake flour
- 2 tsp. cream of tartar
- 1½ tsp. vanilla extract
- ¼ tsp. salt
- 1 jar (10 oz.) lemon curd

MERINGUE TOPPING
- 4 large egg whites, room temperature
- ¾ tsp. cream of tartar
- ½ cup sugar

1. Place egg whites in a large bowl. Sift ½ cup of sugar and flour together twice; set aside.
2. Add cream of tartar, vanilla and salt to egg whites; beat on medium speed until foamy. Gradually beat in remaining sugar, 2 Tbsp. at a time, on high until stiff glossy peaks form and the sugar is dissolved. Gradually fold in the flour mixture, about ½ cup at a time.
3. Gently spoon batter into an ungreased 10-in. tube pan. Cut through batter with a knife to remove any air pockets. Bake on lowest oven rack at 350° until golden brown and the entire top appears dry, 35-40 minutes. Immediately invert pan; cool completely, about 1 hour.
4. Run a knife around the side and center tube of pan. Remove cake; split into two layers. Place cake bottom on a parchment-lined baking sheet. Spread with the lemon curd; replace cake top.
5. For meringue, in a small bowl, beat egg whites and cream of tartar on medium until soft peaks form. Gradually beat in sugar, 1 Tbsp. at a time, on high until stiff glossy peaks form and sugar is dissolved. Spread over top and sides of the cake.
6. Bake at 350° until golden brown, 15-18 minutes. Transfer to a serving plate.

1 piece: 238 cal., 1g fat (1g sat. fat), 15mg chol., 121mg sod., 51g carb. (41g sugars, 0 fiber), 5g pro.

How To Test for Stiff Peaks
Test meringue peaks by lifting the beater from the bowl. The egg white peaks should stand straight up from the beater. Pinch some meringue between your fingers; it should feel silky smooth.

EASY APPLE STRUDEL

HONEYDEW GRANITA

Make this refreshing summer treat when melons are ripe and flavorful. I like to garnish each serving with a sprig of mint or a small slice of honeydew.
—Bonnie Hawkins, Elkhorn, WI

Prep: 10 min. • **Cook:** 5 min. + freezing
Makes: 5½ cups

- 1 cup sugar
- 1 cup water
- 6 cups cubed honeydew melon
- 2 Tbsp. sweet white wine

1. In a small saucepan, bring sugar and water to a boil over medium-high heat. Cook and stir until sugar is dissolved. Cool.
2. Pulse honeydew, sugar syrup and wine in batches in a food processor until smooth, 1-2 minutes. Transfer to an 8-in. square dish. Freeze 1 hour. Stir with a fork. Freeze, stirring every 30 minutes, until frozen, 2-3 hours longer. Stir again with a fork just before serving.

½ cup: 107 cal., 0 fat (0 sat. fat), 0 chol., 17mg sod., 27g carb. (26g sugars, 1g fiber), 1g pro.
Diabetic exchanges: 1½ starch, ½ fruit.

MOCHA MERINGUE SANDWICH COOKIES

MOCHA MERINGUE SANDWICH COOKIES

These crisp, chewy cookies inspired by the famous Concorde cake can be made any size you choose. They're also great with a variety of fillings—try making them with fruit preserves.
—Marie Valdes, Brandon, FL

Prep: 30 min. + standing
Bake: 15 min./batch
Makes: about 2 dozen

- 3 large egg whites, room temperature
- 1 tsp. instant coffee granules
- ½ cup confectioners' sugar
- ¼ cup baking cocoa
- ¼ tsp. cream of tartar
- ¾ cup sugar
- ¾ cup chocolate frosting
  Additional confectioners' sugar

1. Preheat oven to 350°. Place egg whites in a large bowl. In a small bowl sift coffee granules through a fine sieve, pressing with a spoon. Sift together ½ cup confectioners' sugar, cocoa and coffee.
2. Add cream of tartar to egg whites; beat on medium speed until foamy. Gradually beat in sugar, 1 Tbsp. at a time, beating on high after each addition until sugar is dissolved. Continue beating until stiff glossy peaks form. Fold in coffee mixture.
3. Cut a small hole in the tip of a pastry bag or in a corner of a food-safe plastic bag; insert a #11 round pastry tip. Add meringue; pipe 1¾-in. spirals 1 in. apart onto parchment-lined baking sheets.
4. Bake the meringues until set and dry, 12-15 minutes. Cool completely before removing meringues from paper.
5. To assemble, spread about 1½ tsp. frosting onto the bottom of half of the meringues; cover with the remaining meringues. Dust cookies with additional confectioners' sugar.

1 cookie: 76 cal., 2g fat (1g sat. fat), 0 chol., 25mg sod., 15g carb. (14g sugars, 0 fiber), 1g pro.
Diabetic exchanges: 1 starch, ½ fat.

✳

TEST KITCHEN TIP

Cream of tartar is an acid that makes the beaten egg whites more stable. If you don't have it, use 1/2 tsp. lemon juice or white vinegar.

DATE OATMEAL BARS

In no time at all, you can treat your family to these bars. They'll never suspect how light the snacks are.
—Helen Cluts, Eden Prairie, MN

Prep: 20 min. • **Bake:** 20 min. + cooling
Makes: 16 servings

- 1 cup chopped dates
- ½ cup water
- ¼ cup sugar
- 1½ cups quick-cooking oats
- 1 cup all-purpose flour
- 1 cup packed brown sugar
- ½ tsp. baking soda
- ¼ tsp. salt
- ⅓ cup butter, melted
- 1 large egg white, room temperature

1. Preheat oven to 350°. Place dates, water and sugar in a small saucepan; bring to a boil, stirring constantly. Reduce heat; simmer, uncovered, until thickened, about 5 minutes, stirring constantly.
2. In a large bowl, mix oats, flour, brown sugar, baking soda and salt; stir in melted butter and egg white. Press half of the mixture into an 8-in. square baking pan coated with cooking spray. Spread oat mixture carefully with date mixture; top with remaining oat mixture.
3. Bake until lightly browned, for 20-25 minutes. Cool in pan on a wire rack. Cut into bars.

1 bar: 182 cal., 4g fat (3g sat. fat), 10mg chol., 114mg sod., 35g carb. (23g sugars, 2g fiber), 2g pro.
Diabetic exchanges: 1½ starch, ½ fruit, 1 fat.

DATE OATMEAL BARS

PUMPKIN PIE CUSTARD

Instead of pumpkin pie, try this flavorful light holiday dessert. My husband's aunt shared the recipe with us after she brought this treat to a family party. It's wonderful.
—Nancy Zimmerman
Cape May Court House, NJ

Prep: 20 min. • **Bake:** 35 min. + chilling
Makes: 10 servings

- 1 can (15 oz.) canned pumpkin
- 1 can (12 oz.) fat-free evaporated milk
- 8 large egg whites
- ½ cup fat-free milk
- ¾ cup sugar
- ¼ tsp. salt
- 1 tsp. ground cinnamon
- ½ tsp. ground ginger
- ¼ tsp. ground cloves
- ¼ tsp. ground nutmeg
  Sweetened whipped cream and additional cinnamon, optional

1. Preheat oven to 350°. Place ten 6-oz. ramekins or custard cups coated with cooking spray in a 15x10x1-in. baking pan.
2. In a large bowl, beat the first four ingredients until smooth. Add the sugar, salt and spices; mix well. Divide mixture among ramekins.
3. Bake until a knife inserted in the center comes out clean, 40-45 minutes. Cool on a wire rack. Refrigerate custard within 2 hours. If desired, top with whipped cream and sprinkle with cinnamon.

1 serving: 120 cal., 0 fat (0 sat. fat), 2mg chol., 151mg sod., 24g carb. (21g sugars, 2g fiber), 7g pro.
Diabetic exchanges: 1½ starch.

FROSTY WATERMELON ICE

For a different way to serve watermelon, try this make-ahead frozen dessert. It's so refreshing on a summer day...and you don't have to worry about seeds while you're enjoying it.

—Kaaren Jurack, Manassas, VA

....

Prep: 20 min. + freezing
Makes: 4 servings

- 1 tsp. unflavored gelatin
- 2 Tbsp. water
- 2 Tbsp. lime juice
- 2 Tbsp. honey
- 4 cups cubed seedless watermelon, divided

1. In a microwave-safe bowl, sprinkle gelatin over water; let stand 1 minute. Microwave on high for 40 seconds. Stir and let stand 1-2 minutes or until gelatin is completely dissolved.
2. Place lime juice, honey and gelatin mixture in a blender. Add 1 cup of the watermelon; cover and process until blended. Add the remaining watermelon, 1 cup at a time, processing after each addition until smooth.
3. Transfer to a shallow dish; freeze until almost firm. In a chilled bowl, beat with an electric mixer until mixture is bright pink. Divide among four serving dishes; freeze, covered, until firm. Remove from freezer 15-20 minutes before serving.
¾ cup: 81 cal., 0 fat (0 sat. fat), 0 chol., 3mg sod., 21g carb. (18g sugars, 1g fiber), 1g pro.
Diabetic exchanges: 1 fruit, ½ starch.

FRUITY CEREAL BARS

(PICTURED ON P. 229)

With dried apples and cranberries, these crispy cereal bars are perfect for snacks or brown-bag lunches. Store the leftovers—if you have any!— in a covered container.

—Giovanna Kranenberg, Cambridge, MN

....

Takes: 20 min. • **Makes:** 20 servings

- 3 Tbsp. butter
- 1 pkg. (10 oz.) large marshmallows
- ½ cup dried cranberries
- ½ cup chopped dried apples
- 6 cups Rice Krispies

1. In a large saucepan, melt butter over low heat. Add marshmallows; cook and

stir until blended. Remove from heat; stir in remaining ingredients.
2. Press into a 13x9-in. pan coated with cooking spray; cool mixture completely. Cut into squares.
1 bar: 111 cal., 2g fat (1g sat. fat), 5mg chol., 73mg sod., 24g carb. (13g sugars, 0 fiber), 1g pro.
Diabetic exchanges: 1½ starch, ½ fat.

FIRST-PLACE COCONUT MACAROONS

These coconut macaroon cookies earned me a first-place ribbon at the county fair. They remain my husband's favorites, and whenever I make them to give away, he asks me where his batch is! I like that the recipe makes a small enough quantity for just two to nibble on, but you might want to double the recipe.

—Penny Ann Habeck, Shawano, WI

....

Prep: 10 min. • **Bake:** 20 min./batch
Makes: about 1½ dozen

FIRST PLACE COCONUT MACAROONS

- 1⅓ cups sweetened shredded coconut
- ⅓ cup sugar
- 2 Tbsp. all-purpose flour
- ⅛ tsp. salt
- 2 large egg whites, room temperature
- ½ tsp. vanilla extract

1. In a small bowl, combine the coconut, sugar, flour and salt. Add egg whites and vanilla; mix well.
2. Drop by rounded teaspoonfuls onto greased baking sheets. Bake at 325° until golden brown, 18-20 minutes. Cool on a wire rack.
1 cookie: 54 cal., 2g fat (2g sat. fat), 0 chol., 41mg sod., 8g carb. (7g sugars, 0 fiber), 1g pro.
Diabetic exchanges: ½ starch, ½ fat.

FROZEN PINEAPPLE-KIWI POPS

Kiwi, pineapple, sugar and water are all you need to make these easy, breezy freezer pops. What a great treat for a hot day.
—Colleen Ludovice, Wauwatosa, WI

Prep: 20 min. + freezing • **Makes:** 1 dozen

- 3 cups cubed fresh pineapple
- 1 cup water, divided
- 8 tsp. sugar, divided
- 12 plastic or paper cups (3 oz. each) and wooden pop sticks
- 2 cups sliced peeled kiwifruit (about 6 medium)

1. Place pineapple, ½ cup water and 4 tsp. sugar in a food processor; pulse until combined. Divide among cups. Top cups with foil and insert sticks through the foil. Freeze until firm, about 2 hours.
2. Place kiwifruit and the remaining water and sugar in food processor; pulse until combined. Spoon over pineapple layer. Freeze, covered, until firm.

1 pop: 50 cal., 0 fat (0 sat. fat), 0 chol., 1mg sod., 13g carb. (10g sugars, 1g fiber), 1g pro.
Diabetic exchanges: 1 fruit.

ORANGE RICOTTA CAKE ROLL

ORANGE RICOTTA CAKE ROLL

I come from a big Italian family where my mom cooked and baked many delicious meals and desserts from scratch. Now I like to do the same for my family. This magnificent cake is always the finale to any celebration dinner we have.
—Cathy Banks, Encinitas, CA

Prep: 45 min. • **Bake:** 10 min. + chilling
Makes: 12 servings

- 4 large eggs, separated, room temperature
- ¼ cup baking cocoa
- 2 Tbsp. all-purpose flour
- ⅛ tsp. salt
- ⅔ cup confectioners' sugar, sifted, divided
- 1 tsp. vanilla extract
- ½ tsp. cream of tartar

FILLING
- 1 container (15 oz.) ricotta cheese
- 3 Tbsp. mascarpone cheese
- ⅓ cup sugar
- 1 Tbsp. Kahlua (coffee liqueur)
- 1 Tbsp. grated orange zest
- ½ tsp. vanilla extract
  Additional confectioners' sugar

1. Place the egg whites in a large bowl. Preheat oven to 325°. Line bottom of a greased 15x10x1-in. baking pan with parchment; grease paper. Sift the cocoa, flour and salt together twice.
2. In a large bowl, beat egg yolks until slightly thickened. Gradually add ⅓ cup confectioners' sugar, beating on high speed until thick and lemon-colored. Beat in vanilla. Fold in cocoa mixture (batter will be very thick).
3. Add cream of tartar to egg whites; with clean beaters, beat on medium until soft peaks form. Gradually add remaining confectioners' sugar, 1 Tbsp. at a time, beating on high after each addition until sugar is dissolved. Continue beating until soft glossy peaks form. Fold a fourth of the whites into batter, then fold in the remaining whites. Transfer to prepared pan, spreading evenly.
4. Bake until the top springs back when lightly touched, 9-11 minutes. Cover cake with waxed paper; cool completely on a wire rack.
5. Remove waxed paper; invert the cake onto an 18-in.-long sheet of waxed paper dusted with confectioners' sugar. Gently peel off parchment.
6. In a small bowl, beat cheeses and sugar until blended. Stir in Kahlua, orange zest and vanilla. Spread over cake to within ½ in. of the edges. Roll up jelly-roll style, starting with a short side. Trim ends; place on a platter, seam side down.
7. Refrigerate, covered, for at least 1 hour before serving. To serve, dust the cake roll with confectioners' sugar.

1 slice: 169 cal., 9g fat (5g sat. fat), 94mg chol., 95mg sod., 17g carb. (14g sugars, 0 fiber), 7g pro.
Diabetic exchanges: 2 fat, 1 starch.

GRAPEFRUIT, LIME & MINT YOGURT PARFAIT

(PICTURED ON P. 228)

Tart grapefruit and lime are balanced with a bit of honey in this cool and easy parfait.
—Lois Enger, Colorado Springs, CO

Takes: 15 min. • **Makes:** 6 servings

- 4 large red grapefruit
- 4 cups reduced-fat plain yogurt
- 2 tsp. grated lime zest
- 2 Tbsp. lime juice
- 3 Tbsp. honey
  Torn fresh mint leaves

1. Cut a thin slice from the top and bottom of each grapefruit; stand fruit upright on a cutting board. With a knife, cut off peel and outer membrane from grapefruit. Cut along the membrane of each segment to remove fruit.

2. In a large bowl, mix yogurt, lime zest and juice. Layer half of the grapefruit and half of the yogurt mixture into six parfait glasses. Repeat layers. Drizzle with honey; top with mint.

1 parfait: 207 cal., 3g fat (2g sat. fat), 10mg chol., 115mg sod., 39g carb. (36g sugars, 3g fiber), 10g pro.

APPLESAUCE SPICE CUPCAKES

I began making these moist cupcakes when I was in grade school, and I am still baking them today.
—Edna Hoffman, Hebron, IN

Prep: 15 min. • **Bake:** 25 min. + cooling
Makes: 1 dozen

- ⅓ cup butter, softened
- ¾ cup sugar
- 2 large eggs, room temperature
- 1 tsp. vanilla extract
- 1⅓ cups all-purpose flour
- 1 tsp. baking powder
- ½ tsp. baking soda
- ½ tsp. salt
- 1 tsp. ground cinnamon
- ½ tsp. ground nutmeg
- ⅛ tsp. ground cloves
- ¾ cup applesauce
- 1 cup prepared cream cheese frosting

1. In a large bowl, cream butter and sugar. Add eggs, one at a time, beating well after each addition. Beat in vanilla. Combine dry ingredients; add to the creamed mixture alternately with applesauce.

2. Fill greased or paper-lined muffin cups two-thirds full. Bake at 350° until a toothpick inserted in the center comes out clean, 25 minutes. Cool 10 minutes before removing to a wire rack. Frost cooled cupcakes.

1 cupcake: 258 cal., 9g fat (5g sat. fat), 45mg chol., 291mg sod., 41g carb. (27g sugars, 1g fiber), 3g pro.

APPLESAUCE
SPICE CUPCAKES

**HOMEMADE
HONEY GRAHAMS**

CREAMY LAYERED BLUEBERRY ICE POPS

These delicious ice treats can be made with raspberries or blackberries. The rosemary sprig and lemon zest brings another layer of taste. They're quick, easy and kid-friendly.

—Gloria Bradley, Naperville, IL

Prep: 35 min. + freezing
Cook: 10 min.
Makes: 10 servings

- ⅓ cup agave nectar
- ¼ cup water
- 1 fresh rosemary sprig
- 1 lemon zest strip (2 in.)
- 1 Tbsp. lemon juice
- 2 cups fresh or frozen blueberries
- 2 Tbsp. sugar
- 2¼ cups frozen whipped topping, thawed
- 10 freezer pop molds or 10 paper cups (3 oz. each) and wooden pop sticks

1. For lemon syrup, place the first four ingredients in a small saucepan; bring to a boil, stirring occasionally. Remove from heat; let stand, covered, for 10 minutes. Remove rosemary and lemon zest. Stir in lemon juice; cool completely.
2. Place blueberries and sugar in another saucepan; cook and stir over medium heat until the berries pop, 5-7 minutes. Cool completely.
3. To assemble, cut a small hole in a corner of a food-safe plastic bag. Add the whipped topping to lemon syrup, whisking to blend. Transfer half of the mixture to prepared bag; pipe into molds. Layer with blueberries. Pipe the remaining whipped topping mixture over top. Close molds with holders. For paper cups, top with foil and insert sticks through foil.
4. Freeze until firm, about 4 hours. To serve, dip pop molds briefly in warm water before removing.

1 pop: 104 cal., 3g fat (3g sat. fat), 0 chol., 0 sod., 19g carb. (18g sugars, 1g fiber), 0 pro.
Diabetic exchanges: 1 starch, ½ fat.

TEST KITCHEN TIP
Agave nectar, made from the same plant used to make tequila, is a sweetener that can be used like sugar or honey.

HOMEMADE HONEY GRAHAMS

The way my boys eat them, I would spend a fortune on honey graham crackers at the grocery store. So I decided to come up with a homemade version that is less processed. These are even better tasting, and they don't last long at our house.
—Crystal Jo Bruns, Iliff, CO

Prep: 15 min. + chilling
Bake: 10 min./batch • **Makes:** 32 cookies

- 1 cup whole wheat flour
- ¾ cup all-purpose flour
- ½ cup toasted wheat germ
- 2 Tbsp. dark brown sugar
- 1 tsp. baking powder
- 1 tsp. ground cinnamon
- ½ tsp. salt
- ½ tsp. baking soda
- 6 Tbsp. cold butter, cubed
- ¼ cup honey
- 4 Tbsp. ice water

1. Whisk together first eight ingredients; cut in butter until crumbly. In another bowl, whisk together honey and water; gradually add to dry ingredients, tossing with a fork until dough holds together when pressed.
2. Divide dough in half. Shape each into a disk; wrap in plastic wrap. Refrigerate until firm enough to roll, about 30 minutes.
3. Preheat oven to 350°. On a lightly floured surface, roll each portion of dough to an 8-in. square. Using a knife or fluted pastry wheel, cut each into sixteen 2-in. squares. If desired, prick holes with a fork. Place squares 1 in. apart on parchment-lined baking sheets.
4. Bake until the edges are light brown, 10-12 minutes. Remove from pans to wire racks to cool. Store grahams in an airtight container.

1 cookie: 60 cal., 2g fat (1g sat. fat), 6mg chol., 89mg sod., 9g carb. (3g sugars, 1g fiber), 1g pro.
Diabetic exchanges: ½ starch, ½ fat.

CREAMY LAYERED BLUEBERRY ICE POPS

PEPPERMINT MERINGUES

These melt-in-your-mouth cookies are super as a gift or to share with guests.
—Dixie Terry, Goreville, IL

Prep: 10 min. • **Bake:** 1½ hours + cooling
Makes: about 1½ dozen

2 large egg whites, room temperature
⅛ tsp. salt
⅛ tsp. cream of tartar
½ cup sugar
2 peppermint candy canes, crushed

1. In a bowl, beat egg whites until foamy. Sprinkle with salt and cream of tartar; beat until soft peaks form. Gradually add sugar, beating until stiff peaks form, for about 7 minutes. Drop by teaspoonfuls onto ungreased foil or parchment-lined baking sheets; sprinkle with the crushed candy.
2. Bake at 225° for 1½ hours. Turn off heat; leave cookies in the oven with the door ajar until cool, for at least 1 hour. Store in an airtight container.

1 meringue: 32 cal., 0 fat (0 sat. fat), 0 chol., 23mg sod., 8g carb. (7g sugars, 0 fiber), 0 pro.
Diabetic exchanges: ½ starch.

CRAN-APPLE CRISP

CRAN-APPLE CRISP

Cranberries, walnuts, brown sugar and orange peel help give this apple-packed crowd-pleaser its rich flavor. After the first taste, guests will be asking for the recipe... and a second helping.
—Diane Everett, Newton, CT

Prep: 20 min. • **Bake:** 40 min.
Makes: 15 servings

8 cups thinly sliced peeled tart apples (about 5 large)
¾ cup sugar
½ cup dried cranberries
½ cup chopped walnuts
¼ cup all-purpose flour
1½ to 2 tsp. grated orange zest

TOPPING
½ cup packed brown sugar
⅓ cup whole wheat flour
⅓ cup nonfat dry milk powder
1 tsp. ground cinnamon
¼ to ½ tsp. cloves
5 Tbsp. cold butter, cubed
⅓ cup quick-cooking oats

1. Preheat oven to 350°. Place the first six ingredients in a large bowl; toss to combine. Transfer to a 13x9-in. baking dish coated with cooking spray.
2. Mix first five topping ingredients; cut in butter until mixture resembles coarse crumbs. Stir in oats. Sprinkle over the apple mixture.
3. Bake, uncovered, until golden brown and apples are tender, 40-45 minutes.

1 serving: 200 cal., 7g fat (3g sat. fat), 10mg chol., 42mg sod., 35g carb. (28g sugars, 2g fiber), 2g pro.
Diabetic exchanges: 1½ starch, 1½ fat, ½ fruit.

STRAWBERRY MUFFIN CONES

This is a delightful way to serve a cupcake. I share these with the neighborhood kids, who love the ice cream cone look and the ease of eating. Adults who try them say snacking on muffin cones makes them feel like kids again.
—Barb Kietzer, Niles, MI

Prep: 20 min. • **Bake:** 20 min. + cooling
Makes: 20 servings

- 2 cups all-purpose flour
- ½ cup sugar
- 2 tsp. baking powder
- ½ tsp. baking soda
- ½ tsp. salt
- 2 large eggs, room temperature
- ¾ cup (6 oz.) strawberry yogurt
- ½ cup canola oil
- 1 cup chopped fresh strawberries
- 20 ice cream cake cones (about 3 in. tall)
- 1 cup (6 oz.) semisweet chocolate chips
- 1 Tbsp. shortening
  Colored sprinkles

1. In a large bowl, combine the first five ingredients. In another bowl, beat eggs, yogurt, oil and strawberries; stir into dry ingredients just until moistened.
2. Place the ice cream cones in muffin cups; spoon 2 heaping Tbsp. batter into each cone. Bake at 375° until a toothpick inserted in the center comes out clean, 19-21 minutes. Cool completely.
3. In a microwave, melt chocolate chips and shortening; stir until smooth. Dip the muffin tops in chocolate; allow excess to drip off. Decorate with sprinkles.
Note: These muffin cones are best served the same day they're prepared.
1 cone: 253 cal., 13g fat (3g sat. fat), 29mg chol., 196mg sod., 33g carb. (16g sugars, 1g fiber), 4g pro.

GRANDMA'S CHRISTMAS SPICE CUTOUTS

My great-grandma made these, and the tradition was passed down in the family—without a written recipe! Mother would start them the day after Thanksgiving, which was exciting for us kids, as we knew Christmas wasn't far off. They are easy to decorate; my grandchildren always look forward to helping with them.
—Elaine Phelps, Cornell, WI

Prep: 1¼ hours + chilling
Bake: 10 min./batch
Makes: about 7 dozen

- 2 cups molasses
- 2 cups dark corn syrup
- ½ cup shortening, melted
- 2 Tbsp. white vinegar
- 1 Tbsp. cold water
- 10 cups all-purpose flour
- 1 tsp. baking soda
- 1 tsp. powdered star anise
- ¼ tsp. ground cloves
- ⅛ tsp. ground cinnamon
- ⅛ tsp. ground nutmeg
  Dash salt

1. Combine first five ingredients. Whisk together the remaining ingredients; add to the molasses mixture and mix well. Refrigerate, covered, 3 hours or overnight.
2. Preheat oven to 375°. On a lightly floured surface, roll out dough to ⅛-in. thickness. Cut into desired shapes with floured 2-in. cookie cutters; place 1 in. apart on greased baking sheets. Bake until set, 10-12 minutes. Remove cookies to wire racks to cool.
1 cookie: 109 cal., 1g fat (0 sat. fat), 0 chol., 47mg sod., 23g carb. (12g sugars, 0 fiber), 2g pro.
Diabetic exchanges: 1½ starch.

STRAWBERRY MUFFIN CONES

CRINKLE-TOP
CHOCOLATE COOKIES

CRINKLE-TOP CHOCOLATE COOKIES

When I baked these moist, fudgy cookies for the first time, my three preschool children went wild over them! I like them because they're lower in fat and easy to mix and bake.

—Maria Groff, Ephrata, PA

Prep: 15 min. + chilling
Bake: 10 min./batch
Makes: about 3½ dozen

- 2 cups (about 12 oz.) semisweet chocolate chips, divided
- 2 Tbsp. butter, softened
- 1 cup sugar
- 2 large egg whites, room temperature
- 1½ tsp. vanilla extract
- 1½ cups all-purpose flour
- 1½ tsp. baking powder
- ¼ tsp. salt
- ¼ cup water
- ½ cup confectioners' sugar

1. In a microwave, melt 1 cup chocolate chips. Stir until smooth; set aside. Beat the butter and sugar until crumbly, about 2 minutes. Add the egg whites and vanilla; beat well. Stir in melted chocolate.
2. In another bowl, whisk together flour, baking powder and salt; gradually add to butter mixture alternately with water. Stir in remaining chocolate chips. Refrigerate the dough, covered, until easy to handle, about 2 hours.
3. Preheat oven to 350°. Shape dough into 1-in. balls. Roll in confectioners' sugar. Place 2 in. apart on baking sheets coated with cooking spray. Bake until set, 10-12 minutes. Remove to wire racks to cool.

1 cookie: 85 cal., 3g fat (2g sat. fat), 1mg chol., 39mg sod., 15g carb. (11g sugars, 1g fiber), 1g pro.
Diabetic exchanges: 1 starch, ½ fat.

NO-BAKE PEANUT BUTTER TREATS

(PICTURED ON P. 229)

This quick and tasty dessert is perfect for a road trip. The treats won't stick to your hands, so you'll crave more than one. Keep them on hand in the refrigerator for an easy snack.

—Sonia Rohda, Waverly, NE

Takes: 10 min. • **Makes:** 15 treats

CRANBERRY STUFFED APPLES

- ⅓ cup chunky peanut butter
- ¼ cup honey
- ½ tsp. vanilla extract
- ⅓ cup nonfat dry milk powder
- ⅓ cup quick-cooking oats
- 2 Tbsp. graham cracker crumbs

In a small bowl, combine peanut butter, honey and vanilla. Stir in the milk powder, oats and graham cracker crumbs. Shape mixture into 1-in. balls. Refrigerate balls until serving.

1 ball: 70 cal., 3g fat (1g sat. fat), 1mg chol., 46mg sod., 9g carb. (6g sugars, 1g fiber), 3g pro.
Diabetic exchanges: ½ starch, ½ fat.

CRANBERRY STUFFED APPLES

Cinnamon, nutmeg and walnuts add a homey autumn flavor to these stuffed apples, but the slow cooker does most of the work for me.

—Grace Sandvigen, Rochester, NY

Prep: 10 min. • **Cook:** 4 hours
Makes: 5 servings

- 5 medium apples
- ⅓ cup fresh or frozen cranberries, thawed and chopped
- ¼ cup packed brown sugar
- 2 Tbsp. chopped walnuts
- ¼ tsp. ground cinnamon
- ⅛ tsp. ground nutmeg
  Whipped cream or vanilla ice cream, optional

1. Core apples, leaving bottoms intact. Peel top third of each apple; place in a 5-qt. slow cooker. Combine cranberries, brown sugar, walnuts, cinnamon and nutmeg; spoon into apples.
2. Cover and cook on low until the apples are tender, 4-5 hours. Serve with whipped cream or ice cream if desired.

1 stuffed apple: 136 cal., 2g fat (0 sat. fat), 0 chol., 6mg sod., 31g carb. (25g sugars, 4g fiber), 1g pro.
Diabetic exchanges: 1 starch, 1 fruit.

PLUM UPSIDE-DOWN CAKE

The delicate flavor of plums is a pleasing change of pace in this upside-down cake.
—Bobbie Talbott, Veneta, OR

Prep: 15 min. • **Bake:** 40 min.
Makes: 10 servings

- ⅓ cup butter
- ½ cup packed brown sugar
- 1¾ to 2 lbs. medium plums, pitted and halved
- 2 large eggs, room temperature
- ⅔ cup sugar
- 1 cup all-purpose flour
- 1 tsp. baking powder
- ¼ tsp. salt
- ⅓ cup hot water
- ½ tsp. lemon extract
  Whipped cream, optional

1. Melt butter in a 10-in. ovenproof skillet. Sprinkle brown sugar over butter. Arrange the plum halves, cut side down, in a single layer over sugar; set aside.

2. In a large bowl, beat eggs until thick and lemon-colored; gradually beat in sugar. Combine the flour, baking powder and salt; add to egg mixture and mix well. Blend water and lemon extract; beat into batter. Pour over plums.

3. Bake at 350° until a toothpick inserted in the center comes out clean, for 40-45 minutes. Immediately invert onto a serving plate. Serve the cake warm, with whipped cream if desired.

1 piece: 245 cal., 7g fat (4g sat. fat), 53mg chol., 173mg sod., 43g carb. (32g sugars, 1g fiber), 3g pro.

BANANA CHOCOLATE CHIP COOKIES

These soft cookies have a cakelike texture and lots of banana flavor that everyone seems to love. It's one of the best banana cookie recipes I've found.
—Vicki Raatz, Waterloo, WI

Prep: 20 min. • **Bake:** 15 min./batch
Makes: 3 dozen

- ⅓ cup butter, softened
- ½ cup sugar
- 1 large egg, room temperature
- ½ cup mashed ripe banana
- ½ tsp. vanilla extract
- 1¼ cups all-purpose flour
- 1 tsp. baking powder
- ¼ tsp. salt
- ⅛ tsp. baking soda
- 1 cup (6 oz.) semisweet chocolate chips

1. In a small bowl, cream the butter and sugar until light and fluffy. Beat in the egg, banana and vanilla. Combine flour, baking powder, salt and baking soda; gradually add to creamed mixture and mix well. Stir in chocolate chips.

2. Drop by tablespoonfuls 2 in. apart onto baking sheets coated with cooking spray. Bake at 350° until the edges are lightly browned, 13-16 minutes. Remove to wire racks to cool.

1 cookie: 69 cal., 3g fat (2g sat. fat), 10mg chol., 50mg sod., 10g carb. (6g sugars, 0 fiber), 1g pro.
Diabetic exchanges: ½ starch, ½ fat.
* HEALTH TIP * Using ½ cup mashed banana in the cookies instead of starting with more butter saves about 1½ grams saturated fat per cookie.

BANANA CHOCOLATE CHIP COOKIES

BLACK & BLUE BERRY GRUNT

GRAPEFRUIT YOGURT CAKE

We eat grapefruit for breakfast and in winter-fruit salads—so why not for dessert? Here's a sweet-tart cake that's easy, delicious and one of a kind. Oh, and it's healthy, too!
—Maiah Miller, Montclair, VA

Prep: 10 min. • **Bake:** 25 min. + cooling
Makes: 12 servings

- 1½ cups all-purpose flour
- 2 tsp. baking powder
- ¼ tsp. salt
- 3 large eggs, room temperature
- 1 cup fat-free plain yogurt
- ⅓ cup sugar
- 5 Tbsp. grated grapefruit zest
- ¼ cup agave nectar or honey
- ½ tsp. vanilla extract
- ¼ cup canola oil

GLAZE

- ½ cup confectioners' sugar
- 2 to 3 tsp. grapefruit juice
  Grapefruit wheels and fresh mint leaves, optional
  Fresh mint leaves

1. Preheat oven to 350°. Whisk together flour, baking powder and salt. Combine next seven ingredients. Gradually stir flour mixture into yogurt mixture, then pour into a 9-in. round baking pan coated with cooking spray. Bake cake until a toothpick inserted in center comes out clean, 25-30 minutes. Cool.
2. For glaze, mix confectioners' sugar with enough grapefruit juice to reach desired consistency; drizzle glaze over the top, allowing some to flow over sides. Top cake with grapefruit and mint if desired.
Freeze option: Omit glaze. Securely wrap cooled cake in plastic and foil; freeze. To use, thaw at room temperature. Prepare glaze; top as directed.
1 slice: 187 cal., 6g fat (1g sat. fat), 47mg chol., 159mg sod., 30g carb. (17g sugars, 1g fiber), 4g pro.
Diabetic exchanges: 2 starch, 1 fat.

TEST KITCHEN TIP

It's a cross between a pound cake and a sweet quick bread, so is Grapefruit Yogurt Cake a dessert or a breakfast? You make the call!

BLACK & BLUE BERRY GRUNT

If you're looking for something different from the usual cakes and fruit pies, try this old-fashioned dessert. It features a delicious combination of blackberries and blueberries with tender homemade dumplings on top.
—Kelly Akin, Johnsonville, NY

Takes: 30 min. • **Makes:** 8 servings

- 2½ cups fresh or frozen blackberries, thawed
- 2½ cups fresh or frozen blueberries, thawed
- ¾ cup sugar
- ¼ cup water
- 1 Tbsp. lemon juice
- ⅛ tsp. ground cinnamon
- ⅛ tsp. pepper

DUMPLINGS

- 1 cup all-purpose flour
- 2 Tbsp. sugar
- 1 tsp. baking powder
- ½ tsp. baking soda
- ⅛ tsp. salt
- 2 Tbsp. butter, melted
- ½ cup buttermilk
- 1 Tbsp. cinnamon-sugar
  Sweetened whipped cream, optional

1. In a large skillet, combine first seven ingredients. Bring to a boil. Reduce heat; simmer, uncovered, for 5 minutes.
2. Meanwhile, in a large bowl, combine the first five dumpling ingredients. Add the butter and buttermilk; stir just until moistened. Drop batter by tablespoonfuls onto the berry mixture. Sprinkle with the cinnamon-sugar.
3. Cover tightly; simmer until a toothpick inserted in a dumpling comes out clean, 10-15 minutes. Serve warm; if desired, top with sweetened whipped cream.
1 serving: 226 cal., 4g fat (2g sat. fat), 8mg chol., 229mg sod., 47g carb. (31g sugars, 4g fiber), 3g pro.

**APPLE-PUMPKIN
UPSIDE-DOWN CAKE**

APPLE-PUMPKIN UPSIDE-DOWN CAKE

*No matter what time of year it is, we love
the combination of classic fall fruits in this
yummy cake. I bake the apples on the
bottom to keep them plump and moist,
then flip the cake so we can dig in at any
time of day. It's best served warm with
vanilla ice cream.*
—Christina Yahraes, San Francisco, CA

Prep: 15 min. • **Bake:** 30 min. + cooling
Makes: 8 servings

- 2 large eggs, room temperature
- 2 Tbsp. plus ¼ cup softened butter, divided
- 2 Tbsp. plus ¾ cup sugar, divided
- 1 tsp. ground cinnamon, divided
- 2 medium apples (about 10 oz.), peeled and thinly sliced
- ½ cup canned pumpkin
- 1¼ cups all-purpose flour
- 1 tsp. baking soda
- ½ tsp. salt
- ½ cup buttermilk
   Vanilla ice cream, optional

1. Preheat oven to 350°. In a microwave,
melt 2 Tbsp. butter. Stir in 2 Tbsp. sugar
and ½ tsp. cinnamon; spread mixture into
a 9-in. pie plate. Arrange apples in a single
layer over butter mixture.

2. Cream remaining butter and remaining
sugar until light and fluffy. Beat in the
pumpkin. Add eggs, one at a time, beating
well after each addition. In another bowl,
whisk together flour, baking soda, salt and
remaining cinnamon; add to the creamed
mixture alternately with buttermilk; beat
well after each addition.

3. Spread batter over apples. Bake until a
toothpick inserted in center comes out
clean, 30-35 minutes. Loosen sides of the
cake from pie plate with a knife. Cool for
10 minutes before inverting onto a serving
plate. Serve warm and, if desired, with
vanilla ice cream.

1 slice: 278 cal., 10g fat (6g sat. fat), 70mg
chol., 422mg sod., 43g carb. (27g sugars, 2g
fiber), 4g pro.

CHOCOLATE SWIRLED CHEESECAKE

*This cheesecakes looks and tastes rich
and indulgent, but it's a lightened-up
version you can feel good about serving.*
—Kathy Shan, Toledo, OH

Prep: 30 min. + chilling
Bake: 40 min.
Makes: 12 servings

- 2 cups 2% cottage cheese
- 1 cup crushed chocolate wafers (about 16 wafers)
- 1 pkg. (8 oz.) reduced-fat cream cheese, cubed
- ½ cup sugar
   Dash salt
- 1 Tbsp. vanilla extract
- 2 large eggs, lightly beaten
- 1 large egg white
- 2 oz. bittersweet chocolate, melted and cooled
   Fresh raspberries, optional

1. Line a strainer with four layers of
cheesecloth or one coffee filter; place
over a bowl. Place cottage cheese in the
strainer; refrigerate, covered, 1 hour.
Place a 9-in. springform pan on a double
thickness of heavy-duty foil (about 18 in.
square); wrap foil securely around pan.
Coat inside of pan with cooking spray.
Press crushed wafers onto bottom and
1 in. up sides.

2. Preheat the oven to 350°. In a food
processor, process the drained cottage
cheese until smooth. Add cream cheese,
sugar and salt; process until blended.
Transfer to a bowl; stir in vanilla, eggs and
egg white. Remove 1 cup batter to a small
bowl; stir in melted chocolate.

3. Pour plain batter into crust. Drop
chocolate batter by spoonfuls over plain
batter. Cut through batter with a knife to
swirl. Place the springform pan in a larger
baking pan; add 1 in. of boiling water to
the larger pan.

4. Bake until the center is just set and top
appears dull, about 40 minutes. Turn off
oven; open door slightly. Cool cheesecake
in oven 30 minutes.

5. Remove springform pan from water
bath; remove foil. Loosen sides of the
cheesecake with a knife; cool on a wire
rack 30 minutes. Refrigerate overnight,
covering when completely cooled.

6. Remove rim from pan. If desired, top
with raspberries.

1 slice: 187 cal., 8g fat (5g sat. fat), 46mg
chol., 378mg sod., 17g carb. (14g sugars, 1g
fiber), 8g pro.
Diabetic exchanges: 1½ starch, 1 lean meat,
½ fat.

CHOCOLATE
SWIRLED CHEESECAKE

Index

SLOW-COOKED RATATOUILLE